Network+ Certification Success Guide

Network+ Certification Success Guide

Dorothy Cady and Nancy Cadjan

McGraw-Hill

New York   San Francisco   Washington, D.C.
Auckland   Bogotá   Caracas   Lisbon   London
Madrid   Mexico City   Milan   Montreal   New Delhi
San Juan   Singapore   Sydney   Tokyo   Toronto

McGraw-Hill

A Division of The McGraw-Hill Companies

The views expressed in this book are solely those of the author, and do not represent the views of any other party or parties.

2 3 4 5 6 7 8 9 0   DOC/DOC   9 0 4 3 2 1 0 9

ISBN 0-07-135018-7

The sponsoring editor for this book was Michael Sprague and the production supervisor was Clare Stanley. It was set in Usherwood by Patricia Wallenburg.

Printed and bound by R. R. Donnelley & Sons Company.

McGraw-Hill books are available at special quantity discounts to use as premiums and sales promotions, or for use in corporate training programs. For more information, please write to the Director of Special Sales, McGraw-Hill, 11 West 19th Street, New York, NY 10011. Or contact your local bookstore.

Throughout this book, trademarked names are used. Rather than put a trademark symbol after every occurrence of a trademarked name, we use names in an editorial fashion only, and to the benefit of the trademark owner, with no intention of infringement of the trademark. Where such designations appear in this book, they have been printed with initial caps.

 This book is printed on recycled, acid-free paper containing a minimum of 50% recycled, de-inked fiber.

To friends everywhere whose trials and triumphs make their friendships stronger—a lesson the authors had the privilege of learning first hand.

Acknowledgments

The authors would like to take a moment to acknowledge all of the individuals who helped to make this book possible. In particular, we'd like to thank:

Arthur Cadjan (Nancy's husband) who did the dishes, cleaned the house, brought me sandwiches and didn't complain that our Christmas vacation was spent on this book. He makes my dreams possible.

Raymond, Shana, and Ray (Dorothy's spouse and children) who were always supportive, helpful, and patient. They make it all worth doing.

Doug Bastianelli (Network + Program Manager for CompTIA) who answered our questions, encouraged us, and gave us permission to use the important and relative information about Network + certification that CompTIA published.

Judy Brief, Michael Sprague, and Patty Wallenburg, without whom this book simply would not have been possible.

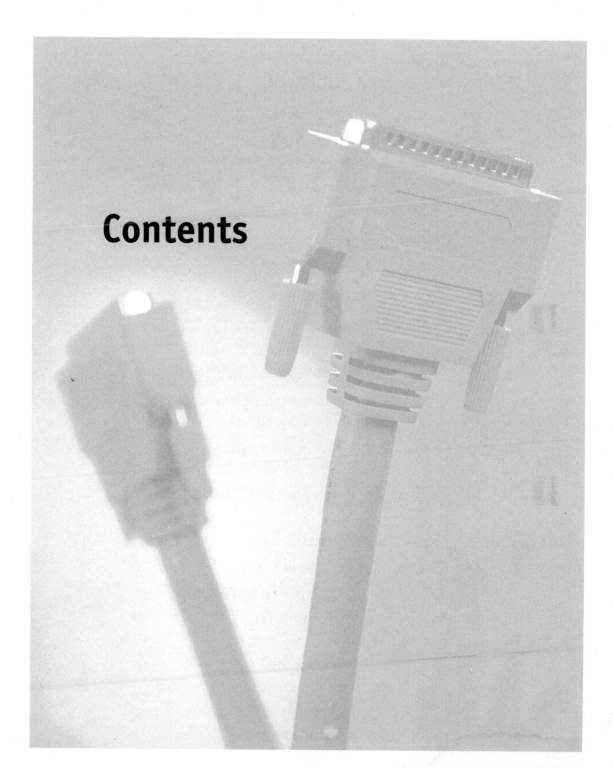

Contents

INTRODUCTION

The IT job market is growing at an unprecedented rate. In the age of Information, those who can facilitate its movement are in high demand. If you're in the industry already, you have a head start. If you are just joining the industry, don't worry. There's plenty of room for you. However, being an IT professional is not a simple thing. It takes work, dedication, and the drive to succeed. If you have these qualities, then you chose the right book.

Why Should You Read This Book

With the mix of various operating systems, hardware, and configurations in today's networks, it is difficult for employers to know that the IT professionals they hire have the knowledge and skills to deal with the complexity of heterogeneous networks. It may also be difficult for IT professionals to represent the skills they have acquired in the networking profession. One way to solve both these problems is to train, test, certify, and license individuals.

Other professions have known and recognized this for years. You cannot become an airline pilot, for example, without years of flight training, testing, certification, and licensing. While IT professionals don't have to be licensed as do airline pilots and professionals in some other industries, there is still a body of required knowledge. Training, testing, and certification have become acknowledged by the IT industry as ways to recognize IT professionals.

To address the need to be able to identify qualified IT professionals, the Network+ Certification Task Force was formed in 1995 by Computing Technology Industry Association (CompTIA), a leading industry association. The Task Force was created to identify, classify and publish skills standards for networking professionals employed in three types of organizations: information technology companies, channel partners, and business-government firms. Companies like Compaq, Digital, Lotus, Microsoft, and Novell have contributed significant time and resources to categorizing the tasks needed to be a network professional. The ability to complete these tasks successfully can now be proven with the Network+ Certification program.

In the past decade, the interest in vendor-neutral certification has grown tremendously because of the need to prove that IT professionals know the basics of any system and are not tied down to working with only one product line. For example, since 1993, approximately 75,000 technicians have taken CompTIA's A+ certification and have proved that they have the necessary skills. A+ was the first certification to allow computer technicians to show that they had the basic skills to succeed in their job. It is the first certification that has given employers and customers a way to be assured that those holding the certification have the necessary skills regardless of the vendor or brand name of the hardware.

The need for the same level of confidence in the networking field grows more apparent as networking systems become more heterogeneous. As the lines between vendors become finer and the need to maintain multiple platforms becomes more critical, IT professionals and employers need to know that you have the skills necessary to deal with complexity. Network + is a vendor-neutral networking certification provided by CompTIA, a non-profit association of more than 7,500 computer resellers, manufacturers, software publishers, distributors, and service companies across the industry. It represents the defining certification for all network professionals. Just as CompTIA's A + Certification has become an industry standard for computer technicians, Network + is on course to becoming the mainstay certification of networking professionals.

If you want to be recognized and rewarded as the true IT professional you are, or if you want to become one of those recognized as an IT professional, you should be aiming for industry certifications. The Network + certification is a good one to obtain. Not only does it tell others that you are an IT professional, but it assures them that you have at least a minimum level of needed knowledge. It also gives you the leverage to ensure that promotions, pay raises, and interesting assignments all come your way.

Who Should Read This Book

Whether you are an experienced networking professional, or just starting out in your career, this book is for you. There's no doubt that the IT industry is one of the fastest growing industries today. You can be part of that growth and reap the benefits it provides if you are prepared to do so. Part of that preparation involves learning the industry, choosing an area of the IT profession which best suits you, then working toward earning respect in that area. With that respect come the money and the benefits.

Part of earning that respect is showing others that you know what you are talking about. You can do that in the everyday way you do your job. You can do that by being a professional. And, you can do that by showing others that you aren't the only one who thinks you know your job. You can do it by obtaining one or more IT profession certifications. The Network + certification is a perfect one to start with. Because it is industry-neutral, it shows others that you know networking, not just how to install a specific vendor's product. While product certification will also win you respect in your profession, a general certification such as Network + shows others that there is more to your knowledge than just a specific vendor's product.

So, if you are looking into becoming an IT professional, are an IT professional who wants others to know it, or just want to get the respect you deserve, you can do that by obtaining the Network+ certification. This book is one of the best to help you do that. It helps you learn what you need to know to obtain the Network+ certification—a first step toward becoming certified.

What This Book Covers

This book is the resource you need to understand why and how to obtain your Network+ certification, and what knowledge is required to pass the Network+ certification examination. It will help you understand why you should become Network+ certified to begin with. It will also help you understand the process you must go through in order to become Network+ certified. As you explore the technical knowledge you need in order to pass the exam and become certified, it also shows you what you must learn that you don't already know, and how to go about getting that valuable information.

In addition, this book offers advice and insight into what you need to know to succeed, both at passing the certification examination, and at working as a professional in the IT industry. It also provides guidance to some of the best resources for the latest information on the networking skills sought by today's companies.

This book contains seven chapters. Although chapters four through seven are the heart of the information you'll need to pass the Network+ exam, the other chapters help you understand additional important details about the Network+ certification program:

❖ Why you would want to become Network+ certified to begin with
❖ What the Network+ certification can do for you as an IT professional
❖ What it's really like to work in the IT profession.

If you already know why you want to become Network+ certified, what the Network+ certification can do for you, and what it's really like to work in the IT profession, then you may want to skip those related chapters and go through only those chapters that help you prepare for the actual test. To help you determine whether that is an appropriate approach for you, as well as what this book is all about and what it can do for you, a brief overview of each chapter and its content follows.

Chapter 1: Becoming Network + Certified discusses the process associated with obtaining the Network + certification. It includes information about what the Network + Certification program is, who sponsors it and why, how it was developed, how long it may take to get the certification, how much the certification testing program will cost, and how to register to take the certification test. It also explains what prerequisites exist for Network + certification. It discusses the actual Network + certification testing process including such related information as how the actual testing process works, and what to expect when you take the test.

Chapter 2: Evaluating Trends in the IT Industry takes an in-depth look into trends in the IT industry and provides discussion of where the networking technology field is going as a whole. This knowledge is critical for professionals who want to be at the forefront of the industry and be a part of making the trends—not just following them. Understanding IT trends gives you the knowledge needed to arrive at the forefront of this industry through Network + certification.

Chapter 3: Valuing Your Network + Certification discusses the value of becoming Network + certified. It explains how the Network + certification can be the basis from which to obtain more specialized certifications such as the MCSE certification offered by Microsoft Corporation. Just as medical doctors begin their training by obtaining a basic degree in medicine, and then go on to obtain more specialized training such as that of an orthopedic surgeon, networking professionals can follow a similar path using the Network + certification as a starting point to a more specialized area of networking technology. This chapter also contains practical advice from a variety of network professionals experienced in the field. Network + supporters and sponsors share their knowledge and advice with Network + certification candidates to help make your entire certification experience a better one.

Chapter 4: Working as a Network Professional profiles the responsibilities and job duties of a typical network professional. It lists and explains each of the 15 job categories around which the Network + certification is based. It details typical job duties for each of these categories, and gives a brief explanation of what it means to perform those typical duties. Where appropriate, the chapter uses real-life examples of how different duties are fulfilled in the daily activities of a network professional. This type of information provides the less-experienced reader with a greater understanding of what it is like to be a network professional and shows how knowledge is effectively used in a real networking job. In addition, this chapter will help the more experienced network professional see how the knowledge and experience gathered over the years applies directly to the Network + certification program.

Chapter 5: Using the Examination Blueprint to Prepare for the Test walks you through the actual blueprint that CompTIA used to create the Network + certification examination tests. This chapter explains and defines each of the 15 categories around which the test questions were written, and identifies the goals and tasks associated with each of those categories. Each area of knowledge on which you may be tested is included in this chapter. So too is additional information to help you understand exactly what types of related knowledge the questions test. After you read this chapter, you will have no doubt about what you need to know to pass the Network + certification exam.

Chapter 6: Studying for the Certification Test provides information about the recommended reading and training available to help you prepare to take and pass the Network + certification test. In addition, this chapter provides basic information on useful study skills, particularly those skills effective for studying and retaining technical material, and information on how to put together your own unique study plan for filling in the gaps in your networking knowledge. Before you can put together your own special study plan, you need to know just what those knowledge gaps are. This chapter also explains the pre-certification assessment test included in Chapter 7, and how to use that pre-certification test to determine in which of the 15 job categories around which the test is based you should concentrate your studies.

Chapter 7: Assessing Your Level of Networking Knowledge contains a 150-question pre- and post-assessment test for you to take in order to determine what your current level of networking knowledge is, and whether you may be ready to take the actual Network + certification test. The test itself contains sample test questions for each of the 15 job categories in which candidates may be tested. To make it easier for you to see what category the test questions relate to, they are arranged by category. In addition, the total number of test questions for each category correlates to the total percentage of questions the actual Network + certification test will have on each of the 15 categories of networking knowledge. As a pre-assessment, this test helps you identify in which of the 15 job categories your current skill and knowledge level are the weakest. These areas are then the ones you should use to develop a personal study plan as discussed in Chapter 6. To help you develop your personal study plan, the answers to the test questions are also provided, along with a brief explanation of why the chosen answer is correct. Once you have taken this pre-assessment test and determined those areas which need more study, you will be able to use the recommended reading from Chapter 6 to locate appropriate books and other networking technology and networking practice study materials.

How To Get the Most From This Book

This book cannot possibly contain all the information that might be useful to an IT professional. Its main goal is to help you focus your efforts toward understanding what it is you need to know to pass the Network + examination, and toward learning how to gain that information. To accomplish that, it not only provides all needed information to help you understand the Network + certification program, process, and test, but it also furnishes lists of information sources such as books and Web sites to use to learn the networking information required.

Step one in getting the most from this book is understanding what it is designed to do for you, as well as what it wasn't intended to do. The next step is to work with this book. If you want to know about the program, the industry, and the benefits to you of Network + certification, read the book from front to back.

If all you want is to know what it takes to pass the test, then concentrate all your efforts on Chapters 4, 5, 6, and 7. Follow the recommendations you'll find in those chapters to create a study plan and prepare for the test. Take the 150-question pre- and post-assessment test as recommended to identify your weaker areas of networking knowledge, and then study, study, study.

The information in this book has been collected from some of the greatest industry vendors, resellers, and trainers as well as from other IT professionals who are familiar with the industry and its future. It provides a look at the IT profession and how to succeed in it, not just what it takes to pass the Network + exam (although it does that too).

The *Network + Certification Success Guide* is the resource for information about the Network + certification program and the exam. It may well be the only resource you need to understand how to pass the exam and obtain a new level of respect in the IT industry. If you do need additional study resources and information to supplement your current networking knowledge-base, however, this book provides a gateway to learning more and exploring the fascinating career of the networking professional. Either way, this book provides the information you need to complete Network+ certification and put your career on the right path.

1

Becoming Network+ Certified

This chapter gives an overview of the Network+ Certification program to help you understand that program and the benefits that Network+ Certification holds for you. It explains what Network+ certification is, who it is for, and what it will do for you. It also explains who sponsors Network+ certification and how the certification was developed. In addition, it covers the information you need to know to obtain the certification, and includes information related to the test, including details about how to register and pay for the test, as well as what to expect when you take the test. Finally, it explains what to expect after you are certified, and how Network+ certification relates to other certification programs.

What is Network+ Certification?

Network+ certification is a way for you as an IT professional to prove your competence by earning a nationally recognized, vendor-neutral networking certification. You receive Network+ certification only after successfully completing the Network+ certification test sponsored by the Computing Technology Industry Association (CompTIA). This certification was created in conjunction with major networking software and hardware companies like Compaq, Digital, Softbank, U.S. Robotics, U.S. West, Wave Technology, Lotus, Microsoft, and Novell. The program is backed by major vendors, distributors, and resellers.

The Network+ certification exam tests your basic knowledge of networking technology and the practice you need to be successful in the IT industry today. The criteria for the test and certification were developed by industry leaders and organizations and categorized into a variety of skills necessary to be successful in three different types of organizations: information technology companies, channel partners, and business-government firms. The test covers a broad range of technology and best-practices policies in 15 different categories, but does not test knowledge of vendor-specific products. The categories are:

- ❖ Operating Network Management System
- ❖ Implementing the Installation of Network
- ❖ Setting Up Standard Operating Procedures
- ❖ Managing Support Efforts
- ❖ Administering Change Control System
- ❖ Troubleshooting the Network
- ❖ Administering the Network
- ❖ Designing the Network
- ❖ Planning a Customer's Job
- ❖ Analyzing/Evaluating the Applicability of New Technology
- ❖ Maintaining the Network
- ❖ Analyzing/Evaluating Network Implementation
- ❖ Implementing Change Control System
- ❖ Developing Documentation (and SOPs)
- ❖ Developing/Coordinating/Delivering Training

Chapter 4 discusses in detail these 15 categories and their 175 related job tasks.

Network + certification is based on a knowledge of the skills necessary for network administration as determined by the industry experts. As noted, these skills have been grouped into 15 categories. Network + certification allows you to prove that you have the skills needed to succeed. It documents your competence in a range of areas of networking such as operating network management systems, installing networks, setting up standard operating procedures, managing support efforts, troubleshooting the network, administering the network, designing networks, and so on.

To become Network + certified, you must pass one test which covers all 15 skill categories. When you pass the test, you are Network + certified and have achieved a vendor-neutral certification that shows you have the necessary knowledge in the areas of networking technology and networking practices.

What Can Getting the Network+ Certification Do For Me?

Network + represents a company-neutral, industry-wide recognition of your networking knowledge. It is a logical next step from the A + Certification as well as a path for entering directly into networking. It means a level of assurance about your abilities that employers have not had before. According to CompTIA, Network + Certification has the following benefits:

- ❖ Increased productivity and competence as employees are given assignments at the appropriate level for information technology professionals' experience, knowledge and expertise
- ❖ Improved recruitment, hiring, retention, retraining, reassignment, and promotion of information technology professional
- ❖ Measurable skills sets that lead to the elimination of redundant, unnecessary and irrelevant training courses
- ❖ Information technology professionals with an identifiable career path
- ❖ Information technology professionals enjoying increased self-esteem as they demonstrate the necessary competencies as defined by experts in the industry
- ❖ Information technology professionals developing a portfolio of industry-supported skills and credentials transferable from information technology to other industries and locations

❖ Pursuit of an intense, dedicated training program so that an information technology professional can acquire the skills necessary to qualify for an excellent job

❖ A common ground for business, education and government to collaborate on training and other needs

❖ Easier identification of qualified resources; when the skills required to perform a job efficiently and effectively are understood, the process of identifying competent resources is simplified.

Because of its ability to provide a baseline standard for employers, customers, and IT professionals, Network + certification plays an important role in the IT industry and provides great benefit to all involved in the complex world of networking. For example, a senior technical recruiter for a national recruiting organization says that she works with some companies that will not interview a candidate who is not certified. Other companies require certification in addition to a 4-year degree. Still others view certification as an asset in addition to the years and depth of experience possessed by the potential employee. For entry-level candidates, this recruiter has noticed that certification is the one factor that puts potential candidates above other entry-level candidates applying for the job.

Network + certification assures high quality among those who sell and service networking products. According to vendor estimates, there are hundreds of thousands of individuals who have received vendor-specific certification. It is estimated that there are over 20,000 Oracle Certified Professionals, 275,000 Microsoft Certified Professionals, and 135,000 Novell Certified Professionals (see Figure 1.1). These numbers do not take into consideration the number of professionals working on their certification. Novell estimates that there are 600,000 people worldwide working on their Novell certification. Because Network + certification covers the basics tested in many vendor-specific training programs, it can dramatically reduce the cost of training professionals who work in heterogeneous network environments.

Customers prefer working with professionals have proved their credentials with an industry-recognized certification. John Ratzan, a technical consultant at IBM's Solutions Practice, in Tucson, AZ., says "IT certifications are effective and beneficial for today's technical consultants." He sees the continued move toward certification as consistent with current industry trends. Although experience is extremely important, Jim Cogliano, Chief Operating Officer of Sullivan & Cogliano, a national IT company based in Waltham, MA.

says that his client companies often request certified candidates. These certified IT professionals command salaries 10 to 15 percent higher than those of non-certified professionals.

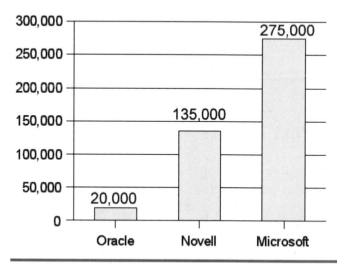

FIGURE 1.1 Individuals who have attained some of the leading vendor certifications

Network professionals find their value in the marketplace and to their customers increases with professional certification no matter where they are employed. Because of rapid changes in technology and stiff competition for network professionals, certification is an essential tool for managers trying to keep their business up and running on the latest technologies and to attract top IT professionals. Training and certification provide companies with a competitive edge in hiring and retaining employees. Companies that invest in their employees help them become more productive quickly. "You just can't not train," says Judy Weller, senior analyst at the Gartner Group. "People are going to learn to do stuff one way or the other."

Today' companies also understand that a certified employee is a better and possibly a more contented employee. Jo Haraf, chief technology officer at Morrison & Foerster, in San Francisco, says, "If people don't get training, there's going to come a time when they're useless to me. I consider it an investment. I upgrade my servers; I had darn well better upgrade my people." The Gartner Group estimates that in 1997, the U. S. spent $5.4 billion on technology training and certification. Of that training, IT professionals received 42 percent—the most of any group of professionals.

Although once mostly used by consultants, certification is increasing in demand in the Fortune 500 companies, according to Weller. "Often when an organization is outsourcing a function, they will try to require the outsourcer to do some formal assessment as a way of judging the quality of the people," Weller says.

Many IT professionals find that with industry-recognized certification, doors to new opportunities, promotions, and higher salaries are opening for them.

What Prerequisites Must I Meet?

There are no specific prerequisites for taking the Network+ test. However, this certification represents that you already have skills and knowledge in the basics of networking and the test is geared to those who already have experience and/or training in networking. According to CompTIA, the target audience for this certification is the networking professional who has 18 to 24 months of experience in the IT industry. CompTIA also suggests that you take the A+ certification exam before taking the Network+ certification, though this is not a requirement. Because of your previous experience in the IT industry, you might be able to take the Network+ certification test with little preparation, while others who are not as experienced might need training or a personal study program to pass the Network+ test. If you have taken the A+ certification, you are well aware that your experience in the industry is quite useful when taking the exam. Unlike exams that are oriented to studying a certain textbook to pass, this exam draws heavily on practical real-world experience. This book will help you understand what areas of experience and learning will be focused on and will give you suggestions on how to strengthen your experience in areas where you feel less than ready for the exam.

Who Sponsors the Test?

CompTIA sponsors the test and administers the resulting certification. (Visit CompTIA's home page for more information about this association. See

Figure 1.2.) You take the actual test through an independent testing association—Sylvan Prometric. For information about Sylvan Prometric, refer to the "Getting Network + Certified" section in this chapter.

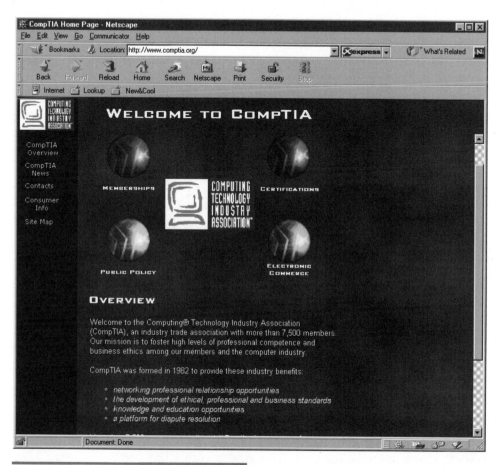

FIGURE 1.2 The home Web page for CompTIA

CompTIA is a not-for-profit international trade association based in Lombard, IL; its members include more than 7,500 computer resellers, manufacturers, software publishers, distributors, and service companies. The mission of CompTIA is to promote high levels of professional competence and business ethics among its members and the computer industry. Members of CompTIA are located in all 50 states and Canada and they represent all major companies in the networking industry. CompTIA committees and task forces address issues that affect the entire computer industry.

CompTIA has a history of leading the way in creating industry-wide standards that are recognized and accepted by all major companies. For example, CompTIA also developed:

❖ The first industry-wide standard warranty reimbursement claim form
❖ The A+ certification program.

The A+ certification program quickly became the industry standard for certifying computer technicians in fundamental service and support skills. It was the first and is the most widely accepted vendor-neutral certification program, and as the interest in vendor-neutral certification has grown, A+ certification has become the certification of choice. Since 1993, approximately 75,000 technicians have obtained A+ certification and have proved that they have the necessary industry skills to do their jobs both competently and effectively. A+ gives employers and customers a way to be assured that a computer technician has the basic skills necessary regardless of the vendor or brand name of the hardware. The Network+ Certification program has similar goals.

Just as the A+ certification has become the standard for computer technicians, Network+ certification is well positioned to become the industry standard for networking professionals because it has the backing of leaders in the industry and is administered by CompTIA, a respected industry trendsetter.

How the Network+ Program Was Developed

With the growing need for vendor-neutral certification and an industry-wide standard for networking professionals, CompTIA set out in 1995 to identify, classify and publish skills standards for networking professionals employed in IT companies, channel partners, and business-government firms. With that goal in mind, CompTIA formed the Network+ Certification Task Force. The Task Force was made up of industry professionals at all levels and in all areas of the networking profession including manufacturers, distributors, resellers, industry associations, and others.

These industry experts committed CompTIA to defining the job tasks of network professionals through sound research. After conducting this research, the Task Force met to formulate the findings into an IT Skills Job Task Analysis. This outlines 175 separate tasks, grouped into 15 categories that make up the work of a network professional. Supporters of the program contributed extensive investments of time, expertise, and financial resources to the creation of the IT Skills Job Task Analysis and the resulting test. In addition to the resources provided by the Cornerstone sponsors, input and support came from other companies interested in creating a standard certification for the networking industry. These participants contributed their expertise to help define the baseline skills and standards to be tested by the Network+ exam.

However, just creating an outline of skills does not mean that you can create a certification program which assures that a candidate has the appropriate skills, knowledge, and abilities to perform a job. To ensure that, CompTIA and the Task Force created the Network+ test-based certification so that a measurable mastery of these skills, knowledge, and abilities could be demonstrated. CompTIA followed up this outline of skills with an extensive survey of industry professionals. The net result was the confirmation by professionals throughout the industry that CompTIA had accurately and adequately defined the responsibilities and job tasks of the networking professional.

Cornerstone members of the program include:

- ❖ Microsoft
- ❖ Novell
- ❖ Lotus
- ❖ US West
- ❖ Computerworld
- ❖ Compaq Computers
- ❖ Digital Equipment Corp.
- ❖ Softbank
- ❖ U.S. Robotics
- ❖ Wave Technologies
- ❖ Banyan

Other highly respected companies and organizations in the networking profession which have contributed to the creation of the Network+ certification program include:

- ❖ Network Professional Association (NPA)
- ❖ Information Technology Training Association (ITTA)
- ❖ Vanstar
- ❖ DataTrain
- ❖ Fluke

Once the results of the IT Job Task Analysis were formulated, they provided the foundation for developing an industry-wide certification program called Network + certification. As the Network + certification testing program was developed, the task force continued to examine and reexamine the information provided by the job task analysis including the definition of the target audience and their job tasks. The task force focused on survey results gathered by CompTIA to set the standards for the program, including the number of tests necessary for certification and the content of the material covered in the test.

In developing the test, the following process was followed:

1. Subject matter experts were identified to develop test objectives.
2. A blueprint survey was conducted to determine the number of test items needed for each objective.
3. The size of the test was determined.
4. Specific items for the test were written.
5. Each of the items was reviewed for technical accuracy, congruence, psychometrics, and grammar.
6. Subject matter experts were asked to rank the importance of the tasks as they apply to networking professionals with 18–24 months experience in the industry.
7. A beta test was conducted and analyzed for test improvement. Test items were then reformatted and improved as needed based on the beta test findings.
8. A cut-score survey was conducted to determine the pass/fail rate and set the test matrix.
9. A final review of each test item and the overall test was conducted. This included an extensive technical edit.

In creating the Network + exam, test developers made extensive efforts to adhere to the Standards for Educational and Psychological Tests established by the American Educational Research Association, the American Psychological

Association, and the National Council on Measurement in Education. Galton Technologies, a national test developing facilitator, consulted on the development of specific test questions. Following the information provided by industry experts and the guidelines for testing set by national education associations has helped CompTIA create a fair and unbiased certification test that will become an industry standard for all networking professionals.

Some people might be worried that taking an adaptive exam like the Network+ exam will automatically lower their score because fewer questions are asked. However, studies have shown that scores for adaptive exams are almost identical to longer exams that test a broader amount of material. The plus to taking adaptive exams is that the amount of time needed to take the exam is significantly reduced (see Figure 1.3). You don't have to spend as much time in the testing center, yet your scores accurately reflect your knowledge.

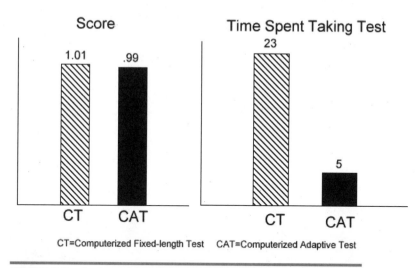

FIGURE 1.3 A comparison of computer aided versus standard testing

Getting Network+ Certified

Network+ certification is open to everyone who would like to take the test; there are no prerequisites. The Network+ certification test is administered by Sylvan Prometric and is computerized. Sylvan offers computerized testing on a continual basis at almost 2,000 sites in more than 70 countries. Scoring is performed on-site immediately after the test is completed. Because of new test design and delivery techniques, the test has an excellent ability to accurately assess skills.

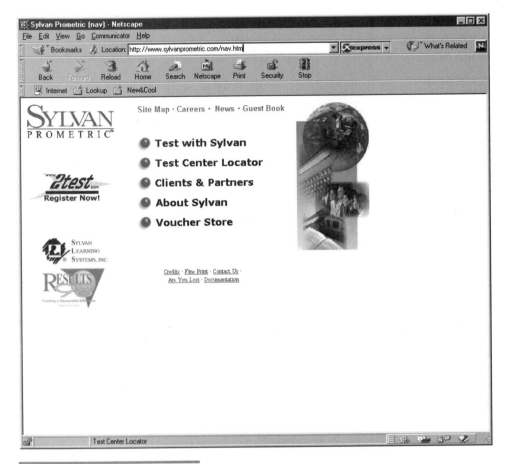

FIGURE 1.4 Sylvan's main web site

Sylvan Prometric's computer-based testing software has many features to optimize the testing experience. The testing software allows you to select answers with the keyboard or the mouse. If you are having difficulty answering a question, you can mark it for later review. The test software remembers and reminds you of questions not fully answered. You can also review any question before the scoring. However, it is usually best to go with your first instinct. Studies show that the first instinct is usually correct. There is also an on-screen clock to remind you of time remaining. Finally, if you have any questions about the testing software, on-screen help is always available during the test. These features give you the best possible testing environment.

The fee for taking the Network + certification test had not been published at the time this book was written. However, certification testing fees for vendor-specific tests cost an average of $80 to $150 per test. The fee for the Network + exams will be similar to the fees charged for taking the A + exam. The A + exam fees are $85 for those employed by CompTIA member organizations and $120 for non-members. CompTIA also will offer bulk pricing for companies that purchase a group of exam vouchers. Before you take the exam, check the CompTIA web site for the current exam price and for details. Or check with your training coordinator to see if your company has purchased exam vouchers.

Sylvan Prometric accepts payment by Visa, MasterCard, American Express, or check. For more information and to pay for the test, contact Sylvan Prometric at 1-888-895-6116.

When you call, make sure you have the following information:

❖ Social Security number (or Sylvan ID number)
❖ Complete mailing address and phone number
❖ Employer or organization name
❖ Date you want to take the test
❖ Method of payment

If you object to providing a Social Security number for test purposes, Sylvan Prometric will issue you a unique Sylvan ID number you can use for all Sylvan tests.

Also, if you are taking the test as a part of your company or organizational accreditation program, your employer might have paid for the test in advance by purchasing a voucher from Sylvan Prometric. If this is the case, you need only present the voucher number when contacting Sylvan to complete the payment.

Once you have paid for the test, you can schedule your test date. If you are paying by check, you will need to call back once the funds have been verified. If you are paying by voucher or credit card, you can schedule your test at the same time you make payment. If you have any need to change the date of the test or cancel it, you can do so by contacting Sylvan at least one business day prior to the test. If you do not do so, you automatically forfeit your payment.

Sylvan operates almost 2,000 testing centers worldwide and their registrars will help you schedule the test at the most convenient location. If this is the first time you will be registering for an exam provided by Sylvan, the registrar will create an electronic file with your information, including the testing center closest to you. Then, as you register for tests in the future, this file will eliminate the need to gather the data each time. If you have taken tests such as the A + certification tests from Sylvan previously, this file has already been created. Once your information is on file with Sylvan, you may be able to use Sylvan's new on-line registration system at their test registration web site (**www.2test.com**) to register for other certification tests (see Figure 1.5). As of the publication of this book, online registration is not available for Network + certification. Sylvan has said that it will be available in the near future.

Preparing for the Test

The main goal of this book is to help you prepare for the Network + certification test. In addition to the chapters in this book that explain the Network + program, several chapters (4–7) concentrate specifically on the test and how to pass it.

Chapter 4 explains in detail the 15 categories of skills you will be tested on. Chapter 5 provides detailed information on the blueprint developed by CompTIA for the Network + test, and is therefore the chapter with the most information about the content of the test. Chapter 6 gives direction on where to find more information on skill sets you feel you need to study before the test. Chapter 6 also explains the best ways to prepare for the test and gives useful tips on creating a personal study plan. Chapter 7 provides a chance to assess your skills with a pre- and post-assessment test.

How much you need to study to pass the Network + certification test depends primarily on the amount of time you have spent in the networking industry. The test was geared for networking professionals with 18–24 months' experience and A + certification. If you have been in the networking profession for a long time, you may not need to do much study or preparation. If you are relatively new in the field or have not worked in a variety of positions, you might find it useful to study the suggested materials in Chapter 6.

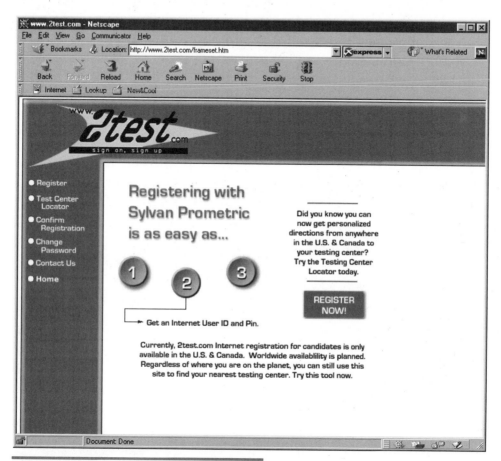

FIGURE 1.5 Sylvan's online registration web site

Because the Network + certification is meant to show a certain level of experience and expertise in the networking industry and not just an ability to study a specific set of course materials and pass an exam, you may find resources that will help you prepare and hone your experience in many different places. Although formal training specifically for the Network + certification has not been announced, it is likely to become available, as A + certification training has. According to CompTIA, several companies are working on material and courses to help prepare for the exam. Check

CompTIA's web site periodically for a list of these companies (see Figure 1.6). Many other courses that contain relevant information are available, even though they are not being identified as applicable for Network+ training. Novell's Course 565: Networking Technologies and Microsoft's Course 578: Networking Essentials and Course 1254: Microsoft Certified Systems Engineer Core Requirements Self-Paced Training Kit are all good examples of the courses and self-paced training available.

It is important to note that most people preparing for the test will need to study many hours and will need to identify and work on areas of weakness in the skills tested in the Network+ certification test. Read and follow the suggestions for setting a personal study plan in Chapter 6 and make sure you come to the test prepared.

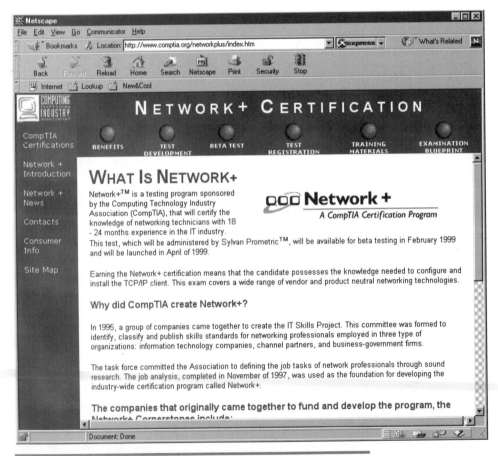

FIGURE 1.6 CompTIA's current information on Network+ certification.

Taking the Test

After you have prepared and registered for the test, you will be ready to take it. Once you are at the Sylvan testing center, the following will be required:

❖ You must show two forms of identification before beginning the test. One must be a photo ID. For example, you could bring your driver's license, passport, student identification, work identification, Social Security card, major credit card, or other form of identification.
❖ You must sign in and out of the log book.
❖ During the test, books, calculators, computers, notepads, or reference materials are not allowed. You will not need pens or pencils because the test is computer-based.

In addition, Sylvan provides the following during the test period:

❖ Proctors will provide you with a dry erase pad or scratch paper that is collected and destroyed after each test.
❖ Proctors actively monitor you during the test. Any suspicious behavior is immediately reported.
❖ Testing software is equipped with question-by-question backup so a test can restart from the point of the interruption if there is a power outage or system failure.

To ensure a good test experience, arrive early to sign in, get settled, and take the online tutorial to familiarize yourself with the types of questions you might be asked on the test. Understanding how the questions will be presented will eliminate much of your test anxiety.

The Network + certification test will take approximately 11/2 hours to complete and will contain approximately 80 questions. These questions will be multiple choice. Most of the questions will have four answers to choose from. If more than one right answer is needed, you will be prompted to choose two or more correct answers. A few number of questions will include graphics.

After the Test

Once you have completed the test, you will see your test results on-screen and will be given a printed copy of the score report. Make sure that the printed copy has been embossed by the test center to indicate that it is an official score report. The report has two pages: a Testing Fee Reimbursement Form and a report of test results. The Testing Fee Reimbursement Form can be used to obtain reimbursement from your employer. The score report shows the score needed to pass the test and your score. It also shows the percentage of questions you answered correctly in each section. The report does not give details about the specific questions you missed.

Once you have taken your test, the test results are sent electronically to CompTIA. No one else sees the results of your test. If you have passed the test, you will be issued a Network+ certificate in two to three weeks. You will also receive a wallet-sized card showing that you are Network+ certified and you are eligible to add the Network+ logo to your business cards. Contact CompTIA about the specific guidelines for using this logo.

If you do not pass the test, you can register to take it again. You can take the Network+ test as many times as necessary. There is no required waiting period before you can retake the test. However, if you did not pass the exam, you will want to study rigorously so that you pass on the second attempt. Use the report you received to gauge the areas on which you should concentrate when studying for the next test. If you have a chance, make notes before leaving the testing center on which questions seemed to give or areas you had trouble in during the test. Doing this during the test might be viewed as "suspicious behavior." Besides, all scratch paper used during the test generally has to be handed in after the test. (Testing centers and test developers don't want individuals copying down test questions and answers to give to someone else later.)

If you find that you missed many questions in one area, refocus your study efforts and look at this first test as a practice run. Use the information in Chapters 4, 5, 6, and 7 to refocus your preparation efforts. If you study well, you will be prepared the next time you take the test.

Once you have earned your Network+ certification, your status in the networking profession increases. Because you have proved your skills in the areas of networking technology and in the practices considered most important by the top companies and organizations, you have proved your value as a networking professional to your customers, employer, future employer, and yourself.

Understanding the value of your Network+ certification and the role it plays in the networking market is important. Chapter 2 explains the most recent trends in the IT industry and discusses where the jobs will be and who will be ready for those jobs. In Chapter 3 you will discover the value of your certification and how it works with other certification programs. This chapter also discusses where the networking technology field is headed today and the trends in IT hiring practices.

Web Sites to Visit

Web Sites for More Test Information

CompTIA—**www.comptia.org**

Sylvan Prometric online registration system—**www.2test.com**

Web Sites of Network+ Cornerstone Partners and Supporters

Compaq—**www.compaq.com**

Computerworld—**www.computerworld.com**

DataTrain—**www.datatrain.com**

Digital Equipment Corp.—**www.digital.com** (Digital and Compaq recently merged. Information about Digital is listed at both web sites)

Fluke—**www.fluke.com**

Lotus—**www.lotus.com**

Microsoft—**www.microsoft.com**

Novell—**www.novell.com**

U.S. Robotics—**www.3com.com** (U.S. Robotics and 3Com recently merged and their web sites have been centralized)

US West—**www.uswest.com**

Vanstar—**www.vanstar.com**

Web Sites of Industry Associations Supporting Network+

Information Technology Training Association (ITTA)—**www.itta.com**

Network Professional Association (NPA)—**www.npa.com**

Articles to Read on the Web

Jacobs, Paula. "The certification debate: Why do IT pros have such passionate opinions about a few tests?" *InfoWorld* Vol. 20, Issue 42 (Oct. 19, 1998). http://www.infoworld.com/cgi-bin/displayCareers.pl?981019cert.htm

Steen, Margaret. "The training imperative" *InfoWorld* Vol. 20, Issue 25 (June 22, 1998). http://www.infoworld.com/cgi-bin/displayCareers.pl?/features/980622training.htm

Corcoran, Cate T. " Putting skills to the test: Skills assessment can help with hiring, but some are wary" *InfoWorld* Vol. 20, Issue 46 (Nov. 16, 1998). http://www.infoworld.com/cgi-bin/displayCareers.pl?981116test.htm

Bednarz, Ben. "Checking out your computer guru..." *Computer Bits* Vol. 8, Issue 6 (June 1998) http://www.computerbits.com/archive/19980600/biz9806.htm

Violino, Bob. "Third Annual Network/IS Managers' Salary and Job Satisfaction Survey" *Network Computing Online*, http://www.networkcomputing.com/careers/relcert.html

Schnaidt, Patricia. "1997 IS/Network Manager Salary Survey" Network Computing Online, Feb. 1,1997 http://www.networkcomputing.com/802/802f3.html

2

Evaluating Trends in the IT Industry

Rapid changes in the Networking technology field may make it hard to understand where the industry is headed and the role Network + certification plays in the future of the industry. Understanding what is happening in the industry today and the projected trends for the future will help you plan your career. Understanding the role of certification in the industry in general, and the specific role of Network + certification, will help you focus your efforts.

The IT industry is changing to meet the challenges of the Information Age and the dawn of the new Millenium. This is bringing about swift changes in the IT industry. There are new trends in hiring practices and policies as well as new jobs being created due to new technological challenges. This chapter discusses the IT industry, current trends in the industry and how these trends affect you. After reading this chapter, you will understand:

- ❖ The current crisis in the IT industry
- ❖ The US and International outlook for the IT industry
- ❖ Projected hiring trends in the IT industry
- ❖ Job satisfaction among IT professionals
- ❖ Where the IT industry is headed

Looking at the Current Crisis in the IT Industry

The world has been rapidly changing in the past decade. The changes in technology and the transformation of our economic base from goods to information have created an atmosphere much like that of the era of the Industrial Revolution. The information-driven revolution of the late 20th century has created a great demand for workers highly skilled in the use of information technology. For example, employment in the U.S. computer and software industries has almost tripled in the last 10 years, and the demand for people skilled in any aspect of technology is not limited to any one industry. It cuts across all areas—manufacturing and services, transportation, health care, education and government. If you can create, apply or use information technology, you skills are in demand.

Information technologies are the most important technologies in the economy today. Approximately 70 percent of the U.S. GDP (Gross Domestic Product), is increasingly information-technology intensive. A shortage of IT professionals could undermine U.S. innovation, productivity, and competitiveness in world markets because IT professionals work in almost all fields and industries in the United States.

Computer-based information systems have become an integral part of managing information, workflow, and transactions in both the public and private sectors. Therefore, a shortage of IT professionals directly affects the ability of a company or organization to develop and implement the tools needed to increase productivity and reduce costs.

The demand for qualified IT professionals is especially prevalent in the United States. After creating the Information Revolution, the U.S. is finding it hard to locate enough professionals to fill all the current and projected open positions.

According to U.S. government estimates, job growth in information technology fields now exceeds the number of people entering the field. Between 1994 and 2005, more than a million new computer scientists and engineers, systems analysts, and computer programmers will be required in the United States. That means that an average of 95,000 jobs per year will be created (see Figure 2.1). new IT workers will fill newly created jobs and replace workers who are leaving these fields as a result of retirement, change of profession, or other reasons.

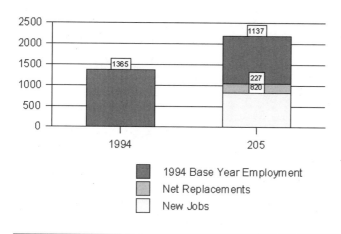

FIGURE 2.1   The projected demand for information technology professionals

In one survey, the Information Technology Association of America (ITAA) estimates that currently there are about 350,000 unfilled IT jobs in the United States today due to a shortage of qualified workers. In another ITAA survey, 50 percent of the information technology company executives surveyed cited the lack of skilled workers as "the most significant barrier" to their companies' growth. These executives viewed the lack of IT professionals as a significantly greater problem than economic conditions, profitability, lack of capital investment, taxes, or regulation.

Surveys by other firms are getting similar results. In a study conducted by Coopers and Lybrand, nearly 50 percent the CEOs of America's fastest growing companies reported that they had inadequate numbers of information technology workers to staff their operations. A survey by Deloitte & Touche Consulting reported that shortages in IT professionals cause many companies to delay information technology projects.

Some of these surveys also point out that as competition for IT professionals increases, rising salary levels increase the cost of doing business. Electronic Data Systems Corporation (EDS) reported that shortages in IT professionals have helped drive up workers' compensation rates by 15 to 20 percent annually. This added cost of doing business must be paid for somehow, so it is often passed on to the consumer, or is offset by layoffs of nonessential, nontechnical personnel.

The U.S. Information Technology Industry Outlook

If you are an IT professional or are considering entering the field, you'll be interested to know that the prospect for all technology professions in the U.S. is good. Across all sectors of business and government, increases in the number of positions available to IT professionals are expected.

Of all industries, the service sector—not including transportation, communications, finance, insurance, real estate, and wholesale and retail trade—is expected to need the most new IT professionals. According to a recent report by the Department of Commerce, the service sector is expected to increase its employment of technology-related professionals by as much as 158 percent. Estimates indicate that positions for computer scientists and engineers will increase by 14 percent, and that by the year 2005, positions for computer programmers will increase by 37 percent.

The most growth in job prospects will come in the field of what the U.S. Department of Commerce termed systems analysis with a growth rate of 158 percent (see Figure 2.2). According to the government's study, a systems analyst (SA) uses his or her "knowledge and skills in a problem solving capacity, implementing the means for computer technology to meet the individual needs of an organization."

In other words, the studies show that the most growth will be in jobs where IT professionals can help companies implement technology and get connected. To do this, these professionals will have to possess a basic understanding of networking because their jobs may include designing entirely new systems, including both hardware and software, or adding a single new software application to harness more of the computer's power.

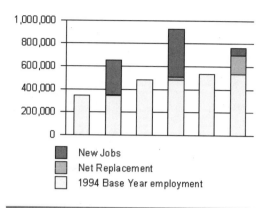

FIGURE 2.2   Projected growth in IT professions

For example, a systems analyst might be called in to help design a new technology infrastructure when two companies with disparate systems, technologies, and practices merge. The systems analyst uses technological knowledge, understanding of networking, and knowledge of business processes to integrate the two companies technologically. This may be as simple as implementing a new software program, or it may require a new network setup.

Or, a systems analyst may help a small company understand various possible technologies and choose the best hardware and software to meet the company's goals at the greatest cost savings. In short, systems analysts will be some of the most important people in the Information Revolution because they will help organizations realize the maximum benefit from investment in equipment, personnel, and business processes.

Private industry is coming up with essentially the same picture of the IT market described in government studies. According to the nation's chief information officers (CIOs), there will be continued strength in the hiring of IT professionals.

In the most recent RHI Consulting Quarterly Information Technology Hiring Index, 26 percent of executives plan to hire additional IT personnel in the next three months while just 2 percent anticipate staff reductions. Seventy-one percent of CIOs plan to maintain their current personnel levels, up from 66 percent in the third-quarter survey (see Figure 2.3).

The Hiring index is an excellent indicator of national trends because it is not based solely on one region. It includes responses from 1,400 CIOs from a random sample of U.S. companies with 100 or more employees. As you can tell from Figure 2.4, although hiring trends vary slightly from region to region, there is a greater than 20 percent increase in hiring across the entire U.S. with a national average of 27 percent.

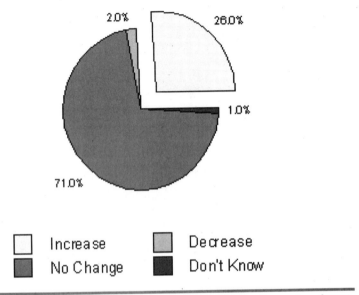

FIGURE 2.3   Projected hiring activities for the fourth quarter of 1998.

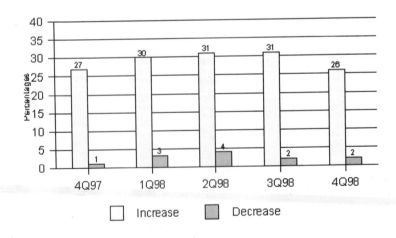

FIGURE 2.4   Quarterly hiring figures

According to Greg Scileppi, executive director of RHI Consulting, "Information technology staffing levels remain high throughout the nation as companies continue to aggressively pursue mission-critical projects, such as systems conversions and Internet enhancements, which cannot be delayed if firms are to stay competitive." He continues, "While the projected pace of hiring is more moderate as technology executives keep an eye on the world's financial markets, the overall atmosphere is one of continued optimism. Demand for networking professionals, database experts, Web developers and other IT specialists is particularly strong." The hiring trend is especially noticeable in the New England states, where there was a 32 percent projected increase in hiring in the fourth quarter of 1998 (see Figure 2.5).

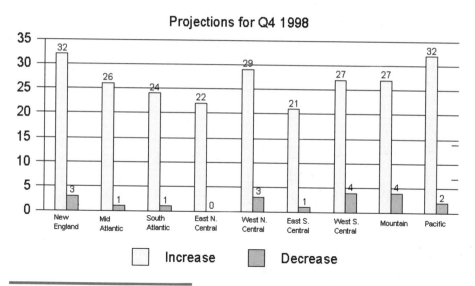

FIGURE 2.5   Hiring index by region

Even with the potential for a downturn in the U.S. economy, Scileppi feels that the "the overall atmosphere is one of continued optimism." Paul Vornbaum, president of Trattner Network, a staffing unit of Norrell, agrees. "There is a shortage of people to do the work, and I see that shortage continuing." Increases in hiring are occurring across all industries including manufacturing (32 percent); professional services (26 percent); retail (25 percent); wholesale (17 percent); finance, insurance and real estate (47 percent); business services(40 percent); transportation (13 percent); and construction (13 percent); (see Figure 2.6).

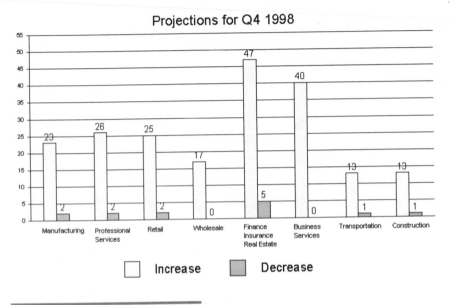

FIGURE 2.6 Hiring index by industry

The International Information Technology Industry Outlook

The shortage of IT professionals is not confined within the borders of the United States. There is a worldwide shortage of IT professionals and industries in other nations are facing problems similar to those faced by their U.S. counterparts. Because other countries are in need of IT professionals, the U.S. cannot solve the lack of IT professionals through increased immigration or foreign outsourcing. It must retain and update the skills of today's IT professionals as well as educate and train new ones.

The European Information Technology Observatory estimates there are 600,000 unfilled jobs in the Information Technology industry worldwide. The Giga Information Group reports that 10 percent of all IT jobs in Europe are never filled.

A 1998 study by International Data Corporation (IDC) and Microsoft unveiled the growing crisis in technology skills in Europe. They estimate that by the end of 1998 there will be 510,000 unfilled jobs in the technology sector in Europe growing to 1.6 million by 2002. According to the study, European businesses are experiencing:

❖ Rising costs due to the shortage in the supply of relevant skills. According to IDC, wages for technical staff during the 12 month period prior to the study increased from 12 percent to as much as 60 percent

❖ Deferred projects due to a lack of resources to implement and manage projects. These indefinite deferrals occur even though they may reduce the organization's competitiveness in the wired marketplace

❖ Poorer overall employee productivity since almost two-thirds of the tasks performed by IT professionals help other employees effectively capitalize on the power of existing IT resources. The lack of trained IT professionals means users are not achieving full productivity gains and businesses are not as competitive as possible with even their existing IT investment.

❖ Increased offshore resourcing as a means to tackle the shortage in skilled professionals. Companies either import personnel on a contract basis or by actually performing projects remotely with contact maintained by communications links.

All of these factors will have a significant impact on Europe's ability to compete in a world where the effective use of IT investment is a growing factor in the competitiveness of business.

Puni Rajah, Director of Services Research, International Data Corporation states that "the most consistent topic of discussion in the IT industry in recent months has been the shortage of necessary skills to manage existing and implement new, IT solutions. Maintenance issues like Year 2000 readiness and accommodating the Euro continue to gather momentum and soak up more and more scarce IT skills. In the meantime the innovative IT solutions designed to take advantage of technology investment and maintain long term competitiveness are being stopped or pushed back by all but the most visionary of organizations. This will significantly affect the competitiveness of European businesses in the global marketplace."

Bernard Vergnes, Chairman, Microsoft Europe, Middle East and Africa further comments that "the IT industry in Europe is a significant employer. According to this research, in 1997 the in-house IT industry alone employed

8.3 million people in Europe. The very positive impact that IT is having on businesses' ability to compete and be successful is growing the demand rapidly." Vergnes feels that Europe has the potential to employ over 12.2 million people by 2002. However, the lack of trained and certified professionals may hinder the increased success of Europe.

A Bright Future in Information Technology

The future of those in IT careers—specifically those in networking-related jobs—is very promising. But IT was not always a profession of choice. Several years ago, networking was a career that most people fell into by accident. You never heard children saying, "When I grow up, I want to be a networking professional." Over the years, the perception and the direction of the technology industry has changed drastically. With the age of information and the onset of the Internet generation, more and more people across the globe are networked to each other. Business, industry, and the private sector are now so interconnected that they depend on networking professionals to keep them safe in the web of today's interconnected world. As you can see in Figure 2.7, this has created a steady need for IT professionals over the past three decades.

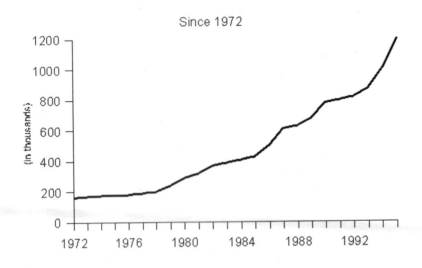

FIGURE 2.7 Employment trend in the IT industry since 1972

A Shortage Means Better Salaries, Bonuses, and Benefits

As a result of all the technological advances in the recent decade, a shortage in IT professionals plagues government and the private sector. The strongest evidence that a shortage exists is the dramatic rise in salaries. A survey conducted by William M. Mercer showed that average hourly compensation for operating systems/software architects and consultants rose nearly 20 percent from 1995 to 1996. In comparison with salary increases in other industries, these increases are quite significant.

For the same time frame, Computerworld's annual survey found that in 11 of 26 positions tracked, average salaries increased more than 10 percent from 1996 to 1997. For example, systems analysts' salaries were up 15 percent, programmer/analysts' salaries were up 11 percent, and directors of systems development received an average increase of 10 percent.

According to a 1997 CIO Institute survey of 1,599 system administrators and security professionals, the demand for network administrators and professionals has consistently outpaced supply in recent years. This has caused salaries for networking professionals to increase at an average of 14 percent.

TABLE 2.1 1997 Salary Average Increase

Range Increase	percent
$20,000 to $29,999	10.33 percent
$30,000 to $39,999	15.99 percent
$40,000 to $49,999	15.72 percent
$50,000 to $59,999	10.87 percent
$60,000 to $69,999	10.25 percent
$70,000 to $79,999	20.94 percent
$80,000 to $89,999	12.77 percent
$90,000 to $99,999	17.12 percent
$100,000 and more	16.13 percent

According to the 1998 *Info World* compensation survey, the trend toward large salary increases seems to have continued in 1998. The report had excellent news for networking professionals—the biggest increases in salaries. The average salary before taxes (excluding bonuses) for these professionals showed an average salary increase of almost 10 percent (see Table 2.2).

TABLE 2.2 Salaries for Networking Professionals Excluding Bonuses

Position	Average Salary
Vice president/director of networking	$80,633
Senior management average	$86,445
Network manager	$53,228
Middle management average	$64,428
Network/systems administrator	$52,450
Staff average	$55,203

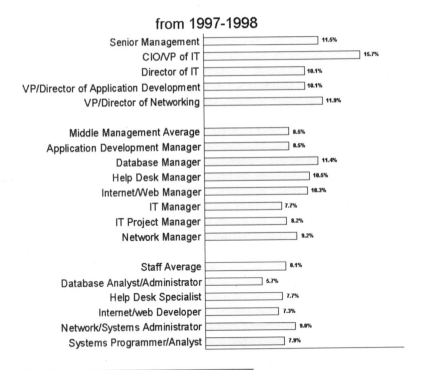

FIGURE 2.8 Average salary increases in 1998

The 1998 InfoWorld compensation survey included responses from 2,257 IT professionals across the market. The vast majority of respondents indicated salary increases. These IT professionals also indicated that in addition to salary increases, they received various types of bonuses (see Figure 2.9) that made their profession even more lucrative, including:

❖ Profit sharing
❖ Personal performance
❖ Certification

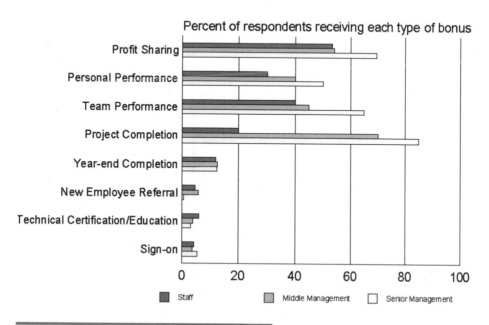

FIGURE 2.9   Bonuses available to IT professionals

In the IT industry, longevity counts (see Figure 2.10). IT professionals who have been in the business for a long time are compensated for their experience. For example, a staff IT professional not in management receives an average salary of $45,092 for up to 5 years' experience. The salary for the same IT professional increases by over $16,000 to an average of $61,000 in approximately 10 years. That is an increase of $1,600 a year. And as the demand for IT professionals increases, this rate of increase will probably also rise.

Satisfaction in the IT Industry is High

Financial reward alone is not the only bright spot for an IT professional. Recent surveys show that IT professionals are extremely happy with their careers whether they fell into them by accident or chose them. According to a survey conducted by Beyond Computing, 98 percent of IT professionals are

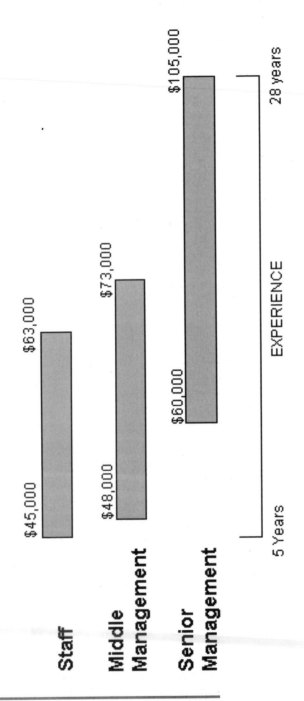

FIGURE 2.10 IT professionals are paid for their experience

happy in their chosen careers. These professionals plan to stay in the IT industry. Over 80 percent of respondents indicated that they do not see themselves changing professions any time soon (see Figures 2.11 and 2.12). Those are phenomenal statistics for industry, but particularly for a computer-related industry as job-changing has long been a customary way in this industry to obtain promotions, higher salaries, and better benefits.

FIGURE 2.11 Career satisfaction

Other studies show that even when salaries are good, if people are not satisfied with their jobs, they leave to find other employment. Few other industries can boast of such levels of satisfaction with career choice.

According to InfoWorld's 1998 compensation survey, IT professionals, for the most part, feel that their compensation and benefits are fair. Approximately 58 percent of respondents not in management positions said that they were fairly compensated. These employees are receiving yearly salary increases, raises for job performance, and personal performance bonuses. In addition to these salary-based compensations, IT professionals receive 401K contribution matches and stock plan options. They also have flexible work hours and other benefits which contribute to overall quality of life.

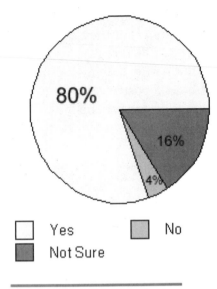

FIGURE 2.12 Future career plans

The Importance of IT Professionals in the Future

We are surrounded by technology that changes our lives and our percep-tions. Technologies such as the latest computer games and computer-gener-ated animation in blockbuster films can bring a new dimension to entertainment and even education. You can now learn to fly one of several types of planes at any of thousands of airports across the U.S. You can shop online and buy books over the Internet or sit in your living room and gaze at the surface of Mars.

There are no signs that the economy's reliance on IT will end any time soon. Even though the information industry barely existed just decades ago, the com-munications and information industries now constitute about 10 percent of U.S. gross domestic product and employ more than 4.5 million people in the United States. According to the U.S. Government "The economic importance of these technologies extends beyond the borders of the communications and informa-tion industries. By making it possible to manage vast quantities of information, these technologies are transforming every sector of our economy—manufacturing and services, transportation, health care, education, and government–and, in the process, changing forever the way people live, work, and interact with one another."

The U.S. Department of Commerce reports that "Technical progress is the single most important factor in generating sustained economic growth, estimated to account for as much as half the Nation's long-term growth over the past 50 years. Technology underpins our fastest growing industries and high-wage jobs, provides the tools needed to compete in every business today, and drives growth in every major industrialized nation."

Today, technological leadership often means the difference between success and failure in the global marketplace—for companies and countries alike. The U.S. Government estimates that technology and advances in knowledge account for approximately 80 percent of growth in the U.S. economy.

You might be concerned that the spotlight on information technology means there soon will be too many people in the field. This is reasonable concern, but there are factors beyond the control of most companies that are drastically driving the need for IT professionals and the specific knowledge they have. Some of those factors are Internet commerce, telecommunications, and the Year 2000 computer bug.

Internet commerce and the growth of the Web in general means more people are networked than ever before. These people need professionals to help them get connected to the electronic world. By the year 2000, over 500 million people, or almost 9 percent of the world's population, will have Internet access. Although currently most people go online primarily to gather information and news, use e-mail, or conduct research, these people are also using the Web to purchase. The growth of the Internet is explosive both within the U.S. and internationally (see Figure 2.13).

A study sponsored by several Fortune 500 companies found that although 97 percent of people logging on to the Internet are doing so to become a more educated consumers. Of these people, 81 percent use the Internet for comparison shopping, and after viewing a Web site or online ad, 46 percent still purchase the products they researched in a store, but 36 percent purchase the product online.

These statistics indicate that there is a huge market for companies who have a Web presence. For example, in 1998, online retail sales during the holidays were around $7 billion for the season. It also means that companies never really thought of as technology-oriented will have to create a Web presence to remain competitive and continue to grow.

Telecommunications and greater integration with the network will continue to provide more access to more people and create a greater global network. That global network will need more and more professionals to run it. If you need proof, just look at the industry in 1998. It is an excellent example of how the telecommunications world and the networking world are increasingly coming together into one.

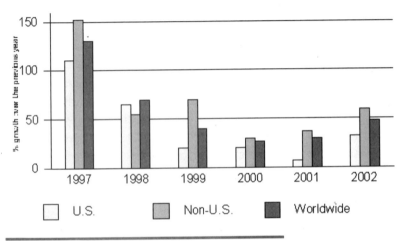

FIGURE 2.13 The international growth of the Internet

AT&T Corp. acquired IBM's Global Network in order to give its AT&T Solutions Inc. network outsourcing unit an immediate opportunity to diversify. It now has the opportunity to provide services such as electronic commerce, Internet access, and SNA management.

In 1998, WorldCom Inc. acquired MCI Communications Corp. to create another telecommunications networking giant. Also, Nortel Networks acquired Bay Networks Inc. to handle data and voice traffic over LANs, WANs and carrier backbones.

The Year 2000 and the problems inherent in updating and replacing legacy computer code in the 21st century provide another good example of the importance of qualified IT professionals. Some of the most important computer software used in industry and government may not work correctly starting in the year 2000 because much of the specialty software running on today's systems was developed to recognize only two-digit dates that represent the year. This means that these computers may not recognize a change to the new century and, thus, may generate erroneous data in a wide range of computer activities, such as financial transactions, logistics, production, and communications.

Although the task to make the needed corrections seems simple, it is not as easy as it sounds, nor is it inexpensive to fix the problem. Industry experts estimate that it may cost as much as $600 billion worldwide to fix the problem. In order to stave off the inevitable difficulties that will occur if the cause is not corrected soon enough (not to mention staving off the lawsuits which will become a reality if the problems aren't corrected), much of the current workforce has been diverted to correct the so-called Year 2000 problem. In 1998, 78 percent of IT executives said that Year 2000 compliance had a moderate to high impact on the rest of their projects (see Figure 2.14).

The Year 2000 problem may even have increased the employment shortage because professionals who previously filled other roles are now concentrating on keeping their companies up and running in the new millennium. As older systems are replaced, a reasonable alternative to fixing the older systems to prevent Y2K complications, the demand for professionals who can run these new systems also increases.

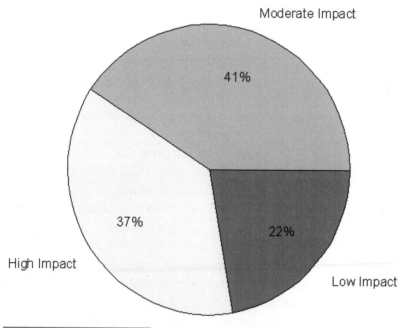

FIGURE 2.14 Impact of Y2K

These same IT executives said they expect that the sharp rise in IT spending due to the Year 2000 problem will not decline after 2000. Of these executives, 50 percent said that they expect their budgets to remain the same, while 35 percent said that they expect their budgets to increase after the Year 2000 work is completed. (After all, the work they are setting aside now so they can deal with Y2K has not gone away. It has just been pushed back into a new budgeting year.)

These three factors alone will generate hundreds of thousands of jobs on top of those jobs created by the move to the Information Age. There is no sign of slowing in the need for IT professionals who grasp the importance of information in today's world and who can help companies, schools, and governments get where they need to go.

Information Technology and Business

In the last 10–15 years, businesses have become increasingly reliant on computer technology to do everything from write a simple letter to automate entire industrial operations. As the reliance on computers grew, so did the need to connect and share the functions of these computers. The result has been the birth of networking and the creation of the networking profession.

Today, businesses share data, concepts, and practices across the company and between companies. For example, the Cox newspaper corporation, which operates several large daily newspapers including the *Atlanta Journal and Constitution,* uses the power of the network to share stories and special features between its newspapers. During the 1996 Olympics in Atlanta, Cox newspapers all over the country were able to use the same special sections originally created for the Atlanta audience because all of the Cox newspapers are networked. This gave readers in other cities, whose newspapers did not have the manpower or the money to report on the Games first-hand, the opportunity to read excellent reporting on an exciting event without the expense of additional on-site reporters.

Networking has created an entirely new way to do business and generate revenue in all sectors. This has resulted in benefits to the companies who take advantage of it, as well as to the companies' employees and customers.

A recent Department of Commerce report showed that companies which use advanced technologies are more productive and profitable than those which don't. The report also shows that it is not only the large industries that are benefiting from technology. Technology is transforming the very basis of competition. Small businesses can now perform high-quality design and manufacturing work that previously required resources that only large businesses possessed.

For example, one engineer working from a networked office in his home can bid on jobs once dominated by large engineering firms. Because of the technology at his fingertips, he can generate proposals and plans that have no less quality than those presented by large firms. If necessary, he can connect to other individuals and form a team using technologies such as e-mail, voice mail, video conferencing, networking, and the Internet to provide all the services his client needs. You can see how technology has led to increases in small business ownership and entrepreneurship.

It is not just the companies and entrepreneurs who are benefiting from technology, however. Employees and customers benefit as well. This same Department of Commerce report notes that in plants that take advantage of these advanced technologies, employment grew 14.4 percent more than in plants that did not use advanced technologies. In addition, production workers' wages were more than 14 percent higher.

This new flexibility for small businesses is occurring at the same time that technology is allowing big businesses to achieve the speed, flexibility, and closeness to customers that were once only possible with smaller companies. Companies are reaching out to customers through the Internet. You can now have an online chat with corporate executives and specialists, or you can get answers or order specific parts direct from the manufacturer.

Technology and the National Defense

One of the greatest ways technology is changing our lives is on the battlefield. The U.S. military uses a wide variety of technologies. Many times, technology can give the U.S. a decisive edge. In recent skirmishes in the Middle East, the U.S. strength in technology allowed the U.S. and other countries to keep troop casualties to a minimum. Whether or not you agree with the U.S. foreign policy toward countries that are considered world threats, it is impressive to see what technology has done to change the face of war. Some of these changes are positive, like the ability to strike targets with increasing accuracy and thus better limit and control the number of civilian casualties.

We cannot ignore the fact that other aspects of the reliance on technology may not be positive, but the U.S. military has no plans to change its increasing reliance on technology as the weapon of choice. According to the U.S. Government, "America's technological superiority has provided our men and women in uniform the wherewithal to protect the freedom, democracy, and security of the United States."

Technology and Quality of Life

Technological advances are improving our quality of life in many ways. They are enhancing communications, making foods safer and better, and facilitating cleaner, safer, more fuel-efficient transportation. Technological advances have also brought drugs and medical therapies that promise new hope for the sick and a healthier life for all. Medical research has resulted in the development of new pharmaceuticals, the advancement of biotechnology, and the creation of medical devices, each of which helps to contribute to less disease and suffering, and in many instances extend the quality and length of individuals' lives.

With the help of technology, environmental research promises cleaner air, water, and soil. Advanced monitoring and forecasting technologies—from satellites to simulation—are helping save lives and minimize property damage caused by hurricanes, blizzards, tornadoes, and other severe weather. The National Hurricane Center uses mathematical computer models to forecast the future motion and intensity of a hurricane. Hurricane forecasters interpret the models to figure out the path the hurricane will take and how intense it will be. Because of advances in information technology and the power of computer processors, the models have improved greatly and forecasts have become more accurate. Based upon this data, public advisories are issued and often, people are evacuated before the wrath of the hurricane is even visible.

Technological advances in agricultural research are producing safer, healthier, and tastier food products that can feed the world's growing population.

Advances in automobile research provide safer, cleaner, more energy-efficient, and more intelligent vehicles. These new cars are saving lives, preserving natural resources, keeping our environment cleaner, and even helping people protect their cars from theft.

You can now purchase a car with the same satellite tracking system used by the U.S. military. These systems are amazing. Not only can they tell you where you are on the earth, but if you are in an emergency, you can ask for roadside assistance. These devices can even keep your car from getting stolen. In a recent car-jacking in Salt Lake City, Utah, a man's car was recovered after being stolen because the global positioning system was able to turn the engine off remotely and bring the thief to a halt.

People across town and across the world are benefiting from today's technological advances in many different ways:

❖ People have become more interconnected. In offices, employees have access to files and devices that can be shared through the network.

Companies save money on equipment and employees have greater access to the tools and information they need to move ahead.

❖ Outside of business, people are becoming more interconnected and the world is shrinking. Families distanced by thousands of miles can share e-mail, photos, and even video and voice through the power of the networked world.

❖ The network crosses political boundaries and racial lines to create a connected world.

❖ Information and telecommunications technologies have enabled instantaneous communications across the globe, allowing employees to telecommute. By eliminating the physical commuting time many employees often face, technology allows many people to spend more time with their families.

New technologies also have the potential to increase our learning opportunities and enrich the learning experience. These technologies provide students with never-before-imagined access to information and tools such as multimedia electronic libraries and museums containing text, images, video, music, instructional software, and simulations.

President Clinton challenged the nation to connect every classroom to the information superhighway by the year 2000 and to provide computers, good software, and well-trained teachers. With this access, students will be able to enter the world beyond the classroom and have access to the best teachers and tools, no matter where in the world they may be located.

However, behind all these technological advances in business, defense, and personal life, there must be someone to make sure the network and the technology are running well. That is the role of the IT professional. Without IT professionals, the Information Age becomes a nightmare of stress and anxiety as non-professionals struggle to keep up with the changing world.

Where the IT Industry is Headed Today

All of this interconnectedness has created a shortage in qualified networking professionals. As people rush to become interconnected, they are often left without the skills and knowledge to do it themselves and they rely heavily on networking professionals with the ability successfully to create the networks they need.

According to a 1998 study by the ITAA, about 350,000 IT jobs remain unfilled because of a lack of skilled workers. To help deal with this shortage of labor, the study showed that 88 percent of 532 companies surveyed retrain existing staff, 40 percent hire immigrants to the U.S., and 16 percent outsource to non-U.S. contractors. Companies are training new and existing employees to make sure the staff has the needed skills. For example, Claremont Technology Group, Inc., a $90 million systems integration company in Beaverton, OR, recently doubled its IT training budget from 2.5 percent to 5 percent of revenue, or about $4.5 million annually.

The situation in the IT industry has not been overlooked by the government either. In the next 10 years, the U.S. Labor Department estimates that another 1.3 million workers will be needed to fill new high-tech jobs. To ease the shortage, the Labor Department has plans to distribute:

❖ $3 million in grants to retrain laid-off workers as programmers
❖ Another $8 million to build an online recruiting site where employers and candidates can post job openings and resumes.

In addition, the Commerce Department will add an additional $17 million to bring technology and training to the poor. And finally, $6 million in government grants will be directed to industry groups that run company internship programs and vocational training for young people.

All of this technological growth and interest in the IT industry has lead to the further development of the networking profession, the continued increase in salaries, and greater levels of respect in the workplace. According to industry experts, job prospects in the field of networking are outstanding. The 1999 RHI Salary Guide, which provides extensive data on salaries and hiring factors in the IT industry to business and government and is frequently used to set compensation levels for employees, shows that the hottest jobs in the coming year will be in networking. The Hot Jobs survey included responses from 1,400 chief information officers in the U.S. and 15 in Canada and showed that networking professionals are in demand across all industries due to the need for companies to create and upgrade their networks (see Figure 2.15).

According to the 1999 Salary Guide, "IT professionals are in strong demand to help firms maintain and expand network infrastructures. Networking skills are also required to incorporate information from company databases, troubleshoot technical problems and train end users on the network."

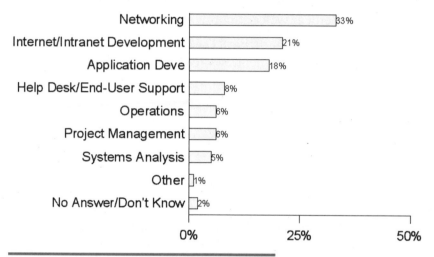

FIGURE 2.15   Information technology's hottest jobs

No matter what you read, whom you survey, or where you look, you cannot help but notice the evidence of the technological revolution all around us. You can see it in the statistics of the U.S. GDP which shows that 70 percent of our gross domestic product is increasingly information technology-intensive. You can hear it in the complaints and statements of CEOs, COOs, and other corporate executives who are desperately searching for enough qualified IT professionals to fill the 350,000 unfilled IT jobs in the U.S. today, and the 90,000 IT jobs expected to be created each year until 2005. If you are an IT professional, you can see it in your annual pay raises, and offers of a variety of bonuses. If you are a recruiter, trainer, or consultant, you can see it in the increasing numbers of open positions to be filled, the percentage of individuals who are almost immediately hired after obtaining an IT certification, and the number of companies seeking you out to do technology consulting for them. Yes. The proof of the need is there. Prospects for the IT industry and networking technology professionals has never been greater.

If you are thinking about certification so that you can help fill the need for certified, experienced, capable IT professionals, then you should read Chapter 3. It will help you determine what the payback can be if you do choose to obtain your Network + Certification.

Articles to Read on the Web

1998 InfoWorld Compensation Survey. http://www.infoworld.com/cgi-bin/displayCareers.pl?98entcar.welcome.htm

"IDC/Microsoft research shows 1.6m critical IT jobs unfilled in Europe by 2002 - 12 percent of the total requirement" Microsoft Web Site (Sept. 22, 1998). http://www.microsoft.com/presspass/features/923idcresearch.htm

America's New Deficit: The Shortage of Information Technology Workers U.S. Department of Commerce Office of Technology Policy. http://www.ta.doc.gov/Reports.htm#USTPS

Technology in the National Interest. U.S. Department of Commerce Office of Technology Policy. http://www.ta.doc.gov/Reports.htm#USTPS

Earls, Alan R., "Certification and the bottom line" *Computerworld* (Apr. 13, 1998). http://www.computerworld.com/home/print.nsf/all/98041341A2

ITAA

"A Call to Action: ITAA's Efforts to Address the Information Technology Skills Gap." http://www.itaa.org/workforce/resources/gwi.htm

"Building the 21st Century Information Technology Workforce: Upgrading the IT Skills of the Current Workforce." http://www.itaa.org/workforce/studies/upgrade.htm

"ITAA Workforce Study." http://www.itaa.org/workforce/studies/hw98.htm

RHI

RHI Consulting Quarterly Information Technology Hiring Index. http://www.rhic.com/jobsRHIC/career/resourcesf.html

3

Valuing Your Network+ Certification

Studies and the statistics they provide have shown us that the trend toward strong growth in the IT profession exists. In fact, studies referenced in Chapter 2, have shown that information technologies are the most important technologies in the economy today, accounting for approximately 70 percent of the U.S. gross domestic product. In addition, studies such as those reported in the most recent issue of the RHI Consulting Quarterly Information Technology Hiring Index seem to indicate that, even while other professions are cutting back on the number of employees, clearly a quarter of executives surveyed stated that they plan to hire additional IT professionals, while only 2 percent anticipate staff reductions.

It appears that both the industry trend and employers' hiring preferences are moving toward certified IT professionals and away from non-certified IT personnel. This indicates that the Network+ Certification is likely to be a decisive factor in whether you get the job, the desired promotion, the pay raises, the benefits, and all of the other perks that go along with being a valued company professional. However, you need to determine for yourself whether the Network+ Certification is worth your time and investment. You should be better prepared to make that decision after reading this chapter as it is designed to help you understand:

❖ The role of certification in today's job market
❖ The specific benefits of Network+ certification
❖ How Network+ certification relates to other vendor-specific certification programs (like Microsoft's MCSE and Novell's CNE)
❖ How to use Network+ certification to put your career at the forefront of the networking technology industry

Approximately 80 certification programs now test technical competency in areas such as networking, databases, enterprise resource planning (ERP), specific software packages, project management, and the Web. Certification is available both from vendors such as Microsoft or Novell and from industry trade organizations, such as CompTIA.

Although there have been no comprehensive, independent studies of the effectiveness and value of certification, several companies have conducted studies on sections of the IT industry and on specific certification programs.

For example, in studies such as those conducted by International Data Corp. and Southern Illinois University, which compared certified professionals to their non-certified counterparts, the certified professionals were rated more productive than their non-certified counterparts. These studies both examined Microsoft Certified Professionals (MCPs), and found that MCPs:

❖ Handled 30 percent more help desk requests than their non-certified counterparts
❖ Decreased IT department costs to employers by over $2,530 per server, per year
❖ Were rated by 84 percent of employers as being more productive than their non-certified counterparts, at least in their area of certification.

In addition, almost a third of companies with certified employees stated that their certified employees were more productive in all areas, not just in their area of certification. Furthermore, the studies show that certification provides increased professional credibility and earning power, with companies paying an average of 20 percent more to individuals who are certified.

Nancy Lewis, general manager of training and certification at Microsoft, says, "Certification makes the difference. The independent studies reinforce the fact that both managers and IT professionals recognize the benefits of certification. Certification helps ensure that individuals are knowledgeable and have the complete portfolio of skills necessary to perform their jobs. In addition, certification is used by employers as one method for evaluating job candidates."

Rebecca Segal, director of services industry consulting at IDC says that the recent study confirms that companies with certified IT professionals experience greater productivity and lower server downtime. "This translates into significant cost savings to employers, which more than compensates for the training, testing and indirect costs associated with certification. The certification process is a win-win situation for both the employee and the employer."

The IDC study also demonstrates that the costs involved in certifying one employee are recouped in less than a year for a company with approximately 10 servers. A company with at least one certified employee saves over $10,000 in downtime costs per year based on an average 11-server company.

The trend seems to be clear—the IT profession is growing, and demand for IT professionals, specifically those with a proven track record and the certifications to show it, is high. What this means for you and certification is that certification has a definite role in the future of networking, and so do those who choose to acquire professional networking certification.

Certification from the IT Professional Perspective

In today's tight job market, IS professionals with the most sought-after skills may think that certification is not necessary because they possess the skills; since there is a shortage in IT professionals, some ask why they should even bother go through the trouble of getting certified. Certification can be an instant ticket to the best jobs, leading to increases in salary offers by as much as $10,000, according to technical recruiters across the country. That makes certification worth the investment.

If you are thinking of becoming or currently are a consultant, then certification is something you need. It provides a tangible measurement you can use to justify billing rates. Osmundo Ray Fernandez, a Visual Basic consultant at Lucent Technologies, in Elizabeth, NJ sees "certification as a way of enhancing my marketability to both clients and employers. Employers feel more comfortable justifying a consultant's rate to a client or customer when the consultant has the academic background, work experience, and certification to back them up."

Certification goes hand-in-hand with experience. You need to have experience, but you cannot hang your experience on the wall. Certification becomes a visible symbol that you know your stuff. Liz Alexander, director of IS at Gardenburger, Inc. in Portland, Ore., underscores this opinion. "If I'm going to hire a consultant, I would expect to see that they are certified — it's like the Good Housekeeping Seal of Approval."

Certification from the IT Employer Perspective

The most common use of certification tests is to screen potential employees or prospective consultants. "We want an objective assessment and measurement of where a candidate sits among their peers," says Karen Frey, director of recruiting at Ciber, a large information systems consulting company in Englewood, CO. Businesses like certification because it has reduced the number of employees who are terminated for inadequate technical skills. It helps companies better match consultants to projects and makes it possible for a company to bring on less experienced, junior people with the confidence that they can do the job.

Certified employees bring a high level of skill and confidence to a job. Prudential Insurance Company of America, believes that "having highly skilled people really improves the performance of the organization," according to Anthony Costa, vice president of IS. "Certification is a cornerstone of a skilled workforce."

The benefits of certification directly affect the company's bottom line in terms of service costs. Studies have shown that certified professionals, bring cost savings and efficiencies to their organizations.

For example, Rich Dellisante, director of Prudential's IS training and development says "Because we have certified people on our staff, one of our outside service providers has reduced our maintenance charges significantly.

We are hoping some of our other key providers will consider doing the same." Certification and the confidence that a company has competent employees makes a great cost-saving difference.

A 1995 survey conducted by International Data Corp. in Framingham, MA., and sponsored by Drake Prometric, IBM and Microsoft Corp., indicated several positives for companies with certified IS professionals. In particular, the study found that companies that supported certification had server downtime half as long and half as expensive as others'. Costs for certification are usually recouped in less than nine months.

However, there are other ways in which certification has become an important part of business. Employers may find that offering potential employees the opportunity to become certified is an excellent hiring incentive. For companies competing for employees, this may be what they need to attract people to the company (see Figure 3.1).

In several recent articles on the growing need for more networking professionals, employers and employees alike commented that money is rarely the primary reason to take or leave a job. IT professionals are looking for a challenge, a job that lets them grow. These articles often cited training and certification as a way to attract and keep talented networking professionals. "Training lets employees increase their skills and gives employers a more skilled workforce. And for companies that aren't able to compete with the sky-high salaries some IT professionals command, training can help compensate for a lower-than-market salary offer."

Paul Lemberg, principal of Lemberg & Co., in San Diego says, "If you compete with your training benefit, that's smart. Not only are you giving people the benefit they want, you're getting better-quality people."

Mark Moerdler, senior vice president at MDY Advanced Technologies, a networking and systems integration company in Fair Lawn, NJ says that "People get turned on when they hear that there's a lot of training going on in the organization."

Certification from the Perspective of Industry Associations

As a simple Internet search will confirm, more and more associations are offering one or more certifications for IT professionals. Most of these associations will tell you that certification is necessary to protect customers and the profession.

For example, the Association of Certified Web Masters' "Standards for Customer Protection" Internet Web page, the URL for which is http://www.fog.nf.net/acwm/standards.html, displays the following statement:

> As with any unregulated profession, some untrained and inexperience individuals attempt to represent themselves as professionals. The goal of this association is to maximize the benefit to the internet customer by ensuring only the highest quality of professionalism in the delivery of web site design, maintenance and promotion. We authorize only those individuals demonstrating the ability to maintain quality and professionalism in the delivery of theses services.

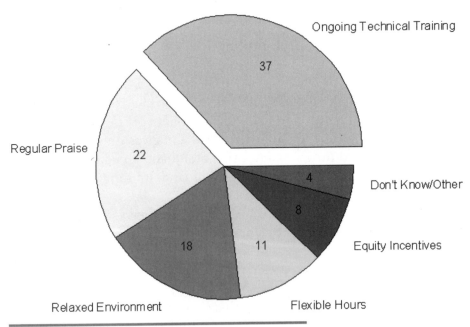

FIGURE 3.1 Effective retention practices (RHI Consulting)

Associations also believe that certification is important enough not only to tout the benefits of certification to its members, but to offer them extra benefits. For example, the Association of Certified Computer Electronics Security Specialists International offers the following benefits to its members. To read this information and related information, see their Web page at **http://home-page.interaccess.com/ ~ accss/app.htm.**

- ❖ Career enhancing Information Security Professional certificate. This distinctive document has been designed to set ISPs apart from uncertified practitioners. Passing the qualifying regimens necessary to reach professional certification represents a valued milestone within this exacting profession.
- ❖ Letters of reference upon request. This one-of-a-kind program offers unparalleled value to members who seek to achieve corporate advancement or expand their employment opportunities. The program is designed to present your professional accomplishments in the most positive of lights, with special emphasis placed upon achieving Information Security Professional certification.
- ❖ Press releases announcing your induction into the Association's professional ranks
- ❖ Registry in the (ISP) section of the International Archive
- ❖ Senior professional status within the ranks of the Association
- ❖ Bona fide credentials that qualify your professional skills.

The Network Professional Association has this to say about their professional certification (see their Web site **http:www.npa.org** for more information about the NPA):

> If you really want to show that you know your stuff (or want to leap ahead in the job market), becoming a Certified Network Professional is your ticket to a better job.
>
> Combining certification from a number of different professional certification programs and adding competency testing of their own, the Network Professional Association's Certified Network Professional is one of the highest and most prestigious certifications anyone in a networking career could have.

After looking at just some of the association Web sites, there's no doubt that various associations strongly believe in certification and its benefits to both the certified professional and the employer.

The Value of Network+ Certification

You need look no further than Wall Street to see the strength in the IT industry in general. Investors are so hungry for technology stocks that a stock can rise from $10 to $150 on the opening day of trading—a trend rarely seen in other industries with the same of regularity.

Investors understand that this is the age of technology and information and the key to this age is controlling the dissemination of this new commodity. Much like the Industrial Revolution, the Information Revolution promises great rewards for those who become involved and provide valuable services.

With the recent resurgence of Novell and the knowledge that the future of networking will most likely be jointly controlled by multiple major companies like Novell, Microsoft, Cisco, and Sun, a vendor-neutral certification is a must. This new multi-platform networking environment is complex, and getting more so. The rate of change in information technology is rapid. This causes frequent changes in skill requirements. Only a few years ago for example, the Internet was a tool used by researchers at American universities. Today the Internet and the World Wide Web are information tools for the masses, driving up the demand for skills needed to create and support online information services. (According to one estimate, 760,000 people are now working at Internet-related companies.) In addition, software makers are constantly under pressure from competition and hardware technology advances to update their programs.

Professionals with a firm grip on the basics of networking technology are better suited to handle the volatile amount of change that can happen when a company upgrades its software or hardware. Having Network+ certification shows that you have the basic networking skills to deal with these changes.

Although certification seems to be the solution to many issues in the IT industry today, it has some drawbacks. One of the main problems with some certification programs is that they can be too expensive. For example, to take the classes and exams for the Microsoft Certified Systems Engineer certification, you could pay between $5,000 and $8,000. Because technology changes so quickly, some programs require further training just to stay current. Those costs add up quickly.

Because much of the certification and training available today comes from vendors who train only on their specific products, the role of vendor-specific certification in strengthening products in the marketplace is also a concern. Critics of vendor-specific certification argue that measurable and transferable industry skills, such as the ones tested in the Network+ certification exam, would be more valuable to IT professionals. These same critics also worry that the emphasis on vendor-specific certification ignores the real value in the ability to learn new technology quickly and apply it across multiple software and hardware configurations.

Network+ Certification from the Perspective of the Networking Professional

Many of today's IT professionals did not enter college with their minds set on their current careers. Instead, these people "accidentally" fell into their careers. Some might have joined the profession out of a love for computing, while others became IT professionals out of necessity. One man, for example, became his college's system administrator while in graduate school because he was teaching technical writing and was fascinated with computers. He taught himself how to become a network administrator by reading books and trying out what he read. With no qualifications other than an interest, he became the one person holding the college's entire network together. Because of his skills in networking, he was able to take a new job working for one of the industry's biggest software developers. During the time he worked for the software development company, he attained several certifications. By obtaining certification, he increased his value in the IT job market and when he was laid off in a recent restructuring, he was able to find a new job at another leading company within one week. That is the power of certification.

Stories like this are commonplace and while many IT workers are successful at acquiring the needed skills through less formal training paths, it is difficult to prove you can transfer such anecdotal learning to other situations, and thus for companies to feel assured that a professional is qualified to run mission-critical networks. People who have entered the profession indirectly and have received several years of on-the-job training benefit greatly from having Network + certification. Not only does certification validate the knowledge they gained through the years, but it also complements any college degree they might have, even if that degree is not in a computer-related field. Network + certification shows employers and employees alike that the holder of that certification has learned what it takes to succeed in the IT profession.

Even if you received a computer science degree in college, having Network + certification increases your value to your employer. According to

Dave Hyatt, sales and marketing vice president at DRA Software Training Center, certificates appeal to IT hiring managers because they represent training that is directly applicable to the workplace.

Although traditional university education is important, it may not be enough to prepare people for the IT profession. Potential employees with degrees are attractive to employers, but many employers have found that sometimes employees who have only a college education need more skill sets. Many college-educated professionals quickly learn that the skill sets they gained in college are lacking the specific experience necessary for the job, particularly considering the pace at which networking and related technologies change.

Companies are looking for IT professionals who can prove their skills in networking. When asked what was the most important consideration when reviewing an IT professional's resume, most CIOs answered that specific technical skills were the most important consideration (see Figure 3.2). Network+ certification shows that you have the skills that managers and CIOs are looking for.

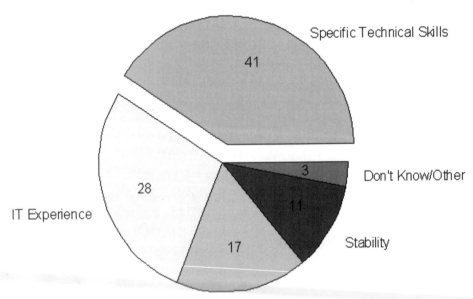

FIGURE 3.2 Importance of technical skills when hiring

Even many college-educated individuals seek certified IT training as a way to increase their value as employees, and their income. One training company reports that 59 percent of its students got a raise after certification and 29 percent of those people got a raise of 10 percent or more. Coupled with other forms of education such as college, certification is powerful.

Network+ Certification from the Employer Perspective

One of the biggest struggles facing IT managers is the struggle to keep up with the rate of change in technology, which has never been faster. This increase in the rate of technology change makes it even more difficult to make the right hiring and training choices. Providing Network+ training and certification helps employers do both without a huge increase in costs.

IT managers are looking for people with the right skills who have the capacity to learn quickly. If employees do not come to a company with Network+ certification, providing the training and the opportunity to receive Network+ certification gives the employer an opportunity to invest in a person who will add significant value to the company. Once properly trained, she will know the basics of any network, and will be able to apply knowledge and skills across the board.

Network+ certification may be required by many companies hiring new employees. Companies who require Network+ certification before employment offers often feel that Network+ certification provides an acceptable level of confidence in employee ability. It is often difficult to tell what a person knows based on a resume. Certification tells the employer that you have at least passed the minimum requirements, and if you have some experience, practically guarantees that you know enough about how to run a network to make their hiring of and investment in you a profitable decision.

Network+ Certification from Customer Perspective

Many companies may also require Network+ certification because it gives their customers a level of assurance that the IT professionals they are working with are trained and accredited. Just as you would not want a root canal from a dentist who had not passed the state exams, customers do not want their networks touched by people without the proper credentials. No company wants its network to be the learning area for a new person. Having Network+ certification shows that you know what you are doing.

Certification is also important in the bid process. Often, RFQs put out by government agencies state that all personnel working on the contract must be certified. Having professionals who are certified helps win a customer's confidence and win the bid for the company. When the RFQ is networking-related, having Network+ certification shows that you are a professional and that you have the skills needed.

How Network+ Certification Relates to Other Certification Programs

Bureaucracy moves slowly, and while some colleges are beginning to offer networking technology programs, the lack of a specific college track for net-working professionals has made professional certification even more impor-tant. However, there are currently so many vendor-specific certification programs that it is often difficult for the IT professional and the employer to know which certifications are the best ones.

In addition, the cost in time, money, and resources needed to attain each of these certifications is often prohibitive. For example, Microsoft requires six classes and exams and estimates that it costs about $6,400 to $10,000 to become a Microsoft Certified Systems Engineer (MCSE). To become a MCSE+ Internet, seven classes and exams are required. To become a Certified Novell Engineer (CNE), it takes seven courses and exams and costs between $8,000 to $10,000. Getting advanced certification is even more expensive. For example, Novell's Master CNE requires five courses and exams and costs about $10,000.

It is only fair to note, however, that these certifications do not require you to take the related courses. If you have gained the required knowledge through experience, self-study, other courses or training, or any combination of these alternatives to training, you can take the required exams to obtain these certifications. If you pass these exams, you become certified. The same is true for the Network+ Certification.

Network+ Certification and Microsoft

Although at the time of the publication of this book, Microsoft had not announced its intentions to accept Network+ certification as equivalent for any of its training, the Network+ certification exam covers the topics in the

Microsoft Exam 70-058: Networking Essentials. This exam covers the topics listed in Table 3.1, which shows which of these topics are covered in the Network+ certification exam.

TABLE 3.1 Material Covered in Microsoft Exam 70-058: Networking Essentials

Area of Focus	Topic Covered by Microsoft	Covered By Network+
Standards and Terminology		
	Define common networking terms for LANs and WANs. Compare a file-and-print server with an application server.	X
	Compare user-level security with access permission assigned to a shared directory on a server.	X
	Compare a client/server network with a peer-to-peer network.	X
	Compare the implications of using connection-oriented communications with connectionless communications.	X
	Distinguish whether SLIP or PPP is used as the communications protocol for various situations.	X
	Define the communication devices that communicate at each level of the OSI model.	X
	Describe the characteristics and purpose of the media used in IEEE 802.3 and IEEE 802.5 standards.	X
	Explain the purpose of NDIS and Novell ODI network standards.	X
Planning		
	Select the appropriate media for various situations.	X
	Media choices include: Twisted-pair cable Coaxial cable Fiber-optic cable Wireless	
	Situational elements include: Cost Distance limitations Number of nodes	
	Select the appropriate topology for various token-ring and Ethernet networks.	X
	Select the appropriate network and transport protocol or protocols for various token-ring and Ethernet networks.	X

continued on next page

Area of Focus	Topic Covered by Microsoft	Covered By Network+
	Protocol choices include:	
	DLC	
	AppleTalk	
	IPX	
	TCP/IP	
	NFS	
	SMB	
	Select the appropriate connectivity devices for various token-ring and Ethernet networks.	X
	Connectivity devices include:	
	Repeaters	
	Bridges	
	Routers	
	Brouters	
	Gateways	
	List the characteristics, requirements, and appropriate situations for WAN connection services.	X
	WAN connection services include:	
	X.25	
	ISDN	
	Frame relay	
	ATM	
Implementation		
	Choose an administrative plan to meet specified needs, including performance management, account management, and security.	X
	Choose a disaster recovery plan for various situations.	X
	Given the manufacturer's documentation for the network adapter, install, configure, and resolve hardware conflicts for multiple network adapters in a token-ring or Ethernet network.	X
	Implement a NetBIOS naming scheme for all computers on a given network.	X
	Select the appropriate hardware and software tools to monitor trends in the network.	X
Troubleshooting		
	Identify common errors associated with components required for communications.	X

Area of Focus	Topic Covered by Microsoft	Covered By Network+
	Diagnose and resolve common connectivity problems with cards, cables, and related hardware.	X
	Resolve broadcast storms.	X
	Identify and resolve network performance problems.	X

Network+ Certification and Novell

The same situation is true for Novell certification. Although at the time of publication of this book, Novell had not announced its intentions to accept Network + certification as equivalent for any of its training, the Network + certification exam covers the topics in the NetWare 5 Course 565: Networking Technologies. This exam covers the basics of computer networking, including terms and concepts. Knowledge of networking technology, contemporary network services, transmission media, and protocols is tested. Knowledge of protocols used in networking implementations from many vendors, especially those most common in today's LANs and WANs is also tested. Table 2.3 lists the topics covered in this course. These same topics are also covered in the Network + certification.

TABLE 3.2 Topics Covered in Novell's Course 565: Networking Technologies

Area of Focus	Topic Covered by Novell	Covered By Network+
Networking Basics		
	Communicating Peer-to-Peer	X
	The OSI Model and All its Layers	X
	Physical Topologies	X
	Logical Topologies	X
	Transmission Media	X
	Physical Device Address	X
	Network Address	X
	Service Address	X

continued on next page

Area of Focus	Topic Covered by Novell	Covered By Network+
	Connectivity Devices	X
	Repeaters and Hubs	X
	Bridges and Switches	X
	Routers	X
	Packet Switching	X
Lower-Layer Protocols		
	IEEE 802.X Series Standards for Interoperability.	X
	IEEE 802.3 and Ethernet	X
	IEEE 802.3u—Fast Ethernet	X
	IEEE 802.5 and Token Ring	X
	The Point-to-Point Protocol (PPP)	X
	X.25 Protocol	X
	Frame Relay	X
	ISDN and B-ISDN	X
	ATM	X
Middle- and Upper-Layer Protocols		
	IPX/SPX Network Design	X
	TCP/IP Protocol Suite	X
	Internet Protocol–IP	X
	Routing Information Protocol–RIP	X
	Open Shortest Path First–OSPF	X
	Internet Control Message Protocol–ICMP	X
	Address Resolution Protocols–ARP and RARP	X
	Transmission Control Protocol–TCP	X
	User Datagram Protocol–UDP	X
	Simple Network Management Protocol–SNMP	X
	File Transfer Protocol–FTP and TFTP	X
	HyperText Transfer Protocol–HTTP	X
	Dynamic Host Configuration Protocol–DHCP	X
	Simple Mail Transport Protocol–SMTP	X
	Obtaining a Registered IP Address	X
	Obtaining a Registered Domain Name	X
Structure of an IP Address		
	IP Address Structure	X
	Identifying the Network Class	X
	Assigning Addresses to Hosts	X
	Host Names, Host Tables, and DNS	X

Area of Focus	Topic Covered by Novell	Covered By Network+
Creating Subnets		
	Subnets and Their Purpose	X
	Using Subnet Addresses	X
	Subnet Masks	X
	Assigning Subnet Addresses	X
Supernetting		
	Purpose of Supernetting	X
	IP Address Criteria for Supernetting	X
	Routing and Supernetting	X
Bridging and Switching		
	Bridging	X
	Types of Bridging	X
	Using Transparent Bridging	X
	Using Switching Hubs	X
	Source-Routing Bridges	X
	Using Token Ring Switches	X
	Comparing Bridges, Switches, and Routers	X
Connecting IPX Networks		
	Routing IPX	X
	Assigning IPX Addresses	X
	Distance Vector Routing: IPX RIP and SAP	X
	Link State Routing: IPX NLSP	X
	RIP/SAP versus NLSP	X
Connecting IP Networks		
	Routing IP	X
	Assigning IP Addresses	X
	Distance Vector Routing: IP RIP	X
	Link State Routing: OSPF	X
Directory Services		
	X.500 Directory Services	X
	Lightweight Directory Access Protocol–LDAP	X
	Domain Name System–DNS	X

Network+ Certification and
Your Company's Certification Program

In addition to vendor-specific training programs, your company may have internal or specialized training programs that you must attend. Often, there are several course in these training programs and the lowest level programs may seem quite easy to those who have been working in the IT profession for several years. Because Network + certification shows that you have mastered the basic skills in networking, it may be accepted in lieu of other training requirements at your company. Remember to check with your training coordinator about this.

As you may know, the A + Certification that CompTIA sponsors has become a standard for its niche of the computer industry. Several companies have implemented CompTIA's A + certification as part of their company's curriculum. It is expected that the same will be true of Network + certification.

Becoming Network + certified makes sense. Whether you are relatively new to the industry and need to prove that you have the skills it takes to get a job or you have been in the industry for a long time and have an excellent track record, Network + provides you with industry-wide, vendor-neutral certification that proves you can do the job.

Since it appears that both the industry trend and employers' hiring preferences are moving toward certified IT professionals over non-certified IT personnel, the Network + Certification may soon be a decisive factor for employers when choosing whom to hire. Whether you get the job, the desired promotion, the pay raises, the benefits, and all of the other perks that go along with being a valued company professional, you will at least attain a new level of professionalism and stature once employers, potential employers, and customers know see that you are Network + certified and realize that your skills have been recognized by a vendor-neutral national association such as CompTIA.

Your next step, therefore, is to prepare yourself to take the Network + Certification examination. At least part of that preparation includes knowing for which job categories and job tasks CompTIA's Network + certification test was developed, understanding what each of those categories and tasks involves, and having a good idea of what it is like to be an IP professional trying to accomplish those tasks as a routine part of your professional life, particularly if you are new to the industry. Chapter 4 is designed to give you this knowledge.

Articles to Read On the Web

Alexander, Steve. "Are you certified to do that?"*InfoWorld* (Aug. 11, 1997). **http://www.infoworld.com/cgi-bin/displayCareers.pl?970811cert.htm**

Corcoran, Cate T. " Putting skills to the test: Skills assessment can help with hiring, but some are wary" *InfoWorld* Vol. 20, Issue 46 (Nov. 16, 1998). **http://www.infoworld.com/cgi-bin/displayCareers.pl?981116test.htm**

Jacobs, Paula. "The certification debate: Why do IT pros have such passionate opinions about a few tests?" *InfoWorld* Vol. 20, Issue 42 (Oct. 19, 1998). **http://www.infoworld.com/cgi-bin/displayCareers.pl?981019cert.htm**

"Microsoft Certification a Home Run for Individuals and Employers: Studies Show Continued Value of Microsoft Certification; Financial and Performance Success Achieved." Microsoft Web Site. October 16, 1998. **http://www.microsoft.com/presspass/press/1998/Oct98/homerun.htm**

Steen, Margaret. "The training imperative" *InfoWorld* Vol. 20, Issue 25 (June 22, 1998). **http://www.infoworld.com/cgi-bin/displayCareers.pl?/features/980622training.htm**

"Training and education: Promoting professional growth" *InfoWorld* Vol. 20, Issue 24. (June 15, 1998). **http://www.infoworld.com/cgi-bin/display Archive.pl?/98/24/z06-24.143.htm**

Other Interesting Web Sites to Visit

Other Web sites of interest are listed by their general topic including current trends in IT and Web magazine articles.

Articles on Current Trends in IT

http://www.microsoft.com/skills2000/headline.htm
http://www.microsoft.com/skills2000/findIT/resource.htm

Collection of Articles from Various Web Magazines

http://www.microsoft.com/skills2000/aboutIT/itnews.htm

CHAPTER
4

Working as a Network Professional

When CompTIA chose to develop the Network+ certification, they wanted to make sure they were looking at the IT industry for what it really is. They wanted to reflect the actual job duties and responsibilities of IT professionals.

To accomplish that task, CompTIA conducted various focus group studies, then used the IT Skills Job Task Analysis (JTA) survey to help validate what they learned in the focus groups. The result was the development of an extensive list of the IT professional's main areas of responsibility, and the duties and tasks associated with those responsibilities. In fact, the list of 175 tasks grouped into 15 categories which resulted from this survey reflects the varied responsibilities and work done by a typical network professional. It is around these 15 job categories and 175 tasks that CompTIA developed the Network+ examination you are planning to take. These 15 job categories and 175 tasks are also what this chapter is designed to present to you.

The 15 categories and 175 tasks are listed in this chapter exactly as CompTIA originally displayed them on their Web site, although if needed, occasional words (such as but, and, etc.) have been added to make statements less cryptic. By seeing them as CompTIA presented them, you will be able to understand what CompTIA and those who participated in the focus groups and surveys originally had in mind. This chapter also provides basic information about the tasks that IT professionals perform so that you can better understand the responsibilities and duties of a networking professional. In addition, this chapter provides real-life examples of how networking professionals carry out some of those tasks in their everyday networking environment. Many of the examples are taken from the authors' experiences within the IT industry, and as both network administrators and network users.

Having this information lets you better understand not only why the knowledge you will be tested on is important and why it was chosen, but also what it is like to be an IT professional. If you are or have been an IT professional, then you will be able to relate to the examples included in this chapter. If you are taking the Network+ exam as an early step in becoming an IT professional, then this chapter will help you better understand what it is like to work in the industry.

By the time you finish reading this chapter, you will:

❖ Know exactly around which job categories and job tasks CompTIA's Network+ certification test was developed
❖ Understand what each of those categories and tasks involves
❖ Understand what information CompTIA used to develop the blueprint for the actual Network+ examination
❖ Have a good idea of what it is like to be an IT professional trying to accomplish those tasks as a routine part of your professional life.

Understanding the 15 Job Categories of the IT Professional

Experienced IT professional or not, you need to understand the 15 job categories (and 175 tasks) around which the CompTIA Network+ certification exam was written. Doing so helps you be better prepared to take the certification exam and helps you relate and better remember information about each of the categories and job tasks.

Each of the 15 job categories of the IT professional has a theme or main idea. The first category is that of operating the network management system. Its main idea is that the network will have problems, and it is your responsibility to manage those problems. You do so by establishing a baseline for your network from which to determine when problems exist, as well as to help you see how much trouble the problem is causing, or could cause, your network. The job tasks associated with that theme are then listed. In this case, the tasks include such things as responding to problems, identifying problems, establishing a baseline, conducting network analysis, reporting on the progress of problem resolution, and so on.

When the committee at CompTIA listed and organized these 15 job categories and the tasks associated with them, they listed the associated tasks in their order of importance. When you are reading through each category and the tasks it contains, it may seem as though the order of the tasks is not logical. Again looking at the first category (operating the network management system), it is not necessarily logical that you would be attempting to establish a baseline for your network only after having responded to problems, identified problems, determined the cause of the problem, then conducted a network analysis. When you look at the order of the tasks, however, you may be able to relate to their order if you consider, as the committee intended, that they are ordered by importance. In other words, it is more important that you respond to network problems when they are brought to your attention than it is that you go around looking at (identifying) other network problems.

Learning About the Job Categories and Job Tasks of the Network+ Certification Examination

The 15 job categories around which the Network+ Certification exam is written are:

- **A.** Operating Network Management System
- **B.** Implementing the Installation of Network
- **C.** Setting Up Standard Operating Procedures
- **D.** Managing Support Efforts

   E. Administering Change Control System
   F. Troubleshooting the Network
   G. Administering the Network
   H. Designing the Network
   I. Planning a Customer's Job
   J. Analyzing/Evaluating the Applicability of New Technology
   K. Maintaining the Network
   L. Analyzing/Evaluating Network Implementation
   M. Implementing Change Control System
   N. Developing Documentation (and SOPs)
   O. Developing/Coordinating/Delivering Training.

Each of the job categories and its associated tasks is discussed in the following sections. As you go through each section, you will notice that some of the job tasks seem to duplicate, or at least closely match, the job tasks in other sections. There is overlap in the work you perform as an IT professional, just as there is also some overlap in the list of job tasks within the different categories.

A. Operating Network Management System

Operating the network management system is a daily task for an IT professional. One of the key tasks you will perform is that of identifying and responding to problems on the network. The Operating Network Management System category contains seven related job tasks (see Figure 4.1), the first of which is responding to problems.

The seven related tasks defined in the operating network management system category are:

   1. **Respond to problems.** For network professionals to respond to a problem, they must first be made aware of the problem. Responding to a problem is often a matter of responding to an individual who has notified you that a problem exists. The response is then determined in part by the problem itself. Some problems are quickly identified and resolved while the user is still on the phone or at your desk. Others require more effort, more troubleshooting, more time, and more documentation.

A. Operating Network Management System

1.	Respond to problems
2.	Identify network problems
3.	Determine if problem is attributed to operator or system
4.	Conduct network analysis
5.	Establish network baseline
6.	Select/use system management and monitoring tools
7.	Report on network system progress

FIGURE 4.1   The seven job tasks of operating network management systems

2. **Identify network problems.** Although the first indication of a problem may be the result of a user-initiated call or complaint, IT professionals frequently find that it is they who first identify a problem within the network. Notification by a users is only one way an IT professional may discover a problem. IT professionals often perform routine checks on the network's components, and may discover problems or potential problems when they do so.

  As an IT professional, you will perform routine checks as well. You may use special equipment such as an ohm meter to measure cable impedance, or special software such as Novell's various management programs to check statistics such as percentage of CPU usage on one or more file servers. A consistently high CPU usage may indicate the need for another server, or replacement hardware that uses dual processors. Whatever monitoring devices and procedures you choose to follow, consistent use of those devices and procedures, along with the initial establishment of a baseline for your network will help you locate problems and potential problems on your network.

3. **Determine if problem is to be attributed to the operator or the system.** Once a network problem is identified, one of the first steps the professional may take is that of determining whether the problem is the result of something the user has done, or something the user should have done but did not do. In other words, the professional must determine if the problem is attributable to the operator or to the system.

Identifying whether the problem is an operator problem often requires that you either attempt to reproduce the problem yourself, or that you observe the operator while he attempts to reproduce the problem. Sometimes, you may have to do both.

4. **Conduct network analysis.** A network analysis can be as simple or as complex as needed. The complexity of the network analysis is determined at least in part by the problem you are trying to resolve. If it is apparently isolated to a single workstation, a complete analysis of packet transmission on the network may not be necessary. A more complete network analysis may be appropriate if you are simply trying to establish a baseline for your network, or making a regular check on its health.

5. **Establish network baseline.** You must know what is normal and regular for your network before you can assess information which may identify when the network is no longer functioning within normal parameters. Thus, you use whatever tools and techniques are appropriate to identify a normal baseline for your network.

   For example, you can measure the impedance of coaxial cable used on your network to see if it conforms to the cables specifications, and to establish a baseline for your network. Periodic measurement of the cable's impedance can then be compared to that baseline to determine whether the impedance has changed. Changes in impedance can indicate specific types of potential problems such as a bad connector or damaged cable. You would not necessarily know that a change in impedance had occurred if you did not first know the normal impedance for your network cable.

6. **Select/use system management and monitoring tools (remote and automated).** There are various system management and monitoring tools you can use to establish a network baseline and then track and monitor network performance. There are software tools as well as hardware tools. For example, you use an ohm meter to measure the impedance of network cabling. You can use network management tools provided as part of the network operating system (OS), such as Novell's NetWare OS. NetWare provides various software tools for system monitoring such as the Monitor NLM (NetWare Loadable Module).

7. **Report on network system progress.** Keeping both users and management informed, of the status of the network, its issues and concerns, and problem troubleshooting and resolution, is an important aspect of the operating network management system job category. For a net-

work administrator or other IT professional, the job and its successes and failures are sometimes quite visible to all company employees. Problems occur with the network which you may have had no way of foreseeing or preventing, but that does not let you off the hook, or make the problem any less visible. As the IT professional, you will be the one to whom everyone looks to correct the problem. Management's and users' confidence in you is important to being a successful IT professional. Thus it is important that you communicate the progress you are making at correcting problems, maintaining the network, improving the network, and generally keeping the network management system in full operation.

Of these seven tasks, the first two are methods for determining that a network problem actually exists. Once the problem is identified, the professional then takes the appropriate steps. If it turns out that the problem is attributable to the operator, the professional can then find a way to carry out one or more tasks associated with the last of the 15 job categories, and ensure the user receives training so the problem is not repeated.

If the problem is not attributable to the operator, the professional must then determine the cause. Many tools and software management options are available to help you establish a baseline for your network, and to then conduct an analysis of your network either when a problem occurs, or just as a matter of maintaining the network in its optimum condition. Once a problem occurs and the cause is determined, you need to resolve the problem and then notify all affected individuals of the problem resolution. Just as often, you may need to ensure everyone knows you are aware of the problem and working on it. They may also need to know that you are simply monitoring the network and that everything is fine or that you have identified potential problem areas.

While I was network administrator for the Federal Aviation Administration, it was my responsibility to see to the installation of the cabling system when we moved into a new facility. Although a company was hired to install the cabling system, I needed to ensure that the maximum cable distances for the type of cabling being installed were not exceeded. If a cable segment is too long for the length for which a cable is rated, network problems result. Sometimes, the entire network is affected, and sometimes only the specific cable segment is affected. Either way, problems can occur.

Once the cabling had been installed in the new building, I used an ohm meter and measured the distance of each cable segment on the network.

Two different cable segments registered lengths greater than that allowed for the cable type. The blueprints for installing the cabling specifically identified the expected length of each cable segment, none of which exceeded the cable's rating. Yet when tested, two of the cable segments were too long.

Further examination revealed that the installers had to reroute these two cables in order to go around some last minute changes made to the building. Doing so caused two of the cable segments to exceed their allowed length. Had I not checked each cable segment to establish that the proper lengths had been used and to set the baseline for the network, problems would have occurred with these two specific segments. It would then have taken a great deal more time later to troubleshoot and resolve the problem.

B. Implementing the Installation of the Network

Although you may not have to perform every specific task each time you implement the installation of a network, there are 13 identified tasks associated with this job category (Figure 4.2).

1. **Install server.** Installing the server involves two phases; the physical installation of the hardware which will be the server and the installation and configuration of the software to make the computer on which it runs an actual server.

2. **Install equipment (award of available working time and access issues).** Even though the server may be physically installed, it is often only a small part of the network. It is an important part of the network, but as far as the number of components is concerned, it is usually a small part, as one server supplies multiple workstations on a network. Many other pieces of equipment must be installed to create a network, including cabling, workstations, and routers.

    Two important issues here involve not only the actual equipment, but also arranging for time and physical access to the areas of the building where equipment must be installed. As an IT professional, you may do some of the equipment installation yourself. However, it is not uncommon for companies to hire out this type of work. Even if you do most of the equipment installation yourself, you will still have to make arrangements for such things as connection to external communication, such as a T1 line.

B. Implementing the Installation of Network

1. Install server
2. Install equipment
3. Manage configuration following installation guidelines
4. Verify that all ordered equipment/software is correct and available
5. Ensure appropriate resources are available for implementation
6. Perform installation QC
7. Conduct pilot test of equipment
8. Establish network management system
9. Set up wiring closet environment
10. Implement fall-back plan
11. Set up timeline for deployment
12. Conduct user pilot
13. Identify group of users for pilot testing new system

FIGURE 4.2   The 13 job tasks performed when implementing a network installation

3. **Manage configuration following installation guidelines.** When a network is installed, its installation is preplanned. Issues such as where the servers will be located, whether drop cables will be centralized to accommodate a pool of network workstations or spaced to individual workstations, and other related issues must be considered. When the servers and workstations are actually configured, the installation plan must be taken into consideration. Thus, managing the configuration of the software and hardware according to the installation guidelines is an important task when installing the network.

4. **Verify that all ordered equipment/software is correct and available (includes vendor coordination).** Both before and after the equipment and software arrive on site to be installed, you need to ensure that the correct equipment and software is ordered, and that it is available. Also, you must ensure before you order each network component that

it is compatible with all of the other network components. You may get all equipment ordered and even some or all of it installed only to find out that some of the equipment is incompatible with other components, or that there is a six-month back order on one or more critical pieces of the network. The entire network may be unusable until the critical piece arrives. Thus you must make sure that not only is the correct equipment and software ordered, but that it will be available when it is to be delivered. Then, once each network component arrives, you must ensure you received what you ordered. You may need to coordinate and work closely with each vendor to ensure that all components are compatible, correctly ordered, and delivered as ordered and when promised.

5. **Ensure appropriate resources are available for implementation (phones, access, etc.).** A network, even if all components are correct, compatible, and on time, must blend successfully with the existing environment if it is to be useful. For example, if you order modems to set up a modem pool for a particular server, but forget to have data lines brought to the server room, your modem pool is useless. Thus, you must consider not only the components of the network, but anything associated with the network as well. You must not only remember to schedule the installation of lines to the server room, for example, but you must also make sure that someone is available to guide the data line installers when they arrive, and ensure they have access to the building as needed.

6. **Perform installation quality control (technical).** When the various components of the network are installed, you need to make sure they live up to the promised standards. You must ensure that the specified quality is met not only for the network components, but also for related components such as data lines. If you ordered a T1 line for example, you need to ensure that the transmission quality meets the specifications for a T1 line.

7. **Conduct pilot test of equipment.** Once the network, or at least an isolated segment of the network, is installed, you should conduct a pilot test of that equipment. The pilot test is conducted to ensure that the network is functioning as intended, and that it does not interfere with other aspects of the company or its daily work. You want to know that the transition to the new or modified network will be smooth and trouble free. Conducting a pilot test of the equipment will help you locate

potential problems and give you the opportunity to solve those problems before you implement the changes across the entire network.

8. **Establish network management system.** You need to determine how the network will be managed. That is, you need to decide what system you will use to monitor the network and ensure it remains at the level of quality you originally intended for the network. Various network management system options are available. It is your responsibility as an IT professional to choose, implement, and maintain the one that is best for your network.

9. **Set up wiring closet environment (power, voltage, etc.; available UPS).** In many networks, particularly those large enough to require one or more in-house IT professionals, wiring for the network often goes into a central location known as a wiring closet. A panel similar to the one shown in Figure 4.3 exists in the wiring closet to keep the mass of cables and other wiring ordered and easy to access, change, and maintain. While you may not be the individual to set up or maintain the wiring closet, you may have to ensure that power is routed to the wiring closet, that sufficient voltage is available, and that one or more UPSs (Uninteruptible Power Supplies) are placed either in the closet or within range.

FIGURE 4.3   Example of a wiring closet

10. **Implement fall-back plan.** Whether you are talking about installing a network or going on vacation, it is rare that everything goes exactly as planned. Having an alternate plan to follow if the first one does not work out is important when installing a network, since many different problems can occur.

     For example, one of the courthouses that was part of the court system network for which I was the network administrator was so remotely located that only six telephone lines were available for the entire town, and two of those lines were already assigned to the courthouse. We implemented a network upgrade that required a direct and dedicated phone line for the courthouse. The phone company for the area was scheduled to install new lines to the town, and for that courthouse, the upgrade of the network depended on the availability of additional phone lines. Unfortunately, the actual installation of those lines was more than one year late. Thus we had to devise a fallback plan that kept this remote courthouse in electronic connection with the network, even though no dedicated phone line was available.

11. **Set up timeline for deployment (pilot, then full).** When installing your network, you should determine what tasks must be completed and put together a plan for when each of those tasks are to be done. You must do the same for many things in life that you want to accomplish.

     For example, the building of a house requires an identified timeline. While you may be able to install the linoleum before you install the carpet, you cannot put the roof on the house before you build the sides. A timeline can help you know whether each step of the network's installation is being done in the correct order, and whether it is within the expected time frame. Whether you are implementing the network as a whole, or implementing only a pilot program, you should establish an appropriate timeline.

12. **Conduct user pilot.** When a new network is implemented or an existing one upgraded, many users are affected. To ensure the implementation goes smoothly, you may want to conduct a user pilot just as you conducted a network pilot. When conducting a user pilot, choose a few users to work on the implemented network initially. Work with those users to find and work out any problems which may be common to all users when the full implementation begins, then when you have worked out the problems, move to the full implementation, or conduct

a second user pilot test to verify that the changes will in fact assist the full implementation to move along smoothly and in a timely manner.

13. **Identify group of users for pilot testing new system.** Whom should you choose when conducting a user pilot? The best answer is often those users who will be typical network users when the full implementation is conducted. However, you may prefer to conduct your user pilot program using only more experienced users. More experienced users are often better at identifying a problem related to the new or upgraded network as opposed to a user mistake common even to the old network.

On the other hand, experienced users may already know how to work around problems, and if those problems crop up during the pilot program, they may not even think to mention them. Then when the less experienced network users encounter the problem during the full implementation, you will not have had the opportunity to identify and correct the problem before the full implementation. The result may be that a greater number of users will be inconvenienced than would otherwise have been necessary.

This in itself may also be a reason to use less-experienced network users for your user pilot. Less experienced users tend to end up pointing out things that you may have considered to be normal and no problem. If they are a problem for your users, then they are a problem you would want to identify and correct before the full implementation.

C. Setting Up Standard Operating Procedures

Standard Operating Procedures (SOP) are documents which define what is to be done given a specified situation. For example, it is now often SOP for all dental personnel to wear gloves when performing any type of examination or procedure in a person's mouth. Only with the widespread advent of AIDS and other diseases did it become SOP to wear gloves in dental offices, but today it is standard practice. Although this particular example of SOP may not be written in procedure form, many SOPs are written down.

For an IT professional, there are 17 job tasks it may be necessary to perform in relation to the category of setting up standard operating procedures (see Figure 4.4). Each of these job tasks involves written documentation of the SOP; the final one involves maintaining those standard operating procedures.

C. Setting Up Standard Operating Procedures

1. Set up SOP for software configuration
2. Set up SOP for data back-up
3. Set up SOP for network
4. Set up SOP for client configuration
5. Set up SOP for disaster recovery
6. Set up SOP for server configuration
7. Set up SOP for fixing a problem
8. Set up SOP for cabling
9. Set up SOP for external access procedures
10. Set up SOP for security internal/external
11. Set up SOP for user accounts
12. Set up SOP for troubleshooting
13. Set up SOP for identifying a problem
14. Set up SOP for approvals for system changes and upgrades
15. Set up SOP for projected changes regarding future growth/capacity planning
16. Set up SOP for peripherals
17. Maintaining standards

FIGURE 4.4   The 17 job tasks related to setting up standard operating procedures

The 17 job tasks associated with setting up standard operating procedures are:

1. **Set up SOP for software configuration.** Software configuration procedures can be established for software installed on the network, as well as for software installed on individual workstations.

   For example, if you are installing multiple copies of WordPerfect on different servers across your network so as to balance the load on the network, you will probably want to configure each copy exactly the same as every other copy. The goal is to ensure the user gets quick access to the software, without having to know or care about where it comes from. If the software's configuration on one server is different from its configuration on another server, the differences may confuse and trouble your network users.

2. **Set up SOP for data backup.** It doesn't matter how you choose to back up your network data, but it does matter that you are consistent about backup. Conducting a full network backup only once a month may be sufficient if data rarely changes during that month, or if regular backups of only the changed data are made during the interim. But whatever method you choose to implement, it is important that the method be consistent and be consistently followed if you are to have the data you need available to be restored should this become necessary. A policy which identifies when and how data are to be backed up should be developed and followed as a standard operating procedure for all networks.

3. **Set up SOP for network.** This job task can encompass anything associated with the network that is not already included in one of the other job tasks. You have SOPs for clients, data backup, software configuration, and so on. There is no specific SOP for the use of UPS devices on your network, for example. So the job task of setting up standard operating procedures for your network could involve identifying where a UPS device is to be used (only on servers, on servers and all routers, etc.), what UPS is the preferred one, what the minimum size of the UPS should be, and so on. Identifying what network SOPs need to be developed in addition to those which have already been identified and developed is part of developing SOPs for your network.

4. **Set up SOP for client configuration.** Different network operating systems have different clients (generally network workstations but other devices such as printers can be network clients as well) and associated software. Certain requirements must be met for the software installed on clients, on workstations in particular, to allow the client to access the network.

   For example, each workstation on a Novell NetWare network requires that special client software be installed. Some configuration of that software is often needed depending on the network topology or operating system (DOS, Windows, etc.) running on the workstation itself. For consistency, ease of troubleshooting, ability of users to access the network from any single workstation, and a variety of other reasons, you may want to establish a standard operating procedure for how specific client workstation software is configured.

5. **Set up SOP for disaster recovery.** No one likes to think it will happen to them, but the one time a network disaster is a real disaster is when you have no disaster recovery plan. If the building in which your network resides were to be demolished by a natural gas explosion or anything else, would you be able to bring the network back up in a reasonable amount of time in a different location? A disaster recovery plan is designed to help you do just that. Questions such as where you should store copies of data so you can install it on replacement hardware need to be answered in a disaster recovery plan. The plan you create defines the standard operating procedure to be followed in the event of a network disaster, natural or otherwise.

6. **Set up SOP for server configuration.** Although most network operating systems are designed to have a default configuration that is optimum for a new server, the optimum configuration for any given server may change with time. Tweaking the server to optimize it is not an uncommon task performed by a network administrator. Once you have configured the server for optimum performance, how do you ensure that configuration is maintained and even used for other servers where appropriate? You document and implement a standard operating procedure for server configuration. That SOP is likely to define software as well as hardware configuration.

7. **Set up SOP for fixing a problem.** The best way to solve a problem, particularly one that occurs more than once in more than one network component, is to document the problem and its resolution. A standard operating procedure is ideal for this purpose. The procedure can identify specific problems and how to correct them, but it can also identify just a standard approach to use in order to identify problems and resolve them. Many standard procedures exist to help you develop an SOP for fixing a problem.

8. **Set up SOP for cabling.** A standard operating procedure for cabling is likely to include information about what cabling is used on the network, what should be done if a segment needs to be replaced, and other cabling related information. The point is to establish a procedure which makes sure that the same level of quality is reached each time an issue related to cabling develops and needs to be solved.

9. **Set up SOP for external access procedures.** External access procedures generally define who is allowed to have access to the network from outside the network, as well as when and how. With so many local area networks now accessing the Internet, it is important that local network security be identified, defined, and described, as well as implemented. An external access SOP is a good tool for identifying, defining, and describing external access procedures.

10. **Set up SOP for security–internal/external.** Closely related to external access procedures are SOPs for internal and external security. You need to ensure network access is restricted to those employees who should have access, and only to those areas or network information that should be accessed. Use a security SOP for defining that access.

    For example, a software testing company may make its Web site available to anyone who wants to see it, but require a password and special access URL for a given company to access the test results on the company's product which the software testing company has posted on the Web site. This provides electronic customer service on a 24-hour basis to the company whose product is being tested, but prevents any of the company's competitors or any unauthorized individual from viewing the posted test results.

11. **Set up SOP for user accounts.** User accounts are set up not only to grant network access, but also to control what an individual user can access. Identifying such things as what groups will be allowed on the network, what access those groups may have, and whether user access is to be restricted to any set days of the week or hours of the day are just some of the items of information you may choose to include in an SOP for user accounts.

12. **Set up SOP for troubleshooting (escalation procedures).** Not all problems may be resolvable with your level of knowledge, or with your limited funds or access to equipment. You may sometimes need the help of others, either externally or internally. When you cannot resolve a problem, you need to know how to escalate that problem so that it can be resolved. You also need to know how to identify when you cannot resolve a problem, and how long you should work on the problem before it is escalated. Issues such as these can be included in an SOP for troubleshooting, and can be very important to a timely resolution of problems.

The lack of an SOP for escalating problems can itself create a problem or make the problem much worse. For example, during the third week I was the network administrator for a WAN which depended heavily on routers, the experienced network administrator I was eventually to replace left on vacation. Two days after she left, two of the network routers went down, leaving two LAN segments without network communication. The only troubleshooting (escalation) SOP this company had was in the vacationing network administrator's head. I was unable to resolve the problem despite all my efforts. (As it turned out, the problem was a software bug in the router itself; something I would never have been able to figure out no matter what troubleshooting and testing I personally conducted as I did not have access to the manufacturer's specifications or software code for the router.) Because there was no troubleshooting SOP, however, I had no way of knowing who should be contacted to assist me with this problem, and I had no way of contacting the vacationing network administrator to find out. The problem was not resolved until she returned from vacation and gave me the escalation procedures.

For two weeks, these two LAN segments had only intermittent network connection. A troubleshooting SOP would have helped me realize after about two days that the problem was not one I could resolve, and it would also have told me exactly whom to call to correct it. The problem would have been resolved in about a week and a half, instead of the four weeks it actually took. The result for the users was a severe backlog of work, whose data input required heavy overtime for the users of those two LAN segments.

13. **Set up SOP for identifying a problem.** As with identifying troubleshooting escalation problems, an SOP should exist to help you identify that a problem exists. Of course, many times you will find out one exists because someone will tell you that they cannot get into the network, or they cannot print, or whatever. But more subtle problems may exist on the network, and without an SOP for identifying those problems you may not discover them soon enough to keep them from causing serious network difficulties. For example, knowing the baseline of network activity and then periodically checking that activity can help you identify segments which are too busy or segments which are underused, potential future problems (you'll notice a trend), or

other issues which simply would not be obvious on a daily basis. A troubleshooting SOP can establish how regularly to troubleshoot your network so that you find problems before your users notice them, and so you find and have the opportunity to plan for and correct potential problems before they become big problems.

14. **Set up SOP for approvals for system changes and upgrades.** Undoubtedly you will eventually have to make changes to your network. You may need to upgrade workstations, servers, printers, or routers. You may need to replace network boards or recable the entire network. How you go about getting approval to do so is excellent material for a standard operating procedure, and in some environments, absolutely mandatory.

    Government facilities are a perfect example. In private enterprise, many IT professionals have some discretion simply to make improvements or changes as needed. In the government sector, however, multiple approvals are often required to make even simple equipment replacement purchases. If you do not follow those procedures exactly, you can end up without the needed equipment, or experiencing a network problem you might have otherwise been able to prevent. SOPs which explain the procedures to follow when system changes or upgrades need to be approved and made can ensure you continue to maintain your network as expected.

15. **Set up SOP for projected changes regarding future growth/capacity planning.** As with procedures for system changes and upgrades, future growth procedures need to exist so that you can be prepared to upgrade or modify your system to accommodate growth before it is desperately needed. Related SOPs can guide you so that you are prepared to implement changes to the system that accommodate growth and capacity planning. Long lead times may be necessary to research growth and capacity options, get management approval, receive budget and purchase authorization, purchase and wait for delivery, pilot test, and then implement system changes. SOPs can help ensure you get an early enough start, and that you follow the needed process for successful implementation.

16. **Set up SOP for peripherals.** How do you replace an older printer? What do you do with the previous printer once it is replaced? What types of printers are you allowed to have on the network? Can you put

a modem on a user's workstation or must all modems be part of a network modem pool? These are just some of the types of questions that a standard operating procedure for peripherals can answer. When you work as an IT professional in this industry, you will come up with questions of your own. If you are not the first network administrator for a given system, SOPs written by others will no doubt point out questions you did not even know you had.

17. **Maintain standards (includes establishing benchmarks and testing them).** Your standard operating procedures should include, procedures which explain how to maintain the standards you have established for your network. If you have set certain benchmarks that must be met for network equipment, then those benchmark standards should be included here. How you maintain those standards, what benchmark tests are to be used and what the minimum acceptable result must be, are important to consider in relation to all of the SOPs you have implemented in your network.

D. Managing Support Efforts

Network users notice two things more frequently than anything else when it comes to the network: whether they can get what they want when they want it and as quickly as they want it, and whether you (the IT professional) are quick and responsive when they do have a problem.

To take care of the first, you have all of the other procedures in place. You have SOPs for installing, setting up, and maintaining the network, and you make every effort to ensure things run smoothly. But problems will occur, and if you can respond quickly and effectively, users will appreciate it. (They will also remember and tell others when you do not.)

It is important then that you have a support system in place to help your network users when they need it. As you can see, managing support efforts is an important IT professional job category. This category contains nine different but related job tasks (see Figure 4.5).

D. Managing Support Efforts

1. Handle customer complaints
2. Apply effective organizational skills
3. Inform users of what is to change and the expected impact on them
4. Transition smoothly
5. Tactfully respond and address new user issues not previously identified
6. Implement support plan
7. Handle issues with regard to company wishes
8. Inform users of the business reason why changes
9. Determine company plan for handling equipment reallocation

FIGURE 4.5 The nine job tasks for managing the support effort

1. **Handle customer complaints.** A user (customer) who has a problem usually lets you know. How you are notified depends on what system you have in place. You may have a policy that requires the user to e-mail a statement of the problem to the appropriate person, or to call a specific phone number. How you respond when the notice comes in is important. So too is what you do once that problem notice comes in. The followup is all part of handling customer complaints and begins with letting the customer know that you have received the complaint, that you will take action, and will report on that action. In other words, good customer service skills are part of handling customer complaints.

   The other part of good customer service is having an established procedure, and following it. SOPs provide the established procedure for you to follow, and help make customer service much easier.

2. **Apply effective organizational skills.** Complaints may dribble in, or you may be deluged by them. Regardless of how many complaints you have at a time, good organizational skills can help you deal effectively with each one.

For example, one organizational skill that is particularly useful is having a single location in which you record everything that is relevant so that you can find that information when you need it, and so that you can make sure you do not forget anything important. When I took over as the network administrator for a local government facility, there had been practically no customer service available. Problems were handled on an emergency-only basis since no staff was available to deal with anything else. One of the first things I did was to set up a notebook into which I could record problems. It included areas for the user's name, telephone number, network connection, user ID and context, description of the complaint, and my own relevant notes. Then as I was taken from user to user and introduced, I questioned each one to determine whether they were having any network or computer problems, and recorded the problems in my notebook. Once I had recorded all problems, I prioritized the problems (another organizational skill/technique), notified those users whose problems were on low priority that it would be a while before I could get to them but that I would be working on their reported problems, and then determined whether any of the recorded problems were similar in nature. Then I worked on the highest priorities first, and solved multiple similar ones at the same time another organization skill—taking care of multiple tasks at the same time.) These combined organizational skills allowed me quickly and smoothly to dispatch two years' worth of accumulated problems in just under a month. Needless to say, the users were all quite happy to have their network problems resolved.

3. **Inform users of what is to change and the expected impact on them.** If you have to make any changes to correct problems or even just to maintain the network, it is important that you let your users know what you are doing. If you do not, you may get neither the cooperation nor the reaction you expected, and the users may be resentful.

Although not a specific network example, I once worked for a company which experienced multiple layoffs over a period of several years. At one point, a large layoff occurred, and the company lost a high percentage of its most experienced and most talented employees. The layoff occurred on a Thursday. The following Monday, all of us who remained in our department came into our cubicles to find brand new chairs waiting for us. No one knew the chairs were coming. If we had been told, we'd have realized that their purchase had been made long before the layoff was ever executed, and that the arrival of the chairs was simply bad timing. As it was, nothing was said about the chairs either before or after their arrival, except by the employees who received them. Most of them needed new chairs, but would have gladly gone without to have their coworkers back. Few people thought management handled that situation very well. In this case, a little communication would have gone a long way.

4. **Transition smoothly.** Do your best to transition from the existing network environment to the upgraded or new network environment. Few people like change, and even fewer have developed the skills and state-of-mind needed to accept change readily, particularly when it is forced upon them. Communication and understanding can help smooth the transition. So can education and training. Consider these factors when a transition is needed, make every effort to ease the transition for your users, and ensure the transition goes smoothly.

5. **Tactfully respond and address new user issues not previously identified.** When users have problems or questions, the IT professional needs to be tactful in response to users, particularly when the problem is a direct result of something the user did incorrectly, or did not do but should have. Applying common courtesy and treating the user the way you would want to be treated if the situation were reversed generally results in good customer service.

6. **Implement support plan.** It may fall to you to implement a support plan that has been developed by someone else, or you may have to develop and implement the company's IT support plan. Either way, you should make every effort to put the support plan into effect based on the plan's guidelines and implementation requirements. That may mean you have responsibility for troubleshooting and making all repairs, or simply for calling in an outside service company to correct problems.

7. **Handle issues with regard to company wishes.** As with implementing a support plan, you should deal with all IT issues based on the company's preferred method. If responsibility for all support issues is to be outsourced, it may be your responsibility to research outsource options, choose one or more outsource service providers, and track the entire service outsource from complaint reporting to satisfactory reso-

lution. Regardless of how support efforts are implemented, you must make sure they are implemented based on the company's wishes.

8. **Inform users of the business reason why changes will occur (results in a list of products).** When you need to make changes to the network, keeping users informed of not just what the changes are, but of why it is necessary to make those changes is likely to make your job easier. Implementing changes often requires the cooperation of users. Even if their cooperation requires nothing more than having them report whether the implemented change was successful, having individual users report noted problems can save you substantial time over having to verify that each change was successfully accomplished for each user.

9. **Determine the company plan for handling equipment reallocation.** Many companies move equipment around from location to location, and from user to user. A software manufacturer may have a policy which allows an employee to work from home on company equipment. That equipment must be moved to the employee's home, then returned when it is no longer needed. The reallocation of the equipment may be short-term such as the overnight use of a laptop, or more long-term such as reassignment of a computer to a different employee. Either way, a plan should be developed and then implemented for handling the reallocation of network equipment.

E. Administering Change Control System

Tracking network inventory and administering a change control system so that additions and upgrades go smoothly is another of the IT professional's responsibilities. In the CompTIA list, eight tasks are associated with the administering change control system job category (see Figure 4.6).

1. **Add/upgrade operating systems.** This job task is like that of installing operating system software. Adding OS software may mean that you are also adding a new workstation. However, you may just be adding software which expands the OS' features, or you may be upgrading an existing version of the OS to a newer version. Also, it can mean that you are partially or completely replacing older OS software with a newer version (upgrading).

E. Administering Change Control System

1. Add, upgrade operating systems
2. Add security changes
3. Add, upgrade the NOS
4. Add, upgrade software to users systems
5. Add, upgrade the servers
6. Add, move equipment
7. Add, delete new users
8. Add, upgrade peripherals

FIGURE 4.6 The eight job tasks which accompany the administration of a change control system

2. **Add security changes.** Adding security changes generally means that for one reason or another, you have determined or been asked to modify the current security system. You may have to modify software security such as adding firewall security because the company is going to allow Internet access, or bring up a Web server. Or you may have to modify one or more users' security access.

3. **Add/upgrade the NOS (Network Operating System).** Just as you may have to add or upgrade workstation OS software, you may also have to add NOS software. When you add a new server to the network, you will have to install the NOS on the server's hardware. You may also have to upgrade the NOS, either with patches or with regular software updates, or to upgrade it from one version of the software to another. In some cases, you may be replacing one NOS with another such as removing Windows NT NOS and installing Novell's NetWare 5 NOS.

4. **Add/upgrade software to user's systems.** You may also have to upgrade various software on users' workstations. The most common upgrade is that of the network client software. However, you may have to upgrade the version of applications software on network servers, or of some special software programs which may have more limited use on the network. In addition, whenever a new workstation is added to the net-

work, the client software will have to be added and configured as well. (If you have SOPs in place for software installation and upgrade, you'll be able to use them to determine the required configuration for the workstation software.)

5. **Add/upgrade the servers.** As noted in job task three of this job category, you may also have to upgrade the server hardware in order to upgrade the server software. Or, you may add another computer to the network so that you can install server software (NOS) on it.

6. **Add/move equipment.** The two types of equipment commonly added to a network are workstations and servers. However, peripherals such as printers and modems, and other network equipment such as routers, may have to be added to the network as well, and doing so is one of the tasks you may have to perform. Network equipment also has to be moved. Sometimes the move is nothing more than loaning a user a backup PC while theirs is out for service. Sometimes the move can be much more extensive.

I recently participated in moving a testing company's computer equipment from one building to another building in a different city. This company had three separate secured labs, two separate specialized testing labs, and a large main central lab. The move involved taking approximately 600 computers from one city to another. The labs and all of the equipment were being moved from the second story of the old building to the first story of the new building.

A special scissor lift had to be rented, and a large picture window removed from one corner of the second story of the old building. Large racks of 15 to 20 computers were wrapped from top to bottom around every PC with special industrial wrap to keep the computers from moving even slightly on the rack. Then each rack was wheeled to the window and out onto the scissor lift. The lift was then lowered to the waiting moving van, and the rack wheeled into it. At the new building, the racks were wheeled off the truck and into the new lab, and the PCs were unwrapped, connected, and tested. The move was very successful, mostly because extensive and careful planning went into the move.

If issues like how to get the racks of computers (which would not have fit into an elevator even if the old building had one) from the second story to ground level had not been well thought out ahead of time, over 600 individual PCs would have had to be carried by hand down a flight of stairs to reach the van. Just the disassembling and reassembling of those 600 PCs would have taken the staff at least two weeks. During that time, no product or software testing would have been possible. As it was, the move took three full days (Thursday, Friday, and Saturday); by keeping the PCs running that weren't to be moved until Saturday, and having all PCs up and running again by the end of the first day, only one day of testing time was lost. (Careful planning of project testing was also necessary to ensure that additional teardown and setup due to the move was not necessary.)

7. **Add/delete new users.** Whenever a new user is added to the company, or an existing user leaves the company, an account must either be created, or removed or disabled. If the user is temporary or expected to return after a leave, the account can be created as a generic account which can be used by temporary personnel filling the position, or temporarily disabled until the user returns.

8. **Add/upgrade peripherals.** Even equipment such as printers and modems becomes quickly outdated with today's fast-improving technology. It is not uncommon for companies to have to replace networking equipment with newer versions in as little as two to three years. Thus, the IT professional must know how to add peripherals to the network, or at least how to upgrade peripherals when upgrading is an option.

F. Troubleshooting the Network

Attempting to troubleshoot a network problem can at first seem like a daunting task. Where do you begin? What do you do if your first attempts at troubleshooting are not successful? Is there a process you can follow to lead you from the initial indication of a problem to its final correction?

The 16 tasks associated with this category (troubleshooting the network) help answer each of these questions. These tasks (see Figure 4.7) provide guidance in network troubleshooting, as well as an overview of what the IT professional must do to successfully troubleshoot a network problem.

When reviewing these 16 tasks, you should note that CompTIA did not to put these tasks in the order in which they would be performed. (For example, task 13 indicates you should implement a trouble tracking system, while step 14 tells you to design a trouble tracking system. It is not generally possible to implement any system which has not first been designed, so if the steps had been in exact order of implementation, these two steps would definitely be reversed.) Instead, CompTIA arranged these steps the same way they arranged the other categories and job tasks—according to their position of importance based on the focus groups conducted, and the survey responses received. To ensure you understand their relative importance in the examination, the order in this chapter is the same order in which CompTIA listed them.

F. Troubleshooting the Network

1. Isolate variables causing the problem
2. Determine if problem is caused by users or system
3. Document trouble call
4. Perform resolution using appropriate equipment
5. Obtain resources (including vendor support)
6. Document solutions
7. Inform other technicians of solutions
8. Identify resources and resolution plan
9. Highlight the symptoms and problem's cause, history, scope, basis in reality, environment
10. Set priorities for problem resolutions
11. Duplicate problem with known state
12. Follow-up to see if solutions stick
13. Implement trouble tracking system
14. Design trouble tracking system
15. Apply all baseline standards (to server, s/w, network, etc.)
16. Teach problem fixes to users, referring back to baseline

FIGURE 4.7   The 16 network troubleshooting job tasks

The 16 tasks associated with troubleshooting the network are:

1. **Isolate the variables causing the problem.** This task requires that you determine what variables are present which may be causing the problem. To accomplish this task, ask questions such as: what was the user

doing when the problem occurred? Can the problem be reproduced? Was there anything else going on then that isn't going on when attempting to reproduce the problem? and Has anything changed since before the problem began?

2. **Determine whether the problem is caused by users or by the system.** Having the users repeat what they were doing while you are watching can help you determine whether they are doing anything which may be causing the problem. If you find that a user is doing something to cause the problem, remember to be tactful when you point out what should be done instead.

3. **Document the trouble call.** Not only should you record the problem, you should also check previous records to see if there is any record of the same or a similar type of problem. If trouble calls are properly documented, you have quick access to problem resolution.

4. **Perform resolution using appropriate equipment (with tenacity).** Once you have determined what the problem is and how to solve it, solve it as quickly as possible. Make sure the user is convinced that the problem is solved and that productivity is no longer affected.

5. **Obtain resources (including vendor support).** You may not always be able to resolve the problem yourself once you have determined what it is. If that is the case, it will be your job to find the resources to solve the problem. That may include seeking out vendors and choosing the best one to hire to resolve the problem.

6. **Document solutions.** Once the solution is determined, you should log the solution with the problem and keep it as part of your network documentation. If the problem seems to be one which occurs regularly, such as network boards going bad, plan ahead to be able to resolve the problem. In the case of network boards going bad, purchasing an extra board or two to keep them on hand is a good idea. Be sure to note in the documentation that extra boards are available.

7. **Inform other technicians of solutions.** If you are not the only IT professional, be certain others are made aware of the problem and its solution. The documentation can be useful for this as well.

8. **Identify resources and resolution plan.** When attempting to solve a problem, you need to know what resources are available, and you should develop a plan for resolving the problem. In many instances, the plan will not be in writing, but if you document the problem's res-

olution, there will be some documentation from which to develop a plan to resolve the problem.

9. **Highlight the symptoms and the cause, history, scope, basis in reality, and environment associated with the problem.** All of these factors should be documented. You can use the documentation of this and other problems to compare these factors.

10. **Set priorities for the problem's resolution.** As with the example I gave about the users who had received only "emergency" support, prioritizing the resolution of a problem helps you keep up with the critical problems on your network. Critical problems are those which prevent a user from doing a job, or which cause corruption of data, or which may ultimately prove disastrous to the network, or its users, or the company's customers. You need to prioritize not only which problems get resolved, but when the resolution of a problem requires more than one task or step, you may also need to prioritize the steps or tasks.

11. **Duplicate problem with known state.** When troubleshooting a problem, you have the user reproduce it for you if possible. You may also find it necessary to reproduce the problem itself. In fact, you may need to attempt to reproduce the problem multiple times. Each time you attempt to reproduce the problem, you may want to do so with different trusted components. If you suspect the network board is bad, then replace it with a known good network board and attempt to recreate the problem. If the problem persists, it is likely that the network board is not the problem. The goal is to control as much of the environment as you can, and test out various aspects of the problem, or pieces of the hardware for defects or potential problem points.

12. **Follow-up to see if solutions stick**. Once you believe the problem is resolved, you need occasionally to check to ensure that it is solved. If the user reported a problem, check back with the user. If you found the problem while conducting network maintenance analysis tests, then continue to watch for reoccurrences or symptoms of the problems when you conduct additional maintenance analysis tests.

13. **Implement trouble tracking system.** Documenting problems, recording the result, and keeping this information for later use is all part of a trouble tracking system. You can also include followup in your trouble tracking system. However you choose to track problems and their resolution, it is your responsibility to take some action to implement a

system. If none exists, you may have to be the one to set it up and implement it. One may already be defined for you. That is, the company may already have a plan and process for tracking problems, and it will simply be your job to implement the plan. As listed under the job category of managing support efforts, determine if there is a company plan, in this case for a trouble tracking system rather than for handling equipment location, then implement it.

14. **Design trouble tracking system.** If no trouble tracking system exists, then you may have to design it, or at least become instrumental in getting the company to design a trouble tracking system. It will make your life as an IT professional easier, and save the company both time and money. It will also save users and often the company's customers a great deal of grief.

15. **Apply all baseline standards (to server, software, network, etc.).** No matter what kind of network problem you are dealing with, having a baseline standard makes all troubleshooting easier and more effective. It is up to you to ensure that baseline standards exist, and that they are applied to all network components, as well as to the network as a whole.

16. **Teach problem fixes to users referring back to baseline.** One way to make your job easier is to teach your users how to fix problems they encounter. I am not suggesting that you turn all your network users into professional troubleshooters, but if problems continue to occur, having the users know what the cause is and what they can do to fix it will substantially reduce the number of trouble calls you receive and respond to. Even if all you can do is teach one user per group of users the baseline for each network component, and then how to resolve basic problems, that user is often more than willing to help others within the group to solve the easier problems when they crop up.

The librarian for the legal library at state offices where I once worked as the network administrator was very interested in computers. It wasn't her job, but she used computers regularly in the library. Periodically, a problem with the computer or the network would occur. If she had not encountered the problem before, I had to troubleshoot it, then resolve the problem. But the librarian always watched over my shoulder, asked intelligent questions, and wanted to know what was going on. Thus, each step of the way I kept her informed about what I was doing and why. I taught her as I did my troubleshooting and resolution. She learned fast. She took notes. As a rule, if the same or a very similar problem occurred to either one of her library computers, or to one of the computers in the office next door, she could usually figure out the problem and resolve it without ever having to place a trouble ticket call. Her efforts reduced my workload, taught others how to resolve their own problems (both the librarian and the others she taught to resolve problems), and made everyone happier. (Her extra efforts also eventually got noticed, and she was promoted to a higher position.)

When looking at the tasks in this job category, you might think that this job category is similar to the first category in this list of 15 job categories (operating network management system) because the first category contains a certain amount of network troubleshooting as well. However, the first category is mostly concerned with network analysis and establishing a baseline as a tool in troubleshooting. The actual network troubleshooting falls instead into this category.

When troubleshooting a network, there are four areas of network troubleshooting that you may have to look at in order to find one or more network problems:

- ❖ Electrical
- ❖ Physical
- ❖ Security
- ❖ Viruses.

Electrical problems such as crosstalk, a problem where the magnetic field generated by one wire interferes with the electrical field of one or more other wires, can result in network packets that are garbled. Packets may be dropped completely, so that the needed information or service request/response is never delivered. In addition, if a packet is received but is damaged, network traffic may increase as the communicating stations attempt to resend and re-receive one or more damaged packets.

Another electrical problem you can encounter on your network is static. A sudden discharge of static buildup can damage equipment. So too can random, high-voltage bursts of current or sudden drops in current that often occur in cities which commonly experience brownouts or blackouts. A UPS (Uninterruptible Power Supply) can help protect against bursts or sudden drops in current.

A somewhat less-noticeable electrical problem is that of line noise. Low voltage, low current electricity, can interfere with your network as well. Other electric devices such as radios, televisions, and even the ballasts in fluorescent lights can be the cause.

Security problems such as inadvertent or deliberate tampering with or destruction of the network's hardware and software should also be considered. You should also determine if any viruses, programs which may be destructive or just a nuisance but which interfere with the programmed and normal processing of information and software, exist on your network.

When troubleshooting your network, consider each of the possible electrical and security problems as well as potential viruses as causes of problems as well as the physical problems, particularly temperature. High temperatures are especially problematic for network equipment.

As the network administrator for a federal office, I had one employee who complained that every afternoon there were intermittent network connection problems. When I examined the user's workstation, I found that the user liked to open the window blinds in the afternoon. That side of the building received indirect sun, so the user didn't think anything of it. However, that indirect sun heated the entire expanse of window on that side of the building. As her computer had been placed so that she could look out the window in the afternoon, and was thus set with its back close to that window, the computer was overheating. If the user turned the computer off for a while, or kept the blinds closed, the difference in the heat was enough to resolve the problem, at least temporarily.

To correct the problem, we rearranged her cubicle so that she could still see out the window in the afternoon, but so that her computer did not sit close to the glass. The intermittent connection problem went away. This was a simple solution to a problem that otherwise might have suggested looking for a bad network card, or a slight break in the cable, or even electrical interference. In this case, knowing that excessive heat is a problem for network components led me to attempt a simpler correction which, as it turned out, was the correct solution.

G. Administering the Network

Network administration includes tasks which range from monitoring the network to implementing failure management. You will usually perform at least one of its associated tasks every day. To define the job duties of a network administrator, CompTIA lists eight different tasks (see Figure 4.8).

G. Administering the Network

1. Perform back-up/failure management (including virus)
2. Monitor network for performance optimization
3. Fine tune network for efficiency and effectiveness
4. Test/implement disaster recovery plan
5. Assign responsibilities for making network changes
6. Coordinate on-going vendor relations
7. Report on server(s) progress
8. Monitor network for appropriate uses in accordance with SOPs

FIGURE 4.8 Network administration's eight associated job tasks

1. **Perform backup/failure management (including virus).** One task you will generally perform daily is that of backing up network data. You may back up only change data on a daily basis, and perform full back-ups only weekly or monthly. Backups done regularly are important to maintaining the network.

   As the network administrator, you may not be the one who actually performs the backup. You may have the daily backup routine assigned to someone else, but it is still your responsibility to see that it is done. You may also sometimes have to restore the data that have been backed up. Viruses creep into networks, and if you keep a sufficient number of backups, you may be able to restore data without the virus, although it will be necessary first to eliminate the virus from the network.

2. **Monitor network for performance optimization.** Monitoring the network to see whether it is maintaining the level of performance you expect is another network administrator's task. Routine analysis of the network pinpoints problems before they become serious. It can also help you see what can be changed to keep your network running at optimum levels.

Monitoring may include such things as using network management utilities provided with the NOS or as separately purchased software to view network details. The monitor utility that ships with earlier versions of the NetWare NOS (see Figure 4.9) allows you to monitor various statistics such as:

❖ Network utilization
❖ Open file activity
❖ Network connection
❖ Memory resources.

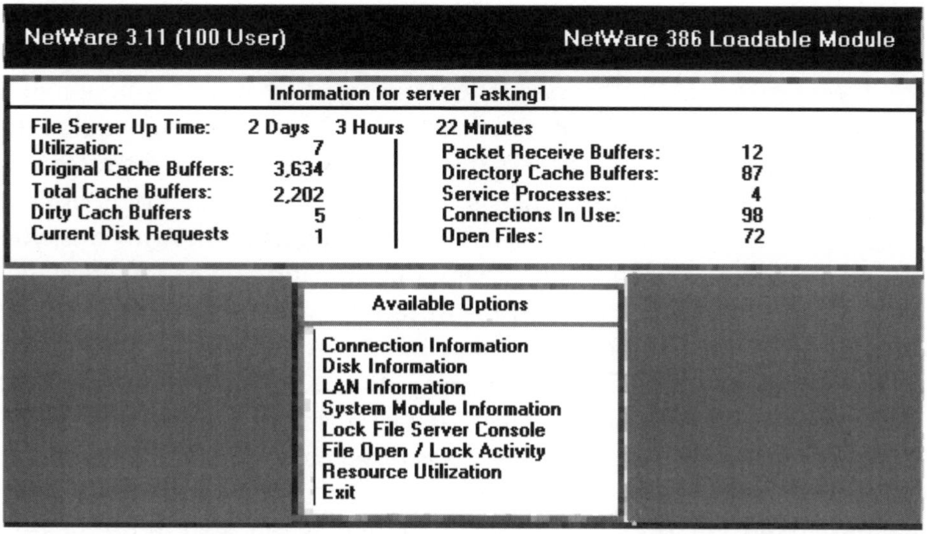

NetWare 3.11 (100 User)		NetWare 386 Loadable Module

Information for server Tasking1

File Server Up Time:	2 Days 3 Hours	22 Minutes	
Utilization:	7	Packet Receive Buffers:	12
Original Cache Buffers:	3,634	Directory Cache Buffers:	87
Total Cache Buffers:	2,202	Service Processes:	4
Dirty Cach Buffers	5	Connections In Use:	98
Current Disk Requests	1	Open Files:	72

Available Options

Connection Information
Disk Information
LAN Information
System Module Information
Lock File Server Console
File Open / Lock Activity
Resource Utilization
Exit

FIGURE 4.9 Example of the Monitor utility that shipped with Novell's NetWare 3. A revised version of this utility also shipped with NetWare 4.

Successfully monitoring the network does not require that you check statistics and run monitoring utilities daily. You must run them initially to record a baseline, then run them periodically, perhaps monthly, for comparison purposes. Differences in the baseline and monthly figures for any given month may not be sufficient to show you whether your network is functioning at optimum capacity, but comparing multiple months' statistics can show you both positive and negative trends.

For example, the initial Novell NetWare monitor utility screen displays the utilization percentage for the file server's CPU. If you check and record this number each month, you may notice an increasing or decreasing trend in utilization. If you notice an increasing trend, you may decide to monitor this particular statistic more frequently. Doing so can give you an idea of how long it will be at the current rate of growth until the server's CPU is functioning at full capacity. This information can help you plan for upgrading the server's hardware, or adding servers to the network.

3. **Fine tune network for efficiency and effectiveness.** The statistics you gather while monitoring the network can also help you fine tune the network to get the most out of it. Also using the Novell NetWare monitor utility as an example, you can track information such as the Directory Cache Buffers statistic. This number indicates how many server buffers are being used to cache data that the server would otherwise have directly to access the hard disk for. Not having to access the hard disk every time it needs the data, reduces the amount of time it takes for the server to provide the requested data. Knowing this, you would also be able to assume that if the Directory Cache Buffers statistic exceeds 100, you need to increase the number of available Directory Cache Buffers to improve the server's efficiency.

4. **Test/implement disaster recovery plan.** The Setting Up Standard Operating Procedures IT professional job category makes you responsible for developing SOPs for a disaster recovery plan. This particular job task shows that you are responsible for testing, and if necessary, implementing, the disaster recovery plan as outlined in the related SOP. Of course, you never really want to have to implement it, but if you do, it had better be a usable plan. The one way to determine whether the plan is usable is to test it before you have to implement it in a real disaster recovery situation.

5. **Assign responsibilities for making network changes (to right person).** As with routinely backing up the network, you may not have to make the actual network changes. However, you are still responsible for making sure that assignment is given to the right person, and that it is successfully carried out. The right person is of course someone who has been trained to do the job properly, and who has the tenacity to follow through.

6. **Coordinate on-going vendor relations (important to know details of service contracts).** The right person for the job of making network

changes may not be a company employee. It may be a vendor you contract with to perform this and other network-related tasks. Developing and then maintaining ongoing, positive, and professional relationships with vendors is an important IT professional's task.

As the network administrator for the Mohave County Courthouse in Arizona, I had the task of coordinating ongoing vendor relations. Vendor relations with several companies had been successfully established by my predecessor. As I had both limited staff and internal equipment for network maintenance and repair, much of the troubleshooting which required special equipment, and parts replacement and repair of workstations was done by one particular vendor. Not only did this vendor provide timely and reasonably-priced troubleshooting repair services, but the relationship established and maintained with this particular vendor always ensured that we received prompt, courteous, and frequently first-priority service.

7. **Report on server(s) progress.** As IT professionals, find it easy to be so busy with daily duties that we forget to keep people informed about the progress of network administration. Reporting to management and users alike of issues related to the network's servers can be important, particularly when it becomes necessary to ask for additional resources (more servers or upgrades for existing servers), or when you need to explain to the users why some scheduled network down time may be necessary.

8. **Monitor network for appropriate uses in accordance with SOPs.** Before you can monitor for appropriate uses, there must be some definition of what appropriate use of the network consists of. This generally comes in the form of company memos or policy statements which outline the dos and don'ts of using the network. For example, if company personnel have Internet access, company policy may restrict that access to business use, or at least require that all personal use be done after network hours. As the network administrator, you may have to monitor this type of usage. Other common usages you may monitor include access to restricted files on the network, the number of users simultaneously accessing each software package, and whether the number of simultaneous users accessing each software package ever exceeds the number of licenses the company owns for that software.

H. Designing the Network

As an IT professional, you may design only a single network for a company by which you are employed. If you do consulting work, you may find that you design hundreds of networks over the years of your career. You may also find that you never work for a company that needs its network designed because it was already designed by someone else. The network design may already be implemented, or you may be hired, as I was by one federal agency, to implement a network that someone else had designed.

The CompTIA job category of designing the network includes the following 18 listed job tasks (see Figure 4.10).

Here you may see some similarities with the job tasks of some of the other categories. For example, the first job task in this category is that of determining equipment compatibility. This is also a necessary part of the fourth task (verify that all ordered equipment/software is correct and available) you perform when implementing the installation of the network. The first place you perform this task, however, is when you design your network.

1. **Determine equipment compatibility**. The best-designed network is of little use if the equipment you use to implement the design is incompatible. When designing the network, you must ensure that all equipment to be used is compatible. With today's open systems architecture, compatibility is not as much of a problem as it has been in the past. That does not mean incompatibility has been completely eliminated.

2. **Translate needs/goals into selection of actual hardware and software.** If you know that your network servers need to handle 250 users each, you would not buy network operating system software that is rated for only 200 users. When choosing hardware and software, know what goals it needs to meet, then make sure your selections meet those goals.

3. **Develop/plan to integrate new with legacy equipment.** Some of the older equipment in today's offices is not very compatible with the newer equipment available on the market. That does not mean you will not be able to integrate the legacy equipment with the new equipment, but it may mean that you have to take extra steps in planning and implementation to integrate that equipment. Carefully planned integration makes the implementation go more smoothly, although it will not necessarily go without problems.

H. Designing the Network

1. Determine equipment compatibility
2. Translate needs/goals into selection of actual hardware and software
3. Develop/plan to integrate new with legacy equipment
4. Cost out the system and option, including equipment, labor, management tools, training, support
5. Design a network according to criteria
6. Set realistic expectations for systems performance
7. Identify equipment availability
8. Develop back-out (if prototype or pilot fails)
9. Create migration coordination plan
10. Create phased-in implementation plan
11. Research specification and conventions
12. Design graphic representation ("network map")
13. Validate specifications and conventions
14. Revise plan as needed
15. Establish (set-up) library for network (licensing, cabling layout, physical floor plan, diskettes, etc.)
16. Design training with network in mind
17. Coordinate with additional vendors
18. Present purchase plan to management

FIGURE 4.10 The 18 job tasks associated with designing the network

4. **Cost out the system and options, including equipment, labor, management tools, training, and support.** When the network is designed, the cost of every aspect of that network must be considered. If you have to integrate legacy equipment, for example, you may find that the special equipment needed to do so is as costly as simply replacing the legacy equipment with newer equipment. Costing out everything

including equipment, labor, management, tools, training, and support helps make sure you have designed a system that meets the company's needs and stays within the budget. Costly overruns are often the result of poor planning, not just price increases from the time you start the planning process to the time you implement the network.

5. **Design a network according to criteria.** Can you imagine trying to build an airplane for a customer without that customer telling you what the airplane is for? You might build a B52 bomber when what the customer wanted was a two-seater Piper Cub. Are both good airplanes? Probably, but they are both useless (and costly) if they aren't what the customer needed. The same thing applies to networks. Find out what the customer needs (the criteria for a network) before you begin constructing it.

6. **Set realistic expectations for systems performance (for users and management, reset as you go along).** Who wouldn't want that $50 cubic zirconia ring to turn out to actually be a $5,000 diamond ring? But if $50 is all you have to pay for a ring (or the equivalent for a network), you cannot expect to get a $5,000 diamond ring (or equivalent network). If you do expect the diamond ring, you will be greatly disappointed. Keep your expectations and those of your users and managers realistic when it comes to what the network can and cannot do for them. Otherwise, when the network you deliver doesn't live up to the one you promised, everyone will suffer.

7. **Identify equipment availability.** When designing a network, make sure you are designing it around equipment that is available. If you design a network that calls for equipment which is not available, due to backlogs, limited technology, or for whatever reason, the implementation of the network will be delayed, and may end up being completely impossible. You look bad. The company suffers. And as often as not, so do the company's customers.

8. **Develop back-out (if prototype or pilot fails).** As has been noted before, everything does not always go exactly as planned. So when designing a network, consider where and how it will be possible to back out of the proposed network if the prototype or pilot program fails and proves that the design itself cannot be successfully implemented.

That is exactly what had to be done when the design for the county courthouse system was developed. (Remember the earlier example about the courthouse in a town so small it only had six telephone lines and the addition of others was a year late?) That implementation had a back out plan. The backout plan consisted of allowing the remote courthouse to continue to operate under its current independent system until the telephone lines were available to add it to the rest of the network. Although this backout system meant the equipment was not being put to its full use, it allowed the rest of the county's courthouses to go forward with the implementation of the network.

9. **Create migration coordination plan.** Data always exist in the old format when you install a new format, whether you are simply changing the filing system, or going from a completely manual processing system to an electronic one. You must develop a migration plan to allow for the smooth transition from one system to the next.

     Again using the country courthouse network as an example, the move to a network was conducted in three phases and extended over a period of two to three years. The first phase allowed for implementation of computers to put all documents online. Older paper documents were kept open and available in an extensive file system until each case was closed. They were stored for a period of time at the local offices, then eventually moved off site to archive storage. New cases were handled by putting them into the appropriate electronic format. The second phase was then to network the computers in each courthouse so that records could be shared within the courthouse. The third phase then networked each LAN (local area network) into a county-wide WAN (wide area network) allowing records to be called up from any county courthouse. Of course, because of the time involved in accomplishing this, the implementation plan included regular upgrades of the LAN hardware in addition to the WAN hardware which was added. Considering the magnitude of the effort, the entire process went fairly smoothly. The fact that it did so was the direct result of the carefully thought out migration plan, and as the next job task identifies, a phased-in implementation plan.

10. **Create phased-in implementation plan.** A phased-in implementation plan is just what it implies—a method of implementing the network that takes into consideration one aspect of implementation at a time. As you saw in the previous job task, the network's design mandated a phased-in implementation plan, and in that case, it was very successful.

11. **Research specification and conventions.** You need to do your research on various aspects of the network when designing it. After you begin to implement the network, it may be too late. If specifications and conventions for one part of the network do not match one or more other parts of the network, you will have to implement your backout plan. Taking specifications and conventions into consideration when designing the network initially is a much better approach.

12. **Design graphic representation ("network map").** Remember the earlier example about the move of a federal office, including its network, from one building to another? When the move of the federal government facility for which I was the network administrator took place, all cabling and server and workstation locations were clearly identified on blueprints and other maps of the new building. These documents were a graphic representation of the network; a network map. That network map ultimately proved very useful.

    When the two network segments which ended up being longer than planned were found, it was a simple task to compare the network map to how the vendor had actually run the wiring. When those graphical documents along with the original blueprints for the building were designed, it was also easy to see that neither the network's designer nor the vendor's installers were really to blame for the problem. The building's architect had not properly positioned on the blueprints every one of the building's supports, so during construction, the contractor had to make modifications to ensure the building did not fall down. There was no argument between the cabling vendor and the network's designer as to who was to blame for the error, so good vendor relations were maintained. In fact, knowing the actual cause of the problem and not "blaming" the vendor resulted in the vendor's voluntarily rerouting the cabling to ensure the cable lengths for those two segments was correct without charging any extra fees. As you can see, a network map is an invaluable aid when designing and when implementing a network.

13. **Validate specifications and conventions.** If it is important to ensure you are meeting specifications and conventions when you design the network, then it is also important to ensure those specifications and conventions are valid. Take the time to validate them when your network's design relies on their being accurate.

14. **Revise plan as needed.** After examining, planning, validating, and all the other tasks you must do have been done, it is not unlikely that you will find changes that must be made. When you do, simply revise the plan, then retest, revalidate, reexamine, and if necessary revise again. Getting the plan right before you begin to implement it is very important to a successful network installation.

15. **Establish (set-up) library for network (licensing, cabling layout, physical floor plan, diskettes, etc.).** When designing a network, you will end up gathering a great deal of information, and creating many documents. Keep all the information you gathered and relevant documents together in a sort of network library. Then, everything you need to know about the network will be available to you, as well as to other technicians and any individuals who may eventually replace you when you are promoted for your excellent work on the network.

16. **Design training with network in mind.** Networks are not a completely new concept, but for many companies and public services, their implementation is. Training will play a big part in making sure their implementation is successful. When you are designing the network, consider what training related to the network will be needed, and design that training with the network in mind.

17. **Coordinate with additional vendors.** No one vendor will be able to supply everything you need. (At least, it will be a very rare occasion if one does, and you will pay a high price for that rare occasion.) Therefore, it is likely that you will have multiple vendors with which to deal. Working closely with each of those vendors, it will be possible for you to coordinate their efforts so that one vendor is done before the next one needs to start, and without too much of a time gap in between. Successful vendor coordination can mean a successful implementation. The opposite is also true.

18. **Present purchase plan (including ROI) to management).** As with just about everything else in business, the design and implementation of a network must prove itself. There must be some type of ROI (return on investment), or a company will not want to spend the money and time, and put its employees and customers through the pain of making such a change. It is your goal when designing a network to be able to show how the purchase of the components (including hardware, software, training, and so on) is to occur, and how the company is to see its return on investment ultimately accomplished.

I. Planning a Customer's Job

An IT professional's customer is the employer company. That may mean you are a regular full-time employee of a company, or it may mean you are contract help, or even a consultant. Any of these situations may apply and should be kept in mind when learning about each of the 23 job tasks (see Figure 4.11) associated with planning a customer's job.

I. Planning a Customer's Job

1. Identify user/management needs and requirements
2. Define existing systems
3. Determine how customer uses current system
4. Study technology options and solutions, pros and cons
5. Identify support needs
6. Determine business process, organization, and communications
7. Establish documentation plan/requirements
8. Establish project goals, functionality, and security
9. Establish time lines
10. Identify training needs
11. Establish contingency back-up plans
12. Allocate resources
13. Determine applicable technology
14. Develop support plans
15. Present report to management
16. Analyze security needs
17. Identify budget parameters
18. Determine risk assessment
19. Develop prototype
20. Present/market the plan to users
21. Evaluate prototype
22. Analyze physical plant
23. Conduct on-site survey

FIGURE 4.11 The 23 job tasks associated with planning a customer's job

1. **Identify user/management needs and requirements.** In this job task, your goal is to determine what the customer needs, and what the requirements are for the network. Companies will not always be able readily to explain to you what their needs are. You may have to perform some systems analysis to figure out what their needs are. Nonetheless, any needs they identify or requirements they put forth must be met. You must strive to meet the needs and requirements that you identify.

2. **Define existing systems (what exists, how it works, current problems, what needs changing).** Again, this job task is often one performed by a systems analyst. Even though your job is not one of a systems analyst, you must still be able to identify the existing system, determine various important factors about it including how it works and what about it does not work, and then figure out what about it should be changed.

3. **Determine how the customer uses the current system.** Part of defining the existing system is understanding how the customer uses it. That also means you need to know what the customer does not use in the current system. For example, a system may be in place, as it was in one retail corporation for which I worked, always to lock the small, valuable items cage in the warehouse whenever no one was there to monitor it. However, it was not uncommon to find that the cage was left unlocked when no one was around. Just because a system is in place, does not mean it is being used. When you determine how the customer uses the current system, you should also be looking for what exists in the current system that the customer does not use, as well as what is used incorrectly.

4. **Study technology options and solutions, pros and cons.** Unless a physician knows what options are open for dealing with a particular medical problem, the patient may never know there are options. Or the patient may choose a less-than-ideal option, unaware that better options exist. The same is true with technology. The IT professional must keep up to date on the existing technology, and what is good and bad about each technology, to be able to present the customer will all appropriate options when it comes time to design, upgrade, or implement networking technology.

5. **Identify support needs.** All technologies need to be supported once they are in place, and often during their design, development, and implementation as well. As the IT professional, it falls to you to identi-

fy where, when, and how the network should be supported, and to point out that information to those who will make decisions about it, as well as to those who will be supporting the network.

6. **Determine business process, organization, and communications.** A company's network is not an isolated business factor. It soon becomes, if it isn't already, an integral part of the company itself. Determining the company's business process, organization, and communications helps you better to understand how and where the network and its technology will fit into the company, and how implementing the technology will best serve the company. Then you can also do a better job of explaining to the company why the technology and the design and implementation you may be proposing is the best one for the company.

7. **Establish documentation plan/requirements.** When planning a customer's job, you should also identify what documentation the company will need, as well as the requirements or specifications for the development of that documentation. Will you be developing the documentation, or will someone else within the company do so? Whatever method is implemented, you need to ensure that the proper requirements are defined and that some plan for developing and providing documentation that meets those requirements is included.

8. **Establish project goals, functionality, and security.** You are also likely to be responsible for setting goals for the project. Those goals will be identified in order to meet the needs and requirements you make a serious effort to define and determine. Then you must define the system's functionality and security to ensure the goals that have been defined are also met.

9. **Establish time lines (includes establishing person hours).** One of the first questions you may hear once you've presented your plan and had it approved by your customers is, "How long will it take?". You will have to determine approximately how many person hours will be required to implement the plan, and then be able to translate that into a workable time line you can present and have approved by your customer. When developing the time line, you will have to consider how many qualified individuals will be available to implement the plan, how many and which vendors will be used, the availability and timing of equipment, how many days a week people will work, whether holidays, vacations, or similar interruptions will have to be accounted for,

and a variety of other factors. Do your best to include anything you think will affect the time required to implement the plan, then present it with honesty.

10. **Identify training needs (end-user; maintainer).** You design and implement systems for users to use. It is therefore, important that the users know how to use the system properly. You must make sure they get properly trained. But training the users isn't enough. You must also make sure one or more employees are trained to maintain the system once it is in place. If you will be the individual to do the system maintenance, the training will come as you implement the system. But you will not always be the one to maintain that system, so how to train a new maintainer is also important to consider. At the very least, plan a method for documenting how to maintain the system so that the documentation can be passed on to the next person taking responsibility for maintaining the system.

11. **Establish contingency back-up plans.** Like backout plans, backup plans are designed to help keep things moving along in the right direction, even when everything does not work out as planned. Your customers will want to know what you plan to do if something goes wrong. A solid backup plan will go a long way to reducing people's natural hesitancy and reluctance to change.

12. **Allocate resources (job roles, people, etc.).** Once you know how many person hours it will take to implement the plan, you will then need to allocate the resources. At the very least, you will have to identify for your customers the types of people (qualifications, skill levels, etc.) needed to implement the plan, as well as possibly make recommendations on who should fill those roles. Your recommendations may be a list of vendors, or it may include or be limited to a list of the company's employees (and why you believe these individuals or vendors to be qualified to handle the job).

13. **Determine applicable technology (evaluation).** You will have to evaluate the available technology. You will need to look at the customer's existing technology, as well as the availability of new technology. That information will then have to be presented to the customer in such a way that the technical aspects of the technology are intelligible.

14. **Develop support plans.** No one wants to jump into a major change without knowing that someone is available to help if required. "Good sup-

port" are two words you can say about any given technology company worth doing business with (although we often end up having to do business with many companies whose idea of good support does not necessarily live up to ours). When planning a customer's job, include plans for supporting the customer during and after the implementation.

15. **Present report to management.** Management usually makes the final decision, so it is management that needs to know that you have considered all the possibilities, planned for eventualities, and are prepared to implement and follow up. A properly drafted report (or series of them) can provide the information that management needs to be comfortable with giving approval to implement the plan.

16. **Analyze security needs (level).** Security seems to be an issue for just about every customer. Consider what level of security the customer needs. Consider whether one level of security is appropriate in some instances, and another level of security in other instances.

   For example, one of the customer service features the county courthouses wanted to provide was a computer in each courthouse with which its customers (the public) could look up certain types of information. They wanted the public to be able to see what the day's court calendar was for any given judge's courtroom. They also wanted the public to be able electronically to fill out certain types of forms like requests for public information. They did not want the public to be able to call up documents about defendants' cases, and they definitely did not want the public to have access to any information which might identify a minor, whether the minor was a defendant, witness, or had any other association with a legal case. A very high level of security was needed for these public-access computers, while a less stringent level of security was needed for court employees who were supposes to have access to these types of information.

   When planning your customer's job, it's important that you know not only generally but also specifically what type of security is needed. In the case of public-access computers for the courthouses, security had to be implemented at the case level, the "participant's" level, access level, and just about every level in between. Detailed research was needed to determine the security requirements in this instance, and is likely to be required for many of the customers with whom you will be dealing.

17. **Identify budget parameters.** Technology is great, but it is also often very expensive. You have to know how much money the customer is prepared to spend in order to make the best suggestions and recommendations for that customer. Therefore, one important task when planning a customer's job is to get from that customer a realistic budget figure with which to work.

18. **Determine risk assessment.** Is there risk associated with accidentally giving out the name of a minor associated with a court case? You bet there is. And as an IT professional, you must determine what risks are associated with the design and development of the network, as well as the storage and retrieval of information contained on that network. In the court's case, you need to be familiar with the laws associated with public (and private) information in order to determine the risk associated with your proposed design and implementation of the network and the information it contains. You do not necessarily have to be the expert, but at least you have to get the customer to provide you with a knowledgeable individual who can help you assess the risk, particularly in situations such as that of public access to court information.

19. **Develop prototype (reality; on paper).** A prototype is a sample of how the final system should work. In spacecraft development, a prototype is usually a model of the spacecraft, and may include such things as wind tunnel demonstrations of the model to prove its ability to fly. In networking, a prototype can consist of a smaller version of the proposed network, with test data and a few trained individuals to run it. The prototype can also be developed on paper, rather than by actually purchasing limited versions and quantities of the software and hardware needed, if that is sufficient to satisfy your customer that the design will work as planned once it has been implemented.

20. **Present/market the plan to users (turn needs into wants).** The design you develop may or may not be exactly what the customer had in mind. Or the customer may not be as receptive to implementing it as you had expected. It may be necessary for you to sell the plan to the customer. That is, you may have to prove not only that the need for what you have designed, but that the customer wants it as well. This requires a certain ability to market and develop your ideas. In other words, even though you know you are giving the customer exactly what is required, you may have to sell the plan.

Do you remember ever hearing the story about the salesman who decided to sell refrigerators to Eskimos? Why would an Eskimo ever require a refrigerator, even though the refrigerator is an obviously great invention? The salesman knew that Eskimos needed refrigerators, but what he had to do was sell the idea to them. He simply showed them that having a refrigerator would keep their fish fresh but not frozen solid so that they would need less time to prepare their fish when they wanted to eat it. (As I understand the story, the salesman made a great deal of money selling refrigerators to Eskimos.) You too may have to sell the equivalent of refrigerators to Eskimos.

21. **Evaluate prototype.** You probably will want to make sure that any prototype you develop does what it was intended, maybe even before you present it to management. Thus, you need objectively to evaluate the prototype you develop. The prototype should prove that the concept will work as intended, and provide the benefits as well as fulfill the customer's needs and wants.

22. **Analyze physical plant.** Analyzing the physical plant means that you must take a look at what exists in order to determine whether your proposed solution is feasible. For example, if your proposed solution involves recabling the entire building, you need to have enough information about the building itself to be able to determine whether recabling is even possible. The same is true with any other aspect of your plan.

    Again, remember that courthouse that was in a town with only six telephone lines? At one time, it was proposed that communication for this courthouse be established using a site-to-site communication system. It didn't take long to rule out this possibility, however, because anyone who had actually seen the physical location of the town and thus of the courthouse realized that it was completely surrounded by mountains. Site-to-site communications were not possible. Had we gone ahead with the planning based on using site-to-site communications for that remote courthouse, we would have wasted time and money. An analysis of the "physical plant" will often quickly reveal flaws in your planning.

23. **Conduct on-site survey (written; observation).** An on-site survey is just what it sounds like. You go to the site and observe what is going on, where it's going on, and write down what you learn. An on-site survey of the remote courthouse made it obvious that site-to-site com-

munication was not possible. While your on-site survey may not reveal anything so obvious, it will often help you see little things that can potentially become big problems.

J. Analyzing/Evaluating the Applicability of New Technology

Computer and networking technology changes frequently. Components get small, faster, and in many instances cheaper. They also quickly become outdated and replaced by better, sometimes completely different, technology. For example, cable TV used to be available only as an analog signal. Now digital cable TV is available. (You can see technology improvements are not limited to business computers and networks.)

As an IT professional, you need to keep up with new technology. You need to be aware not only of its existence, but of its benefits and drawbacks. Also, you need to analyze and evaluate new technology in and of itself, but also in relation to whether implementing the new technology is in your customer's best interest.

There are nine specific job tasks associated with the job category of analyzing/evaluating the applicability of new technology (see Figure 4.12).

J. Analyzing / Evaluating the Applicability of New Technology

1. Determine how new technology will integrate with existing technology
2. Identify capabilities of new technologies
3. Obtain justification for management approval
4. Determine cost factors
5. Identify unmet business needs for new technology
6. Identify sources for new technology
7. Conduct beta-testing of new technology
8. Determine timeframe for beta-testing
9. Obtain new prototype hardware/software

FIGURE 4.12 The nine job tasks associated with analyzing/evaluating new technologies

The nine job tasks associated with analyzing/evaluating the applicability of new technology for use on your network are:

1. **Determine how new technology will integrate with existing technology.** This job task makes you responsible for deciding whether a new technology you are considering implementing will successfully integrate with the technology being used. Even if the technology can be added, you should also consider whether it enhances and improves the customer's environment, particularly when you consider the cost of implementing new technologies versus expanding with existing technologies.

2. **Identify capabilities of new technologies.** Unless you know what a new technology is capable of doing, you cannot properly assess whether that technology can benefit your customer. You should attempt to identify the positive as well as the negative capabilities of new technologies. The technology of the Internet for example (although not totally new, just improved and basically new to most businesses), has pros and cons associated with its capabilities. It is true that the Internet is capable of allowing companies with offices around the world to communicate frequently, to share information, and to open the company up for international expansion. However, it is also true that adding Internet capabilities to a company increases the potential for security violations by anyone, anywhere in the world. Consider the negatives as well as the plusses when identifying the capabilities of a new technology.

3. **Obtain justification for management approval.** As has been previously noted, few customers implement any kinds of suggestions, particularly those which involve major changes or costs, without management approval. To get management approval, you must be able to justify the proposed changes to management's satisfaction. When you present your design and implementation plan, be certain you have also gathered information sufficient to prove that implementing your design is justified.

4. **Determine cost factors.** I asked when the last time was that something cost you more than you planned, you could probably give at least one example from just the past few days. Your story would probably be tinged with a bit of unhappiness. Few of us enjoy spending more than we planned, and in many instances, few of us are financially prepared to do

so. It is the same with business. Before a company makes a decision about implementing any change to an existing or new system, it must know what that changed or new system will cost. You are responsible for determining what cost factors are involved. Without that information, how could you possible figure out how much the actual cost would be?

5. **Identify unmet business needs for new technology.** Most companies do not spend much time thinking about what new technology they can go find and throw into their business. Their concern is generally for how to meet one or more specific needs. As an IT professional, you can identify business needs that customers have, then help them see how new technology can solve those needs. It is true that existing technology may be able to solve one or more unmet business needs as well. If that existing technology will carry the company into the future and provide a sufficient return on investment while ensuring the company remains competitive, then an existing technology may be what you should recommend. Since technology changes so quickly, existing technology is often not as effective as new technology, particularly if you want that technology to continue to meet business needs for a period of time into the future. The goal, is to identify the business need that is not being met, then see how technology can meet the need, and show that to the customer.

6. **Identify sources for new technology.** New technology generally comes from other businesses. Much of today's technology exists because of the efforts made by government organizations such as NASA. Does that mean you need to look to NASA for new technology? Not really. What it does mean is that you have to find companies to provide the new technologies to your customers. (If NASA is offering a technology for sale, then buy it from NASA.) Realistically, you will be looking at companies around the world to provide the technologies that will help businesses move forward and survive in the competitive world of today and tomorrow.

7. **Conduct beta testing of new technology.** There are many reasons to test a new technology before you implement it into an existing environment. Software and hardware manufacturers routinely beta test their technologies before they offer the final product for sale. One reason these companies beta test products is because of the cost involved in preparing and delivering a product to market, as well as the legal implications and costs of recalling and/or replacing "bad" products. As

an IT professional, you would not want to provide a customer with a product that did not function as expected. Even though you may not have the beta testing opportunities that a hardware or software manufacturer does, you can still beta test products and proposed solutions.

Testing companies exist which will, for a fee, set up an environment to your specifications, then introduce into that environment the design or product you want to beta test. They will run the product or implement the design, put it through its paces, and find the problems for you. They will often assist you in working out the problems, or in creating satisfactory workarounds for the problems.

If you are a consultant or an IT professional within a corporate IT department and you want to upgrade or replace existing technology, it may be in your and your company's best interest to beta test the new technology. Testing of this type can also be referred to as proof-of-concept testing, particularly when what it is designed to accomplish is to prove that the new technology or design lives up to its promises.

One company trying to sell its product (network technology solution) to another company approached a testing company and asked them to help them prove that their solution for this customer would not only work as promised, but would benefit this company if implemented. The testing company set up a lab which duplicated as closely as possible, the potential customer's existing network environment. Then the testing company introduced the new technology to the existing environment, and ran battery after battery of defined tests on the system. The result was not only that the company's network technology solution worked as promised, but the data gathered made it possible for the selling company to provide statistics to prove to the buying company that implementing the new system would save the buying company money. It was not difficult for the management at the buying company to make up their minds about this product.

8. **Determine time frame for beta testing.** Of course, beta testing does not have to be as extensive as described in the previous example. Beta testing should be designed so that it meets the needs of the customer. Conducting the beta test within a specified time frame is also important. A beta test with no end is not only costly, but also likely to be of limited use. You must establish a time frame for the beta test, not just set up and run the beta test.

9. **Obtain new prototype hardware/software.** If you are recommending new technology, then of course you should obtain a prototype. A prototype may be a model or example of the technology. If the new technology is complete, the prototype can be the actual technology, but implemented in a limited manner. Either way, obtaining the new prototype hardware and/or software is likely to be necessary, as well as beneficial.

K. Maintaining the Network

A great deal of time, effort, and money go into the design, development, testing and implementation of a network. All that will soon be wasted if the network is not maintained. For an IT professional, it is an important job to see to it that the network is properly maintained. This job which can consist of up to eight different job tasks (see Figure 4.13).

K. Maintaining the Network

1.	Establish need(s) for patches fixes, upgrades, etc.
2.	Test software patches, fixes, upgrades, etc.
3.	Research/locate the vendors' patches, fixes, upgrades, etc.
4.	Develop maintenance schedule (software patches, etc.)
5.	Monitor usage to prevent problems and make corrections
6.	Implement maintenance schedule
7.	Analyze relationship between users and system
8.	Identify standard maintenance requirements

FIGURE 4.13 The eight job tasks required for proper maintenance of the network

To maintain a network properly, complete the following eight job tasks:

1. **Establish need(s) for patches, fixes, upgrades, and so on.** You must have some way of identifying when a patch (software fix for a specific problem, usually one which is critical or at least very troublesome in nature), a fix (software repair for one or more problems, generally not critical problems), an upgrade, or other changes or improvements to

the network are needed. Each customer may have rules which define when patches, fixes, etc., should be implemented. You may be the one who helps the customer to establish the need for such changes.

2. **Test software patches, fixes, upgrades, and so on.** If a patch, fix, upgrade, etc. is to be implemented, test it before you implement it throughout the network. You can use any appropriate method to test the modification. You can hire a testing company, you can isolate a segment of your network and test it on that, or choose any other method which is appropriate. The important thing is to test the patch, fix, etc. in an environment which does not endanger the entire network and its data, and least inconveniences the users.

3. **Research/locate the vendors' patches, fixes, upgrades, and so on.** Once you are aware that a patch, fix, etc. is needed, you must determine whether one is available. The Internet has become particularly useful in this regard. You can often go to manufacturers' Web sites and find out whether a fix or patch exists; often you can also download the fix or patch for free. You can also usually contact the company using e-mail, traditional mail, or by phone to learn what you need to know, then have the fix, patch, etc., sent to you through the mail.

4. **Develop maintenance schedule (software patches, fixes, upgrades, and so on).** All software eventually changes or becomes obsolete. That means you will constantly be fixing, patching, or upgrading some aspect of your network's software. To help these updates go smoothly, it is best to plan a schedule for making the updates. Once you develop this maintenance schedule, it is also helpful to make your customer and the users aware of the schedule, then follow it as closely as possible.

5. **Monitor usage (current state) to prevent problems and make corrections (load balancing).** Just as it is useful to monitor network statistics for troubleshooting purposes, it is also useful simply to monitor the network's usage to determine whether the network's load is properly balanced, and whether corrections need to be made to the network.

6. **Implement the maintenance schedule.** Developing a maintenance schedule is of little use if you do not implement that schedule. As with developing the schedule, keep your users notified of the maintenance schedule, and particularly of any variances from that schedule.

7. **Analyze the relationship between users and system.** Look at the network and the interaction of users with it as a whole system. Consider how the users use the network, what it provides them in the way of

benefits, and what difficulties or hardships it may cause them. Consider the relationship between users and the network as you consider ways to improve the network. The better the relationship between the users and the network, the more cooperation you will get from the users, the more satisfaction the users will get from the network, and the more productive the company will be as a whole.

8. **Identify standard maintenance requirements.** Most systems, regardless of what they are (dishwashers, cars, networks, etc.) have some standard requirements for regular maintenance. Manufacturers generally recommend that you change the oil in your car every 3,000 miles, for example. Network components have maintenance requirements as well. For example, Novell generally recommends that you upgrade your network clients whenever an upgrade is available, or whenever upgrading server software (at a minimum). You should be aware of what the standard maintenance requirements are for each component on the network, and then work to meet those maintenance requirements.

L. Analyzing/Evaluating Network Implementation

As you implement the network, you need to analyze the feedback and evaluate the success of the implementation. If the implementation is not providing the network and resources you expected, as you expected them, you may have to revise your strategies and implement changes.

Whatever approach turns out to be necessary, there are six tasks associated with analyzing/evaluating the implementation of the network (see Figure 4.14).

L. Analyzing/Evaluating Network Implementation

1. Get feedback from users on network
2. Acquire appropriate sign-off
3. Re-evaluate system after initial goals are met
4. Revise all strategies
5. Determine/document lessons learned
6. Lead the second team of implementers (quality control)

FIGURE 4.14 The six job tasks required successfully to analyze/evaluate the network

The six tasks you perform when analyzing/evaluating the implementation of a network are:

1. **Get feedback from users on network (proactively ask them).** The network is not fully operable until the users are satisfied with it. Make sure they are satisfied by asking them. If they provide negative feedback, make every effort to correct whatever problems they have identified, then ask again.

2. **Acquire appropriate sign-off (includes pay-off).** Once you believe the system to be in place and functioning properly, get the customer's approval, in writing. Also, collect any payments still due. Then the appropriate sign-offs will be complete.

3. **Reevaluate system after initial goals are met.** Take another look at the system. Does it meet all of the defined goals, and does it meet them to the level of quality expected? If so, the system is complete.

4. **Revise all strategies.** There are two main reasons to revise your strategies. First, you want to revise your strategies when the ones you are using are not having the desired result. Second, if your strategies have been successful, then followup and followthrough are the next logical steps. You will need to revise your strategies to be successful at both.

5. **Determine/document lessons learned.** As you know, every experience in life provides some lessons. It is also commonly said that we learn from our mistakes. If mistakes were made, or decisions were not the best ones, then you should document that fact. You should also document what was successful about the design and implementation. In other words, you should document both the good and bad lessons learned.

6. **Lead the second team of implementers for follow-up; the quality control team.** Revised strategies can help make the followup successful. A team of quality control personnel will do most of the followup. You may be responsible for leading that team, and the revised strategies that you developed may help you be successful.

M. Implementing Change Control System

A change control system is important to tracking modifications made to the network. If all that is available for future use is the original documentation, wrong decisions may be made. Wrong decisions lead to problems with the network, increased expenses, and may ultimately result in a network that has to be completely revamped, or worse, abandoned. Therefore, implementing a change control system is an important category; it contains eight specific job tasks (see Figure 4.15).

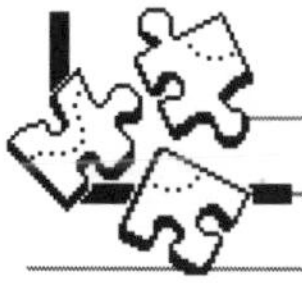

M. Implementing Change Control System

1. Tracks the adds/upgrades of operating system
2. Track the adds/upgrades of software to users systems
3. Track the additions to security changes
4. Track the adds/upgrades of NOS
5. Track the adds/upgrades of servers
6. Track the addition/moves/removals of use equipment
7. Track the addition/deletion of new users
8. Track the adds/upgrades of peripherals

FIGURE 4.15 The eight job tasks that must be completed if you are successfully to implement a network change control system

Perform the following eight tasks when implementing a change control system:

1. **Track the adds/upgrades of operating system.** Every change made to the system needs to be recorded and tracked. That includes changes made to the changes, as is sometimes necessary.
2. **Track the adds/upgrades of software to users systems.** If users' systems software is changed, new systems or new software are added, that too must be documented and tracked.
3. **Track the additions to security changes.** Whenever security is modified, regardless of which level of security is changed, or how minimal the change is, the change must be recorded and tracked.
4. **Track the adds/upgrades of NOS.** The network operating system software is the heart of the network. When changes, additions, or upgrades are made to it, they must be documented and tracked.

5. **Track the adds/upgrades of servers.** When other servers are added to the network, the network map and all accompanying documentation need to be recorded and tracked.

6. **Track the addition and moves, removals of equipment for users.** Keep a record of where equipment is located. If it is moved or taken out of the system completely, or new equipment is added, record and track those changes.

7. **Track the addition/deletion of new users.** Users come and go. Their addition to or removal from the network and the directory services database must be recorded and tracked.

8. **Track the adds/upgrades of peripherals.** Even relatively benign equipment such as peripherals should be recorded on the network map and tracked. If they are moved, that should be noted, along with where they are moved to. Any changes or additions of peripherals should be recorded and tracked for future reference.

N. Developing Documentation (and SOPs)

Throughout the lists of job tasks in this chapter, you may have noticed that documentation has been at least a small part of most of the tasks that need to be performed. Developing documentation, including standard operating procedures to be followed for just about every aspect of the network is also the IT professional's responsibility, and generally includes six job tasks (see Figure 4.16).

N. Developing Documentation (and SOPs)

1. Create troubleshooting documentation
2. Document the system changes
3. Document system (include how parts interact)
4. Provide input for documentation of corporate user support, policies, etc.
5. Document details of service contracts and vendor relations
6. Document the distribution of documents

FIGURE 4.16 The six job tasks of developing documentation and SOPs

There are six specific job tasks associated with developing documentation and SOPs:

1. **Create troubleshooting documentation.** What the problem is, what its symptoms are, when it was noted, what efforts were made to correct it, as well as what was successful and what was not are all part of the troubleshooting documentation you should create. In addition, standard procedures for troubleshooting any network problem should be included in the documentation.

2. **Document the system changes.** This job task was covered in great detail in the implementing a change control system job category. If you simply took the tasks listed in that job category, and put them into this description of this job task, you would have a thorough description of the task of documenting system changes.

3. **Document system (include how parts interact).** Not only should you document each of the components of the network, but you should also record information about how they interact. For example, the county courthouse system I administered had a UNIX-based system which held the database of court records. Access to the UNIX system was through multiple NetWare 4 servers, using Novell's directory services software. An understanding of how these separate systems functioned and interacted in this network was an important piece of the system's documentation.

4. **Provide input for documentation of corporate user support, policies, etc.** Be proactive when it comes to the development of corporate policies regarding user support and other factors which affect the network. Use your technical expertise to help ensure the policies are realistic and appropriate.

5. **Document details of service contracts and vendor relations.** In the situation I described earlier where the network administrator I was replacing had gone on vacation and the routers went down, there was no documentation available to me regarding the different service contracts that had been signed. If there had been, I would have been able to contact the appropriate vendors and have the situation resolved much more quickly. Therefore, when you document service contracts and vendor relations, be sure to include information about which situations are appropriate for which vendors to respond to.

6. **Document the distribution of documents.** Network documents can be extremely valuable and very confidential. If you keep more than a single copy of any network-related document, be certain that you also keep a record of who has those documents. Also, make sure those individuals know the documents are confidential, not to be copied and otherwise distributed, and that you track each one. When you give someone an updated version of a network document, get the previous version back, and see to it that the old version gets shredded. You may want to keep a single copy of each previous version of any given document, however, as it also provides a historical record of your network.

O. Developing/Coordinating/Delivering Training

As you read through the following list of 19 job tasks associated with this job category, it will become apparent that the order in which these job tasks are listed is not necessarily the best order in which to execute them. These 19 job tasks (see Figure 4.17) are instead arranged according to the priority that CompTIA's focus groups and survey results indicated. Because that priority affects the percentage of questions on the Network + examination related to any given category or job task, their order has not been changed here.

The 19 job tasks associated with developing/coordinating/delivering training are:

1. **Determine training wants and needs.** This first step is an information-gathering process. How you go about it is up to you, but there are a few common approaches. You can choose to talk to each employee or department manager and ask what they believe to be their individual or department's training needs. You can develop and distribute a survey (use paper copies, e-mail, or put it on your corporate internal Web site). You can take the information handed to you by management or other personnel. You can assess what software and hardware the network's users have, review each user's knowledge level, then make your own assessment. Whichever method you choose, the end result must be an accurate accumulation of information about training wants and needs from which to make appropriate plans.

2. **Analyze training requirements.** Once you have gathered the appropriate information, you must then review it and determine what the true

needs are. If a large percentage of the users tell you they need training in the use of a specific software application, that should indicate to you that there is a specific need. Once you have identified the areas where training is needed, part of analyzing the training requirements is that of prioritizing the training you believe should be provided.

O. Developing / Coordinating / Delivering Training

1. Determine training wants and needs
2. Analyze training requirements
3. Define training content
4. Update users, help desk, technicians
5. Determine if trainer has network-related competencies
6. Prepare a training plan
7. Develop installer training
8. Prepare a training outline
9. Evaluate training
10. Develop user, support, maintainer training
11. Coordinate support training
12. Design effective training methods for a training solution
13. Design a training needs survey
14. Design effective evaluation strategies for a training solution
15. Conduct a training task analysis
16. Coordinate user training program
17. Design effective instructional strategies for a training solution
18. Develop a training evaluation instrument
19. Write a training target population description

FIGURE 4.17   The 19 job tasks of developing/coordinating/delivering training

3. **Define training content.** As you analyze training needs and wants, you will begin to define what each training option should contain. For

example, if training on a specific software package takes a high priority, then you need to determine what that training should consist of. You need to determine if the training is for basic uses of the software, or more advanced uses.

4. **Update users, help desk, technicians.** When training is warranted and the content defined, you then need to let others know what training is planned. Users, help desk personnel, and technicians should all be made aware of what training you are proposing and planning for so that they know what to expect. This also gives these individuals an opportunity to validate your analysis, or steer you in a different direction if for some reason your defined training content is not just what they believe to be needed.

5. **Determine if trainer has network-related competencies to deliver certification training.** Once you know what you are going to implement for training, you need to determine who is going to do the training, and whether the chosen trainer(s) have sufficient knowledge of networking to provide that training. You have several options for trainers. You can choose an individual in your company who is an expert in the area, and make that individual the trainer. This may be sufficient in many cases, but just because an individual has the knowledge, it does not mean the skill successfully to convey that knowledge is present. You can hire an independent trainer, but again you want to make sure the trainer is competent both in the information you want taught, as well as in how that information can be affected by a network environment. You also want to make sure the trainer has the skills needed to be effective. Another option is to hire an outside professional training firm to provide the training, either in-house or at the training company's facility. Whatever option you choose, the goal is to make sure your users learn what they need to know, and that your company's training budget can handle the expense.

6. **Prepare a training plan.** As with any other major task you may undertake, it is more likely to be successful if you develop a plan to implement that task. In the case of training, you need to develop a training plan. The plan can include information not only about what you want the training to accomplish, but also who should attend (not individual names but job titles or group/department names). It can also include information about how you want to provide the training, and who will provide it.

7. **Develop installer training (includes special training documentation).**
If the needed training is for equipment, software, hardware, or anything else on the network that may require installation, you may have
to develop training to teach others how to do that installation. You may
also need to teach individuals how to install the training program
itself, if appropriate.

8. **Prepare a training outline.** A training plan gives you the basic information about the types of training to be conducted, who should
attend, who will provide it, and other related information. The training
outline can include a schedule of when the training is to take place,
and a general overview of what the training will cover. The training
plan and the training outline are closely intertwined. You may find
that the training outline itself is a natural addition to the training plan,
at least when it is being presented for management approval.

9. **Evaluate training.** You will want to make sure that the training you
have arranged for is doing what you intended it to do. You can evaluate
the training and its success in any of several ways. You can interview
attendees after they have taken the training to see how helpful they
believe the training was. You can track trouble calls for issues related
to the content of the training and determine whether trouble calls
have been reduced. You can spend time watching one or more select-
ed users do their jobs both before and after they have had training and
see if there is a noticeable improvement in performance after the
training. How you choose to evaluate the training is less important
than the fact that you do evaluate it.

10. **Develop user, support, maintainer training (includes special training
documentation).** Developing the training itself can range from creating course outlines to writing all training materials. It can also be as
limited as working with a professional trainer or training company to
develop training that meets your users needs. You may also find that
you need to develop training for individuals who will be responsible
for supporting the users once training has been conducted, as well as
for maintaining the training program until its completion.

11. **Coordinate support training.** Most companies have some type of internal support. It may only be one or two individuals who provide that support, or it may be an entire staff of people who help with anything from
figuring out how to set up a new PC as a workstation, to advanced soft-

ware applications or network maintenance and upgrade. Regardless of the level of support your company provides internally, those providing that support will need training as well. They may need training not only technically, but in the support process. You must coordinate that training.

12. **Design effective training methods for a given training solution.** Once you've chosen the training solution, you may need to design the best method for implementing that training. Internal training classes may be suitable, but external training may also be needed. Hands-on, on-the-job training may work, but sending employees away to classes may also be suitable. The goal is to design the training method most effective for meeting the company's training needs.

13. **Design a training needs survey.** As mentioned in the first job task listed here, designing a training needs survey is one way to determine the training needs and wants of the company. You can use this method early in the process to create an initial list. You can also use this method to refine your training plan, or to see how effective your training efforts have been.

14. **Design effective evaluation strategies for a given training solution.** In order to evaluate training, you need an evaluation strategy, maybe more than one. Designing an evaluation strategy that tells you whether or not the chosen training solution has been effective is your responsibility.

15. **Conduct a training task analysis.** One of the best ways in which to develop or refine a training strategy is to conduct a training task analysis. To meet this job task successfully, you should evaluate what the users most need to be able to do in the course of their regular day. Conducting a task analysis, just as you might do to perform basic systems analysis, can tell you what areas the training needs to concentrate on for your particular users.

16. **Coordinate user training program.** This particular task may be the easiest one you have to perform. Then again, it may be one of the more difficult tasks you have to perform. The determining factor may well be how effectively you determined training wants and needs, conducted training task analysis, analyzed the training requirements, developed the training plan, chose certified training personnel, and implemented the training program. If you were successful at each of these tasks, coordination should be a matter of scheduling training so as not to interfere with daily work production, or to leave a particular

department or group too short-handed during the training period. Coordination may also require scheduling training rooms, instructors, and other applicable issues such as refreshments during breaks. It could also mean following up with a professional training company you hired to ensure the training is done the way you intended.

17. **Design effective instructional strategies for a given training solution.** Designing instructional strategies does not mean you have to start from scratch to come up with some way to teach all those users everything they need to know. Acres of documentation must exist on instructional strategies. It will be your job either to choose instructors or training companies to implement a strategy you feel is most appropriate to meet the training needs of your users and your company, or to review the possibilities and make and implement the most effective choice. You may decide that a self-study course is best for most of your beginning users, and in-house or external training is best for your advanced users. The end result should be that all users received the training they need and can then do their jobs better and more efficiently than before because they received that training. In other words, choose what you believe is the best strategy for your company's users, your company's network, and your company's training needs and wants.

18. **Develop a training evaluation instrument.** You need some way to measure the success of the training program you have designed, developed, and implemented. You need some instrument of measurement. What you choose should be the most representative for your company, and should be determined by what it is you wanted to accomplish with the training program. For example, if you wanted to reduce the length of time it takes your users to input and process one or more specific documents, then timing the processing of those documents by one or more users both before and after the training can be an effective instrument for evaluating the success of the training program.

19. **Write a training target population description.** This document is simply a description of those the training is designed to help. Various training and educational development books are available for you to use to help develop this document as well as the other documents you may need to write while developing, coordinating, and delivering training.

These 15 job categories and the 175 associated job tasks are the core of the work associated with being an IT professional. You may not do all of these tasks at each job you hold as an IT professional, but if you stay in the field for a while, and hold a variety of positions or responsibilities, you are likely to perform many of them at one time or another. Therefore, these categories and tasks are the ones upon which the blueprint for the Network + Certification examination was based, and around which it was designed.

The following chapter contains the blueprint for the Network + Certification examination. Along with each item of required knowledge included in the blueprint is information to help you better understand what each area of required knowledge can include. The blueprint and accompanying information in the next chapter will help you get started at determining whether you have sufficient knowledge to take and pass the Network + Certification exam. It is also designed to help you see where you need to learn more, and what you should study in relation to each of the areas of knowledge.

Using the Examination Blueprint to Prepare for the Network+ Certification Exam

This chapter presents the examination blueprint: the outline CompTIA used to develop the actual questions created for the Network+ Certification exam. The blueprint provides the prioritized outline of the topics on which the Network+ examination is based, as well as information about the relative importance of each topic, although the percentage assigned to each of the topics is approximate. In addition, the blueprint identifies what you are expected to understand about each topic, (although the information is not accompanied by much explanation).

For example, the blueprint lets you know that you are expected to have basic knowledge of networking technology. The additional information the outline provides in this category explains that you should be able to demonstrate an understanding of basic network structure. The topics associated with basic network structure, of which you should have sufficient knowledge, include:

❖ Characteristics of the star, bus, mesh, and ring topologies
❖ Each topology's advantages and disadvantages
❖ Characteristics of network segments and network backbones.

As stated, the blueprint gives an outline of what you need to know about any particular category of networking information if you want to pass the Network + Certification exam. Knowing what you need to understand about network structure lets you determine whether you already have sufficient knowledge of network structure, or whether you should concentrate your studies on those topologies. The blueprint is designed to help you make those determinations, but the outline will not tell you exactly what it is you need to know.

For example, the outline tells you that you need to know the four topologies as well as their advantages and disadvantages. We will assume you already know what each of the four topologies looks like, but you do not really know the advantages and disadvantages of each. The blueprint does not tell you what those advantages and disadvantages are. For that information, you have to draw on your own experience, look up the information in one or more reference books, ask someone who knows, or obtain a Network + Certification study guide written specifically to provide the more detailed information about each topic listed on the Network + Certification examination blueprint.

Regardless of where you find the information you need, you first need to know what examination-related knowledge you do not have. Once you determine that, you should research on those topics. As with the case of the topology topics listed above, you would want to research the advantages and disadvantages as part of your study plan. (Chapter 7: discusses study plans and how they can be used effectively to prepare for the Network + Certification examination.)

Use the blueprint as outlined in this chapter to help you:

❖ Identify what you already know about networking
❖ Identify what areas of networking you need to learn more about
❖ Establish a study plan
❖ Locate the information you need to learn or review
❖ Prepare yourself for taking the Network+ Certification examination.

You should also use the blueprint to help determine which areas of knowledge are the most important when it comes to test questions. To help you do that, the initial percentages assigned by CompTIA to rank by importance the various aspects of IT networking technology and networking practices are included in this chapter as well. If your study time is limited, use these percentages to help you determine on which areas of information you should spend most of your time.

The CompTIA blueprint was given to this book's authors by CompTIA's Network+ Program Manager, Doug Bastianelli. As some of the wording in the initial CompTIA examination blueprint was a little cryptic, the following outline (blueprint) has been modified to correct that. However, the outline itself and the percentage assigned to each area are the same as the original examination blueprint.

To help make sure you understand what is meant by each item of information listed in CompTIA's Network+ Certification examination blueprint, definitions of various terms, and brief explanations or extrapolations are included for many, but not all, of the items of information included on the blueprint. We included this extra information to help make sure you are headed in the right direction when you create your study plan and begin researching the information you still need to learn.

The CompTIA examination blueprint is divided into two main areas of knowledge networking technology and networking practice.

The networking technology area accounts for approximately 67 percent of the test questions on the Network+ certification examination. The networking practice area accounts for the balance (see Figure 5.1). Within each of these two areas, the topics are further divided.

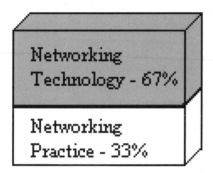

FIGURE 5.1 A graphic displaying the percentage of test questions associated with each area of networking information included on the Network+ Certification test

This chapter is organized to follow the blueprint of the CompTIA Network+ Certification examination. After reading this chapter, you will be able to:

❖ Understand the overall design and organization of the certification exam
❖ See where your knowledge of networking technology and networking practice is weakest
❖ Prepare a study plan according to the suggestions in the following chapter, and base that study plan on your current level of networking technology and networking practice knowledge as compared to the level of knowledge you will need in order to pass the certification exam.

Understanding the Networking Technology Knowledge You Need to Pass the Examination

As the examination will contain approximately 90 questions, roughly 60 of those questions will cover the following nine defined areas of networking technology.

Figure 5.2 displays the percentages for each of the following nine networking technology categories:

❖ Basic knowledge
❖ Physical layer

❖ Data link layer
❖ Network layer
❖ Transport layer
❖ TCP/IP fundamentals
❖ TCP/IP suite
❖ Remote connectivity
❖ Security.

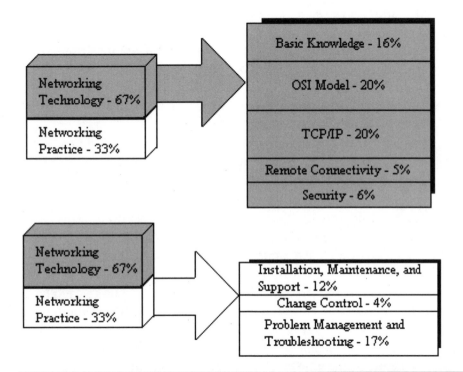

FIGURE 5.2 A graphic displaying the percentages of potential questions which relate to each of the nine categories of networking technology knowledge

As you can see from the list, the second through fourth areas of knowledge relate directly to the OSI (Open Systems Interconnection) networking reference model. The next two areas in the list relate to TCP/IP (Transmission Control Protocol/Internet Protocol), while the remaining three areas have individual importance.

Basic Knowledge

Questions on basic networking knowledge account for approximately 16 percent of the CompTIA Network+ Certification examination. To successfully answer test questions related to basic networking knowledge, you should be able to:

❖ Demonstrate an understanding of basic network structure. This includes knowledge of the characteristics of star, bus, mesh, and ring topologies

❖ Understand the advantages and disadvantages of each of these topologies

❖ Understand the characteristics of network segments and network backbones

❖ Identify the three major network operating systems: Microsoft Windows NT, Novell NetWare, and UNIX

❖ Identify the directory services of these major operating systems

❖ Identify the clients that best serve these specific network operating systems and their resources

❖ Associate IPX, IP, and NetBEUI with their functions

❖ Define mirroring, duplexing, stripping (with and without parity), volumes, and tape backup, and explain how each of these terms relates to fault tolerance or high availability

❖ Define the layers of the OSI (Open Systems Interconnection) model and identify the protocols, services, and functions that pertain to each layer

❖ Recognize and describe the characteristics of networking media and connectors. The characteristics about which you must have sufficient knowledge are: the advantages and disadvantages of coax, Cat 3, Cat 5, fiber optic (see Figure 5.3), UTP, and STP cable, and the conditions under which they are appropriate; the length and speed of 10Base2, 10BaseT, and 100BaseT cable; the length and speed of 10Base5, 100Base VGAnyLan, and 100Base TX cable; and the visual appearance of RJ 24 and BNC cable, and how they are crimped.

❖ Identify the basic attributes, purpose, and function of various network elements: full- and half-duplexing; WANs and LANs; server, workstation, and host server-based networking; peer-to-peer networking; cables, NICs (Network Interface Cards), and routers; broadband and baseband; and gateways, both as a default IP routers and as methods to connect dissimilar systems or protocols.

FIGURE 5.3 Example of one of many different types of fiber optic cable

Understanding the basic structure of the star, bus, mesh, and ring topologies begins with knowledge of their physical design. For example, the bus topology's physical design is generally linear (see Figure 5.4). Workstations use a single connector to attach to the network cable through which they can both transmit and receive. Ethernet systems using T-connectors and coaxial cable are physically structured in the bus topology.

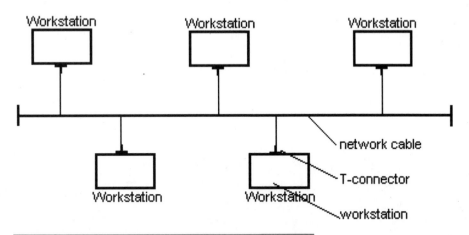

FIGURE 5.4 Diagram of the bus topology's physical design

Understanding the basic structure of different topologies also means that you know about the types of available network cabling compatible with these topologies: coaxial, 10Base-2, 10Base-T, FDDI, etc., (see Figure 5.5), and that you understand other related concepts and facts such as polling, token passing, contention, performance, capacity, and so on.

Type	Max. Segment Length	Main Advantage
10Base2	185 meters	Cost
10Base5	500 meters	Longer cable lengths than 10Base2
10BaseT	100 meters	More reliable and flexible

FIGURE 5.5   Comparison of characteristics of some of the 10base-x cabling types

You should also understand the advantages and disadvantages of each of the basic network topologies, particularly of those listed in this section. For example, for the ring topology, you should know that it is generally the best one to use when high data throughput on a heavily used network is important. You should also be aware that this topology guarantees each workstation will have the opportunity to use the token, and that some systems allow you to give one or more network devices priority access to the network. Each of these examples is an advantage of the ring topology.

You need to understand each topology's disadvantages as well. For example, if one workstation on a star network has a problem, that problem can cause other workstations on the network to have problems as well.

Knowledge of various network components such as network interface boards, the connectors used to attached them to the network (see Figure 5.6), and other related information is also required.

Basic knowledge of networking technology includes an understanding of the different available network operating systems, particularly the three major ones: Microsoft Windows NT, Novell NetWare, and UNIX. Related basic knowledge also means an understanding of the clients used on these networks. For example, Windows NT servers use Windows NT Workstation client software, while Novell NetWare servers use Novell NetWare client software. However, you should also understand that the addition to the network of special software also makes it possible for other clients to access these servers.

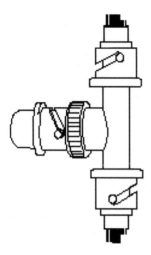

FIGURE 5.6 Example of a BNC connector used to attach an Ethernet network interface card (NIC) to the network

Basic knowledge of networking technology includes an understanding of IPX, IP, and NetBEUI, as well as an understanding of their functions. For example, you should know that IPX stands for Internet Packet Exchange, and that it is a communications protocol that defines how two network nodes communicate. You should also have a basic understanding of what fields make up the packets associated with each technology (see Figure 5.7).

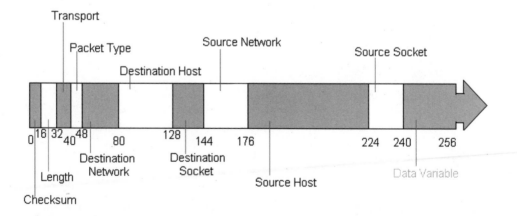

FIGURE 5.7 The fields of an IPX packet

An understanding of the OSI model is also important and includes knowing what each of its layers are, the function of each layer, and a variety of other related information (see Figure 5.8).

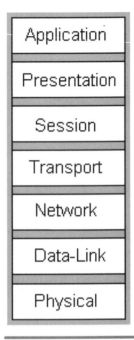

FIGURE 5.8 The OSI model

Understanding basic networking technology requires that you understand each of many different terms and acronyms associated with networking, some of which are mirroring, duplexing, fault tolerance, media, cable, duplexing (see Figure 5.9), WAN, LAN, server, workstation, gateways, routers, bandwidth, and so on. (A good networking dictionary or glossary can be useful for this.) You must also know how those terms and acronyms relate to each other. Therefore, you need a good understanding of the basics of networking.

Physical Layer of the OSI Model

Questions on the physical layer of the OSI model account for approximately 6 percent of the CompTIA Network+ Certification examination. To successfully answer test questions related to the physical layer of the OSI model, you should be able to:

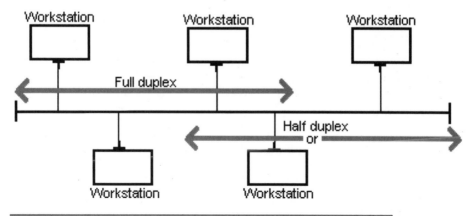

FIGURE 5.9   Diagram of the difference between half-duplex and full-duplex

❖   Given an installation, configuration, or troubleshooting scenario, select an appropriate course of action if a client workstation does not connect to the network after installing or replacing a network interface card, and explain why a given action is warranted

❖   Answer related questions using your knowledge of how the network card is usually configured, including EPROM, jumpers (see Figure 5.10), and plug-and-play software.

❖   Answer related questions using your knowledge of the use of network card diagnostics, including the loopback test and vendor-supplied diagnostics, and of how to resolve hardware resource conflicts, including IRQ, DMA, and I/O base address.

❖   Identify the use of and differences between specific network components including hubs, MAUs, switching hubs, repeaters, and transceivers.

As explained in the previous section, you need a fairly thorough knowledge of the OSI model, which defines standards for networking. When developers use the OSI model as the base to create network components, those components can then successfully work with other components created by other developers. The intent is to make sure networks of different types and designs can all interconnect and share data and resources.

The physical layer is just one of seven layers of the OSI model. It defines the mechanical characteristics and rules associated with the transfer of bits across the network. For example, the physical layer of the OSI model deals with the types of connectors used, the settings for the pins on connectors, voltage characteristics of pins, and so on.

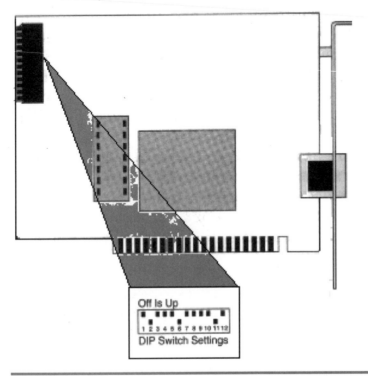

Off Is Up

1 2 3 4 5 6 7 8 9 10 11 12

DIP Switch Settings

FIGURE 5.10 Example of a NIC that uses jumpers to configure settings

Data-Link Layer of the OSI Model

Questions on the data link layer of the OSI model account for approximately 5 percent of the CompTIA Network + Certification examination. To success-fully answer test questions related to the data link layer of the OSI model, you should be able to:

❖ Describe the data-link layer concept of bridges, including what they are and why they are used
❖ Describe the 802 specification, including the topics covered in 802.2, 802.3, and 802.5
❖ Describe the function and characteristics of MAC addresses.

A bridge is a device which connects multiple networks with similar topologies. The data-link layer of the OSI model concerns itself with how bridges make the connection (see Figure 5.11). To be certain that you understand this OSI model layer, you need to understand associated concepts like bridges and how they function, as well as the 802 specification.

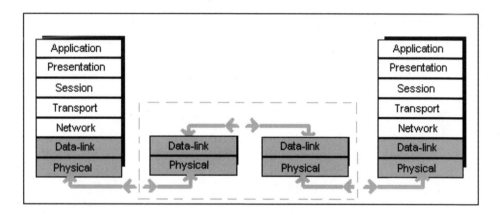

FIGURE 5.11   A bridge functions at the data-link layer of the OSI model

Network Layer of the OSI Model

Questions on the network layer of the OSI model account for approximately 5 percent of the CompTIA Network + Certification examination. To successfully answer test questions related to the network layer of the OSI model, you should be able to:

- ❖ Explain the concept of routing and how it occurs at the network layer
- ❖ Describe the difference between a router and a brouter
- ❖ Describe the difference between routable and nonroutable protocols
- ❖ Define the concept of default gateways and subnetworks
- ❖ Explain the reason for employing unique network IDs (identifications)
- ❖ Describe the difference between static and dynamic routing.

Routing is the delivery of network packets from one network node to another. To route packets, networks require addresses for the sending and receiving nodes. Packets can be routed to nodes on networks which utilize the same topology and protocol as the sending network, or to networks that use different topologies and protocols.

Different network devices are used to ensure the successful routing of packets. Some of these devices are more "intelligent" than others in that they can dynamically determine the best route over which to send network packets. Other devices create a list of routes they can use to send packets, and do not change those routes unless forced completely to recreate their routing table. Intelligent or not, routers function at the network layer of the OSI model (see Figure 5.12), and you should be familiar with routers and other devices related to the network layer of the OSI model.

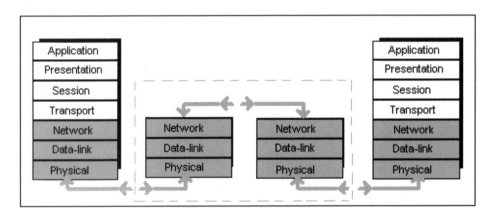

FIGURE 5.12   A router functions at the network layer of the OSI model

Understanding routing, the devices which conduct it, the differences between these devices, and other associated concepts such as the use of unique identification numbers (IDs) and routing tables, will help you attain the knowledge required for passing the Network+ certification test.

Transport Layer of the OSI Model

Questions on the transport layer of the OSI model account for approximately 4 percent of the CompTIA Network+ Certification examination. Successfully to answer test questions related to the transport layer of the OSI model, you should be able to: explain the distinction between connection-less and connection transport and state the purpose of name resolution, either to an IP/IPX address or to a network protocol.

The transport layer of the OSI model is responsible for making sure that units of information are delivered and reliable. One way reliable delivery occurs is through the ability of the network to verify that delivered information was correct. Delivery can use either a connection or a connectionless transport. Name resolution is required to make certain that packet delivery is made to the correct node. Understanding how the transport layer contributes to the successful delivery of information, and associated concepts such as connectionless transport, connection transport, and name resolution will help enable you to answer Network + test questions regarding the transport layer of the OSI model.

TCP/IP Fundamentals

Questions on TCP/IP fundamentals account for approximately 12 percent of the CompTIA Network + Certification examination. To answer test questions related to TCP/IP fundamentals, you should be able to:

❖ Demonstrate your knowledge of the concept of IP default gateways

❖ State the purpose and use of DHCP, DNS, WINS, and host files

❖ Identify the main protocols that make up the TCP/IP suite, including TCP, UDP, POP3, SMTP, SNMP, FTP, HTTP, and IP

❖ Explain the idea that TCP/IP is supported by every operating system and millions of hosts worldwide

❖ Explain the purpose and function of Internet domain name server hierarchies (how e-mail arrives in another country)

❖ Demonstrate your knowledge of the fundamental concepts of TCP/IP addressing, including the A, B, and C classes of IP addresses and their default subnet mask numbers, the use of port numbers (HTTP, FTP, SMTP) and port numbers commonly assigned to a given service

❖ Demonstrate your knowledge of TCP/IP configuration concepts, including the definition of IP proxy and why it is used

❖ Identify the normal configuration parameters for a workstation, including IP address, DNS, default gateway, IP proxy configuration, WINS, DHCP, host name, and Internet domain name.

You will be able to learn a great deal about TCP/IP just by learning the terms associated with it. Many glossaries of networking terms are available (see Figure 5.13).

DNS (Domain Name System) The online distributed database system used by Internet to map names into IP addresses. DNS servers throughout the connected Internet implement a hierarchical namespace that allows sites freedom in assigning machine names and addresses. DNA also supports separate mappings between mail destinations and IP addresses.

FTP (File Transfer Protocol) The TCP/IP standard, high-level protocol for transferring files from one machine to another. Usually implemented as applications level programs, FTP uses the Telnet and TCP protocols. Full duplex - A channel capable of transmitting in both directions at the same time.

TCP/IP (Transmission Control Protocol/Internet Protocol) The suite of protocols developed and used by DAR PA and the US DOD. They build up to Laye r Four of the ISO OSI model, but there is no direct correspondence layer for layer. Three main protocols sit above TCP/IP: Telnet, FTP and SMTP.

DNS (Domain Name System) The online distributed database system used by Internet to map names into IP addresses. DNS servers throughout the connected Internet implement a hierarchical namespace that allows sites freedom in assigning machine names and addresses. DNA also supports separate mappings between mail destinations and IP addresses.

FTP (File Transfer Protocol) The TCP/IP standard, high-level protocol for transferring files from one machine to another. Usually implemented as applications level programs, FTP uses the Telnet and TCP protocols. Full duplex - A channel capable of transmitting in both directions at the same time.

TCP/IP (Transmission Control Protocol/Internet Protocol) The suite of protocols developed and used by DAR PA and the US DOD. They build up to Laye r Four of the ISO OSI model, but there is no direct correspondence layer for layer. Three main protocols sit above TCP/IP: Telnet, FTP and SMTP.

FIGURE 5.13 Sample of some TCP/IP terms and their definitions as found in Brewton-Parker College's Networking Glossary at http://www.bpc.edu/glossary/glossary.htm

Of course, you really need to do more than just look up TCP/IP related terms, but knowing the terminology is a good start. Make sure you understand what is meant by terms such as default gateway, POP3, SMTP, SNMP, FTP, HTTP, IP and others. Also, understand the concept of TCP/IP addressing, and how it functions on a network so that you can successfully answer Network + test questions related to TCP/IP fundamentals.

TCP/IP Suite Utilities

Questions on TCP/IP suite utilities account for approximately 8 percent of the CompTIA Network+ Certification examination. To answer test questions related to TCP/IP suite utilities, you should be able to:

❖ Explain how and when to use various TCP/IP utilities to test, validate, and troubleshoot IP connectivity
❖ Be familiar with the ARP, Telnet, NBTSTAT, Tracert, NETSTAT, ipconfig/winipcfg, FTP, and ping utilities.

Whether you are setting up your network or maintaining it, utilities can help you make sure your network is running as efficiently and effectively as possible. They can also help you troubleshoot problems and track information for determining the optimum configuration of your network.

Some TCP/IP utilities are more complex than others, but all have their uses. For example, the ping utility is a simple one. Its purpose is to let you know whether one network node can see another network node. Other TCP/IP utilities such as NETSTAT are capable of telling you more about your TCP/IP network than just whether one node can see the others.

As an IP professional, you should be familiar with the main TCP/IP utilities, particularly those listed on the Network+ Certification examination blueprint.

Remote Connectivity

Questions on remote connectivity account for approximately 5 percent of the CompTIA Network+ Certification examination. To answer test questions related to remote connectivity, you should be able to:

❖ Explain the distinction between PPP and SLIP
❖ Explain the purpose and function of PPTP and the conditions under which it is useful
❖ Explain the attributes, advantages, and disadvantages of ISDN and PSTN (POTS)
❖ Specify the modem configuration parameters that must be set to enable dial-up networking, including serial port IRQ, I/O address, and maximum port speed

❖ Specify the requirements for a remote connection.

As with other aspects of networking technology, you must understand remote connectivity and the terms associated with it. For example, you should know that PPP stands for Point-to-Point Protocol, and that it is an addition to the Internet protocol suite designed to enable connection of network devices in a network environment where dissimilar transport protocols are used.

You also need to understand the advantages and disadvantages of remote connectivity issues such as using ISDN (Integrated Services Digital Network) versus PSTN (Public Switched Telephone Network) or POTS (Plain Old Telephone Service). Some of the differences and the advantages and disadvantages are obvious. For example, ISDN is digital and designed to carry data, facsimile, graphics, and video transmissions as well as voice. However, the PSTN has somewhere around 300 million telephone connections, so you can take advantage of it from even some of the most remote locations around the globe.

In order to understand remote connectivity, you also need to understand modem configurations (settings which may have to be set manually on the modem or configured using software) for dial-up networking, and other requirements for remote connection. For example, you can use the modem option in Control Panel on a Windows 95 workstation to configure modem settings (see Figure 5.14).

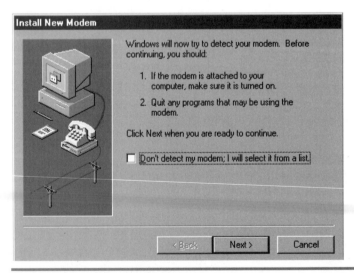

FIGURE 5.14 First window which opens when you run setup for the modem configuration on a Windows 95 workstation

Security

Questions on security account for approximately 6 percent of the CompTIA Network+ Certification examination. To successfully answer test questions related to security, you should be able to:

- ❖ Identify "good practices" associated with selecting a security model at both the user and share levels
- ❖ Identify standard password practices and procedures
- ❖ Explain the need to employ data encryption to protect network data
- ❖ Identify "good practices" associated with the use of a firewall.

Knowledge of security requires that you understand what "good practices" are associated with security models and with the use of firewalls. It also requires that you know the standard practices and procedures for passwords, what data encryption means, and when you should use it to help protect your network.

For example, setting a minimum required length for a password and requiring users to change the password at regular intervals would both be considered standard password practices and procedures. So would instructing network users to not use names of family.

Understanding the Networking Practice Knowledge You Need to Pass the Examination

Knowledge of networking practice accounts for approximately 33 percent of the questions on the CompTIA certification examination (see Figure 5.15). As the examination will contain approximately 80 test questions, roughly 26 of those test questions will come from the following five areas of networking practices knowledge:

- ❖ Implementing the installation of the network
- ❖ Administering the change control system
- ❖ Maintaining and supporting the network
- ❖ Identifying, assessing, and responding to problems
- ❖ Troubleshooting the network

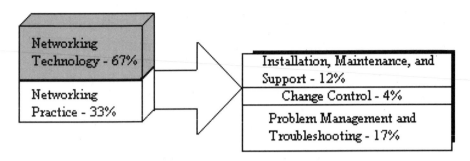

FIGURE 5.15   Percentage of Network+ Certification test questions that will cover networking practice knowledge

Implementing the Installation of the Network

Questions on implementing the installation of the network account for approximately 6 percent of the CompTIA Network+ Certification examination. Successful answers to test questions related to implementing the installation of the network, require that you be able to:

❖ Demonstrate awareness that administrative and test accounts, passwords, IP addresses, IP configurations, relevant SOPs (Standard Operating Procedures), etc., must be obtained prior to network implementation

❖ Given a network installation scenario, explain the impact of environmental factors on computer networks including identifying unexpected or atypical conditions that could either cause problems for the network or signify that a problem condition already exists. Examples include room conditions such as humidity and heat, the placement of building contents and personal effects such as space heaters, TVs, and radios; computer equipment, and error messages.

❖ Recognize (visually or by description) common peripheral ports, external SCSI (especially DB-25 connectors), and common network components including print servers, peripherals, hubs, routers, and brouters.

❖ Given an installation scenario, demonstrate awareness of compatibility, cabling issues, and consequences associated with trying to install an analog modem in a digital jack

❖ Given an installation scenario, demonstrate awareness of compatibility and cabling issues associated with how different cabling results in different uses of RJ-45 connectors

❖ Given an installation scenario, demonstrate awareness of how patch cables contribute to the overall length of the cabling segment.

This category covers more hardware than software issues. Being able physically (or by description) to recognize common peripheral ports and network components such as print servers, peripherals, hub, and others is covered under this category.

If you were shown the picture in Figure 5.16, would you recognize it as a category 5 patch cable? While it might be difficult to say for certain that it was a category 5 patch cable, would you be able to choose that option if your other choices were RS-232, parallel printer cable, or something similar?

The important point here is that you need to be able to understand what the basic components of a network are. You also need to understand how to care for those components. For example, you should be aware of the damage that static electricity and heat can do to various network components.

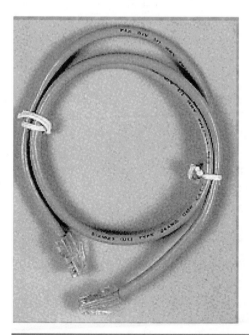

FIGURE 5.16   Example of a category 5 patch cable

The category 5 patch cable shown in Figure 5.16 is from Components Express, Inc.'s online catalog found at **http://www.networkcable.com/category.htm**.

Administering the Change Control System

Questions on administering the change control system account for approximately 4 percent of the CompTIA Network+ Certification examination. Successful answers to test questions related to administering the change control system require you to be able to:

❖ Demonstrate awareness of the need to document the current status and configuration of the workstation (i.e., providing a baseline) prior to making any changes

❖ Given a configuration scenario, select a course of action that would allow the return of a system to its original state

❖ Given a scenario involving workstation backups, be able to select the appropriate backup technique; choices include: tape backup, folder replication to a network drive, removable media, and multi-generation

❖ Demonstrate awareness of the need to remove outdated or unused drivers, properties, etc. when an upgrade is successfully completed

❖ Identify the possible adverse effects on the network caused by local changes. (Adverse affects can include version conflicts, overwritten DLLs, etc.)

❖ Explain the purpose of drive mapping

❖ Given a network scenario, identify the drive mapping that will, using the Universal Naming Convention (UNC) or an equivalent feature, produce the desired results

❖ Given a network scenario, explain the purpose of printer port capturing and identify properly formed capture commands

❖ Given a network scenario where equipment is being moved or changed, decide when and how to verify the functionality of the network and critical applications

❖ Given a scenario where equipment is being moved or changed, decide when and how to verify the functionality of that equipment

❖ Demonstrate awareness of the need to obtain relevant permissions before adding, deleting, or modifying users

❖ Identify the purpose and function of the networking profiles

❖ Identify the purpose and function of the networking rights

❖ Identify the purpose and function of the networking procedures/policies

❖ Identify the purpose and function of the networking administrative utilities

❖ Identify the purpose and function of the networking login accounts, groups, and passwords

Change control systems are a method by which to document and track just about everything you do to modify your network configuration. Change control begins when you first install and configure network components; for the IT professional it generally ends only on the day someone else becomes responsible for the task.

Change control systems ensure that a record of the network exists. They contain historical as well as current information. When using a change control system, you generally record information such as:

❖ Name (of individual making/recording the change)
❖ Contact information (such as e-mail address, street address, mail stop, etc.)
❖ Date change was made (and possibly the time it was made as well)
❖ Where the change was made (may specify a building, a network segment, etc.)
❖ Description of the change
❖ Other related information (such as whether the wiring in a wiring closet was affected, and if so which device name was involved; what host connection changes such as IP address and host name were made, and so on).

You can see that changes can be widespread or confined. The important issue is that you record all changes that affect the network, no matter how small.

How you record those changes is not important as long as you are consistent. You can keep the change information on a note pad in your desk drawer (although this isn't exactly what most professionals would consider a change control system), or you can enter all changes into a database. You can type it up on your computer, or have all IT technicians submit the change information using e-mail (see Figure 5.17).

This figure is part of a form found at: **http://www.scd.ucar.ecu/nets/ Forms/netchange.html**.

Effectively managing change control systems requires more than just recording changes. You also need to know much about the system itself, and for the purposes of the Network+ exam, you need to be able to choose the best approach to take when given a specific network scenario.

Network Change Control Form

Instructions

The following form is meant to be completed before or after a network change has occurred. Please fill out all the fields that apply. Required fields are in bold. When finished, click on the "MAIL FORM" button.

Your email address:

The next three fields refer to the person making the change.

- **Name:**
- **Email address:**

FIGURE 5.17 Example of a portion of an electronic version of a network change control form

For example, you should be able to identify the appropriate drive mappings needed, understand the purpose of printer port capturing and be able to format capture commands, and know when and how to verify the functionality of the network equipment and its critical applications when equipment is to be moved, so that you can make sure it is all functioning properly after the move.

Maintaining and Supporting the Network

Questions on maintaining and supporting the network account for approximately 6 percent of the CompTIA Network + Certification examination. Correct answers to test questions related to maintaining and supporting the network require you to be able to:

- ❖ Identify the kinds of test documentation usually available regarding a vendor's patches, fixes, upgrades, etc.
- ❖ Given a network maintenance scenario, demonstrate awareness of standard backup procedures and backup media storage practices
- ❖ Given a network maintenance scenario, demonstrate awareness of the need for periodic application of software patches and other fixes to the network

❖ Given a network maintenance scenario, demonstrate awareness of the need to install anti-virus software on the server and workstations

❖ Given a network maintenance scenario, demonstrate awareness of the need frequently to update virus signatures.

Although maintaining and supporting the network only accounts for 6 percent of the Network + certification examinations, in some instances it can be your entire job. In many cases, network maintenance and support is such a large task it requires an entire staff to handle all of the related issues.

Key issues with which you will have to deal when you are responsible for maintaining and supporting the network (and when you are answering related Network + certification test questions) include such things as how to utilize vendor's patches, fixes, and upgrades; when a specific network situation exists (given a network scenario), being able to implement standard backup and media storage practices; and utilizing anti-virus software to protect the network.

Identifying, Assessing, and Responding to Problems

Questions on identifying, assessing, and responding to problems account for approximately 6 percent of the CompTIA Network + Certification examination. Successfully answering test questions related to identifying, assessing, and responding to problems will mean you should be able to:

❖ Given an apparent network problem, determine the nature of the action required to resolve the problem. Examples include identifying when simple user "hand-holding" is appropriate, when providing information is the appropriate approach, and when the problem requires providing technical service.

❖ Given a scenario involving several network problems, prioritize them based on their seriousness.

This network category deals almost exclusively with how to determine the level of the problem that exists, and thus the best way to solve it, as well as how to prioritize the tasks you must perform in order to solve the problem. You should also be aware that sometimes network problems consist of several problems that together appear to be a single network issue. You must be able to research the situation sufficiently to recognize such a network problem, and be able to determine the processes needed to handle it, as well as be able to prioritize the tasks you need to perform in order to solve the individual problems contributing to the whole.

Troubleshooting the Network

Questions on troubleshooting the network account for approximately 11 percent of the CompTIA Network+ Certification examination. Successfully answering test questions related to troubleshooting the network will mean you should be able to:

❖ Identify which steps constitute a systematic approach to identifying the extent of a network problem. The steps with which you should be particularly familiar are:
   1. Determine whether the problem exists across the network
   2. Determine whether the problem is workstation, workgroup, LAN or WAN
   3. Determine whether the problem is consistent and replicable
   4. Use standard troubleshooting methods.
❖ Given a problem scenario, select the appropriate next step based on this systematic approach
❖ Identify steps which constitute a systematic approach for troubleshooting network problems. The steps with which you should be particularly familiar are:
   1. Identify the exact issue
   2. Recreate the problem
   3. Isolate the cause
   4. Formulate a correction.
❖ Given a problem scenario, select the appropriate next step based on the defined systematic approach
❖ Identify steps which constitute a systematic approach for determining whether a problem is attributable to the operator or to the system. The steps with which you should be particularly familiar are:
   1. Have a second operator perform the same task on an equivalent workstation
   2. Have a second operator perform the same task on the original operator's workstation
   3. See whether operators are following standard operating procedures.

❖ Given a problem scenario, select the appropriate next step based on the defined systematic approach

❖ Given a network troubleshooting scenario, demonstrate awareness of the need to check for physical and logical indicators of trouble. Indicators for which you should check include: link lights, power lights, error displays, error logs, and performance monitors

❖ Identify common network troubleshooting resources, three of which are knowledge bases on the World Wide Web, telephone technical support, and vendor CDs

❖ Given a network problem scenario which includes a list of symptoms, determine the most likely cause or causes of the problem based on the available information

❖ After determining the most likely cause or causes of the problem, select the most appropriate course of action based on your determination of the cause(s). Consider including the following:
1. Recognizing abnormal physical conditions
2. Isolating and correcting problems in cases where there is a fault in the physical media (patch cable)
3. Checking the status of servers
4. Checking for configuration problems with DNS, WINS, and the HOST file
5. Checking for viruses
6. Checking the validity of the account name and password
7. Rechecking operator login procedures
8. Selecting and running appropriate diagnostics.

❖ Specify the tools commonly used to resolve network equipment problems

❖ Identify the purpose and function of common network tools, including the following:
1. Crossover cable
2. Hardware loopback
3. Tone generator
4. Tone locator (fox and hound).

❖ Given a network problem scenario, select appropriate tools to help resolve the problem. For each tool, understand how to implement the correction, and how to test to verify that the correction worked. Document the solution and provide feedback to the appropriate individuals (usually those who were affected by the problem, and sometimes one or more individuals who are "higher up in the chain of command". Tools which you may use and whose use and function you should understand include:

1. Bridges
2. Patch panels
3. UPS systems
4. Network Interface Cards (NIC)/Network boards
5. Token ring media filters.

Of all of the categories of network knowledge outlined in CompTIA's Network+ certification test blueprint, this category may be the most thorough. It does a fairly good job of outlining network troubleshooting and describing what you need to know about troubleshooting in order to pass the test. The most important study thought you should derive of this category is that you can expect to see questions which give you problem situations, and then be asked to choose from the provided list of tools to use, steps to take, possible causes of the problem, and so on.

One particularly good way to study for this category then would be to research common networking problems, review their causes, understand what it takes to correct them, and what tools (both software and hardware) may be available for you to use. In addition, you should know what the steps of a standard troubleshooting process are, and what tools exist to help you troubleshoot network problems.

For example, assume you are attempting to troubleshoot a communication problem on a network that uses the bus topology. Knowing that a single break in the cable can cause a problem on both sides of that break helps you to understand that it may be difficult for you to isolate that break. On the other hand, if the network utilizes ring topology, finding a cable break is much easier as the repeating function makes it possible for workstations on one side of the break to continue to function.

Having this knowledge helps you know which testing approach is the best one for each topology. In the ring topology, for example, testing the downstream and upstream neighbors of the devices not receiving communication can help you quickly to pinpoint the problem. In the bus topology, however, both a cable break and improper termination of the cable can cause transmission interference.

On a new network or one which has not experienced any recent changes, you may be able to rule out improper termination. But having done so, finding the actual cable break may require that you physically test each cable on the network until you find the one that registers a problem.

If the network problem is not related to the hardware itself, then it may be related to network configuration. As this category points out, you should know how to determine the most likely cause or causes of a network problem and select the most appropriate course of action based on your determination of the cause(s). Once you determine the problem is not a physical one, then you should consider other possibilities including but not limited to the following:

- ❖ Checking the status of servers
- ❖ Checking for configuration problems with DNS, WINS, and the HOST file
- ❖ Checking for viruses
- ❖ Checking the validity of the account name and password.

You should also be aware of the variety of software diagnostic utilities available. You need to know not only that they exist, but what they are and what they are capable of doing. You also need to know whether they are available to you.

Manufacturers of software diagnostic utilities generally attempt to keep them up to date so that they function with the latest networking software and hardware technologies. If you have access to software diagnostic utilities, they need to be ones capable of working with the software running on your network. If your network is using Novell NetWare 3 servers and clients, diagnostic utilities designed for Novell Netware 4 servers and clients may not be of any use if they are not designed to work with older technology.

If you are unfamiliar with diagnostic software, Internet research will help you learn about what diagnostic software is available. There are many to choose from. Check It Pro can give you a quick list of basic facts about a computer's operating system, as well as its hardware. You can even use this particular software to develop a benchmark for system components against which you can perform future analysis for troubleshooting purposes.

The types of tools you use for troubleshooting a network should be chosen based on the network. The most useful tools are often recommended by the hardware and software manufacturers themselves. Therefore, it may be useful for you to check with the leading hardware and software vendors for their recommendations.

For example, if you are working with a Novell NetWare network and ask Novell, Inc., for suggestions or recommendations of tools and information useful for troubleshooting a Novell NetWare network, they are likely to recommend that you get NSEPro. NSEPro is Novell's Network Support Encyclopedia. Its main use is to help you find answers to questions frequently asked by Novell network administrators, and help you protect your network against outdated software (particularly driver software).

If you need to learn about computer hardware, then the Micro House Technical Library (MHTL) is an excellent reference. It is a resource for helping you find specific and recommended configuration and settings information for almost every computer hardware product available. You can use it to obtain detailed information about hard drives, system boards, BIOS settings, and other relevant information.

Regardless of which types of resources you use, the point is that you need to know there are many different ones available, and what they are. You need to know why or when you might choose one particular resource over another. You need to have an understanding of how to use those resources to help troubleshoot network problems, and resolve them.

A great deal of time, effort, and knowledge go into troubleshooting a network. Although the troubleshooting-related questions on the CompTIA Network+ examination only account for 11 percent of the test's total questions, you may have days, perhaps even weeks, as an IT professional when it seems as though all you do is troubleshoot and resolve network problems. If you know the general procedures recommended for troubleshooting network problems, understand what types of problems commonly occur on networks, know what symptoms point to the possible cause of any given network problem, and understand the tools (both software and hardware) available to help you troubleshoot network problems, troubleshooting and maintaining your network will not be quite as daunting a task as it might otherwise seem.

Knowing the general procedures recommended for troubleshooting network problems, understanding what types of problems commonly occur on networks, and so on, will also help you successfully answer the Network+ Certification test questions related to troubleshooting networks.

With all this information about the Network+ certification examination blueprint, you now know the exact outline that CompTIA used to develop the actual questions for the test. This blueprint provides you with the prioritized outline of the topics on which the Network + examination is based, and helps you understand the relative importance of each topic. The blueprint and the explanations and examples included in this chapter should have given you a fairly thorough understanding of what you are expected to know about each of the test topics presented by the CompTIA Network + Certification examination outline.

You might like it if CompTIA had also told you all the detailed information you need to know. But then, you'd simply be able to memorize and recite what CompTIA provided. Would that really prove that you were a competent IT professional? Probably not. You can still be a competent IT professional and not know all there is to know about every one of the topics covered in the Network + Certification blueprint and examination. But how would anyone know? Consequently, as an IT professional, you need to be able to do your job, do it well, and prove to others that you do in fact know what you are doing. That is, you need to be able to prove to others that you are competent.

Yes, you may be able to prove to your present employer and co-workers that you are a competent IT professional by simply by showing up for work everyday and doing your job; by keeping the network running smoothly. But what if you don't yet have that IT job, or you want a promotion or to work for a different company? Becoming Network + certified can help you prove your competency and get the recognition and respect you need to accomplish your goals.

Try not to be overwhelmed by what may seem an enormous amount of required knowledge. The truth is, if you have been working in the industry for any reasonable length of time, you have already acquired much of the knowledge that you need. The two biggest problems you must overcome now are: the fact that the industry changes so rapidly that you must work at keeping your knowledge up to date; and that answering someone else's idea of a series of reasonable questions designed to test your networking knowledge may not be your strong point. Perhaps that is even why you bought this book.

Now that you have come this far and know what the Network + Certification examination is going to cover, take the next step. Go on to Chapter 6 and let it help you prepare to pass that test.

Chapter 6 gives information about some of the study materials available to help you learn the IT professional's job duties, and thus to help you prepare to take the Network + Certification exam. It also explains basic study skills, particularly those useful for preparing to take a technical exam. Applying those recommended study skills which seem to work best for you, along with those you know have been useful to you in the past will help you get ready to prove your acquired knowledge by taking and passing the Network+ Certification examination.

Chapter 6 will also help you prepare a plan to meet your specific study needs. The customized study plan you create with the help of Chapter 6 helps assure that the limited time you have available to study for the Network+ certification exam is put to the best possible study use. But with all that Chapter 6 is designed to help you do, it still takes you to do it. You have read this far and seen just how much information an IT professional needs to know, and how much work an IT professional actually does. Because you still want to become Network+ certified, I have no doubt that you will succeed. Good luck; go for it!

6

Studying for the Certification Test

This chapter is designed to help you prepare to take the Network + Certification examination. It specifically complements Chapters 3 and 4.

Chapter 4 profiled the tasks and duties of an IT professional and presented you with examples from the authors' experiences. It was designed to give you an understanding of what IT professionals deal with on a daily basis, as well as to help you better understand why the Network+ Certification examination includes the types of questions that it does.

Chapter 5 presented the outline for the Network+ Certification examination test that CompTIA developed. It provided information about what CompTIA believes to be the relative importance of each topic, and identified what you are expected to understand about each topic. By doing so, that chapter gave you a detailed overview of what you need to know to pass the Network+ Certification exam. It did not, however, tell you how to go about preparing to take the certification test, the first step in which is understanding the certification testing process.

Now that you understand what it is like to be an IT professional, and how passing the Network+ Certification exam depends on the typical information an IT professional needs to know you are ready to begin preparing for the test. This chapter provides three relevant items of information. After reading this chapter, you will:

- ❖ Know about some of the study materials available to help you learn the IT professional's job duties, and thus to help you prepare to take the Network+ Certification exam
- ❖ Learn about basic study skills, particularly those useful for preparing to take a technical exam
- ❖ Be able to prepare a study plan that meets your specific study needs.

Choosing Study Materials for Preparing for the Network+ Certification Examination

You could randomly search for and choose study materials to help you pass the Network+ Certification exam, but such an approach is likely to be hit and miss. What might work better is an understanding of what CompTIA believes to be relevant study materials. To give you this information, we spoke further with Doug Bastianelli, the CompTIA Network+ Program Manager, who explained that much of what the examination covers is the type of information an IT professional gathers while working in the field.

That does not mean that the IT professional does not study and read, however. So, while Mr. Bastianelli did not provide a specific list of recommended materials, he did indicate that the test questions could be answered with knowledge gained from experience, as well as from many technical books and courses on the related subjects.

As a general rule, most of the leading reference materials for the topics on which the Network+ Certification examination is based will be excellent sources of information. There also are many books and courses on the materials that the exam covers, even though they may specifically state that they are designed to help you pass the Network+ test. There is no doubt that several such books and courses will be on the market shortly after the Network+ Certification test is released.

To help you narrow the list of references you may want to read, this section provides a list of available materials, along with a brief overview or review where applicable. Both available books and Internet references are listed. The list of books comes from multiple sources to ensure that you have a variety from which to choose. Books listed may have been recommended by professionals in the field, or listed on one or more online booksellers such as Amazon.com (see Figure 6.1), Barnesandnoble.com (see Figure 6.2), and the McGraw-Hill Bookstore (see Figure 6.3) found by accessing the McGraw-Hill Web site. More information about each listed reference and where it was found is included with the sections containing the references.

If you have experience in the IT profession, you may need to study only some areas of networking instead of all exam-related areas. For example, you may be very familiar with TCP/IP and basic networking technology, but not with network troubleshooting techniques and concepts. To make it easier for you to choose research materials that will help you narrow your studies, this section, as are the sections in other chapters of this book, is divided based on the areas of knowledge required to pass the Network+ Certification Examination.

In addition to offering suggestions for study materials by knowledge area, this section also discusses where the information for the suggested study materials was found. When a review or information about a specific book is provided, the author or source of that review is also identified. For example, books listed from Amazon.com or Barnesandnoble.com, include a brief statement about the book. Unless otherwise noted, synopses, overviews, etc. included after the relevant reference information for the book also came from the same Web site.

FIGURE 6.1 Amazon.com's Web page

FIGURE 6.2 Barnesandnoble.com's Web page

McGraw-Hill Bookstore

Professional Books of all Publishers

SAVE, STUDY, & PASS!
WITH NEXT GENERATION TRAINING

Buy any New Riders MCSE product and get a 20% rebate on its suggested retail price.

Click here for New Riders rebate offer!

Bookstore Home
Contact Us
Online Ordering
Sitemap

Search Catalog

How to search: enter the Title, Author, Subject, ISBN (without dashes), or a combination of keywords and click on "Search Catalog".

Welcome to the McGraw-Hill Bookstore. We are the retail bookstore of the McGraw-Hill Companies. We have specialized in scientific, technical, computing and business books from **all publishers** since 1961.

Our selection of over 30,000 titles reflects our thirty-five years of experience serving the information needs of professionals from New York City and around the world, leaders on the cutting edge of business and technological developments.

1221 Ave. of the Americas
New York, NY 10020

800-352-3566
or
212-512-4100
(phone)
212-512-4105
(24-hr fax)

Hours:
10AM-5:45PM

FIGURE 6.3   McGraw-Hill's online bookstore Web page

As you now know, knowledge of networking technology accounts for approximately 67 percent of the questions on the CompTIA certification examination, and includes nine of the 15 job categories the test covers. Knowledge of networking practice covers the other 33 percent of the questions, and includes six job categories. The suggestions for study and reference materials are divided in a similar manner. However, because these 15 categories fall into natural groupings (see Figure 6.4)—such as the four named layers of the OSI model all belonging to a grouping call the OSI model—the suggestions for study and reference materials are put into these natural groupings so as not to duplicate suggested references.

You should also be aware that some publishers are preparing to release Network+ Certification guides that will cover all of the 15 job categories on the exam.

As noted earlier, most of the suggested resources in this chapter came either from general Web searches for a specific topic, or from topic searches on a particular Web site. General Web topic searches including terms such as networking technology, OSI model, and TCP/IP were used to locate references on these topics. When specific references were found that did not point to online bookstores or to a publisher's Web site, but included specific information (such as a description of the OSI model), the full reference is included.

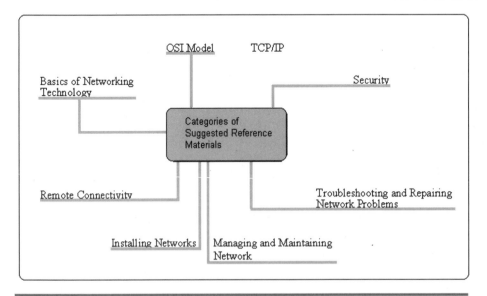

FIGURE 6.4 The groups under which the suggested reading materials have been arranged

References that pointed to an online bookstore or publisher's Web site were further searched to locate the exact book titles, authors, publishers, and other related information. When the books and information about them were located, and the references were included in this chapter, the exact reference is given for the book; the name of the Web site on which the reference and its description or overview were found are also included. To ensure you can find these books, however, we have listed the Web sites for each of the online bookstores and the publishers from which the suggested resources were taken. You have the information you need about each suggested resource, as well as the review or overview of the resource itself that the referenced resource provided.

The references in this chapter are divided by the categories of information you need to know in order to pass the Network+ Certification exam. References within each of those categories identify the online bookstore's or publishing house's Web site from which the book listing was located. However, the exact URL to the Web page for each specific book is not included. Each of the online bookstores has a search engine that allows you to locate any book by its title, or to find all available books by the author. You then need only go to the online bookstore's URL and search for the book's title or author to bring up the specific Web page from which you can read more about the book, and then place an order for it if you choose to do so.

The two online bookstore Web sites used for researching suggested resources are:

❖ The Barnes and Noble online bookstore: **http://www.barnesand noble.com**

 The Barnes and Noble online bookstore provides a brief overview, synopsis, or description of each listed book. In some cases, it also provides one or more reviews written by individuals who have purchased the book. When an overview, synopsis, description, or review was provided with the book's listing, that information has also been included in this chapter along with the book's title, author, publisher, date published, and ISBN number.

 Barnes and Noble sometimes provides a sample chapter (without graphics) of a listed book. This is a particularly nice feature of the Web site which gives you the opportunity to see the writer's style, and to determine whether the level of information the book contains is as in-depth as you are looking for. Also, if the particular chapter chosen does contain specific information you need, you can read it and actually use it to help you study (see Figure 6.5).

❖ The Amazon.com online bookstore: **http://www.amazon.com**

 The Amazon.com online bookstore does not always provide a brief overview, synopsis, or description of each listed book. In some cases, it does provide one or more reviews written by individuals who have purchased the book (see Figure 6.6). When an overview, synopsis, description, or review was provided with the book's listing, at least one of these items of information has also been included in this chapter along with the book's title, author, publisher, date published, and ISBN number. When no description or other details were included about the book on the Amazon.com Web site, either no description is included, or the description has been written by one of us and that fact has been noted.

The following is from <u>Networking for Dummies</u> by Doug Lowe. The URL for this page is:
http://sho.barnesandnoble.com/booksearch/IsbnInquiry/.asp?userid

Chapter 13
Fast as Fast Can Be (or, The Jackalope's Guide to Network Performance)

In This Chapter

- Understanding network bottlenecks
- Tuning your network
- Making your network server faster
- Making your network clients faster

It really is true that there's no such thing as a free lunch. When you network your computers, you reap the benefits of being able to share information and resources such as disk drives and printers. But there are also many costs. There is the cost of purchasing network cards, cable, and software, plus the cost of the time required to install the network, learn how to use it, and keep it running.

There's another cost of networking you may not have considered yet: the performance cost. No matter how hard you try, you can't hide the ugly truth that putting a computer on a network slows it down. It takes a bit longer to retrieve a word processing document from a network disk than it does to retrieve the same document from your local disk drive. Sorting that big database file takes a bit longer. And printing a 300-page report also takes a bit longer.

FIGURE 6.5   One page of a sample chapter from a book displayed on the Barnes and Noble Web page

The online bookstore equivalents for the individual publishing houses used for researching suggested reference materials are:

- ❖ **McGraw-Hill.** McGraw-Hill's online bookstore is at **http://www.bookstore.mcgraw-hill.com**
- ❖ **New Riders publishing.** New Riders is a division of Macmillan Publishing, and therefore some of the references may come from the Macmillan Publishing Web site. The New Riders URLs is **http://www.mcp.com/publishers/new_riders/**. To access the product catalog, click Product Catalog on this Web page, or go directly to this URL: **http://www.mcp.com/catalog/** (see Figure 6.7).

Networking Essentials : Second Edition
by Microsoft Corporation

List Price: ~~$99.99~~
Our Price: $79.99
You Save: $20.00
(20%)

Add to Shopping Cart
(you can always remove it later)

Try express shopping with
1-Click℠ and Gift Click

Availability:
Usually ships
within 24 hours.

Paperback - 800 pages 2nd Bk&cdr edition (November 5, 1997)
Microsoft Press; ISBN: 157231527X ; Dimensions (in inches): 2.50 x 9.54 x 7.55
Amazon.com Sales Rank: 1,125
Avg. Customer Review: ★★★⯪☆
Number of Reviews: 29

Customer Comments

Average Customer Review: ★★★⯪☆ Number of Reviews: 29

A reader from Texas , October 30, 1998 ★★★★★
Excellent book for passing the Networking Essentials exam!
I took the Networking Essentials test first and passed it on the first try with
this book. I found out that the test had been changed from standard to
adaptive testing only 3 days before taking the test. I still went for it and
passed. I strongly recommend this book for the exam. I also used the MS
Prep exam software.

FIGURE 6.6 Sample of a buyer's book review as posted on Amazon.com's Web page

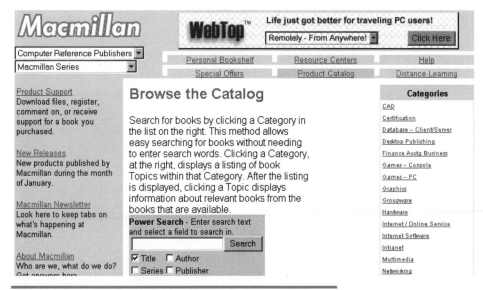

FIGURE 6.7 The Macmillan Publishing product catalog Web site

Suggested Reference Materials for Learning About the Basics of Networking Technology

The following suggested basics of networking technology reference materials were found on the Barnes and Noble online bookstore Web site. When provided on the Web page, the review, synopsis, etc., of the reference material is also included in the following list of suggested reference materials.

❖ Lowe, Doug. *Networking for Dummies*. Foster City, CA: IDG Books Worldwide; 1998. ISBN: 0-764-50346-4.

"Connecting the computers, printers, and other peripherals of your business, school, or other organization can make a huge improvement in productivity and the quality of everyone's work. *Networking For Dummies, 2nd Edition*, provides a practical networking guide that everyone can understand. Author Doug Lowe gives you the solid information and sound advice you need in order to select the right networking software and hardware for your situation. Plus, if you already have a network installed but need to expand or troubleshoot it, you can find expert tips to save you both time and money. From connecting mixed Windows and Macintosh environments to understanding the latest buzzword, intranet, *Networking For Dummies, 2nd Edition*, is an indispensable guide for network administrators."

❖ Maran, Ruth and Marangraphics. *Teach Yourself Networking VISUALLY*. IDG Books Worldwide; 1997. ISBN: 0-764-56023-9.

"Starting with an introduction to networks, network structure, and hardware, Ruth Maran and her team of graphic experts provide concise coverage of the networking universe. Plus, *Teach Yourself Networking VISUALLY* includes vital information for network certifications including Microsoft, Novell, Sun Java, Sun Solaris, and A + certification....

With over 300 pages in full color (600 illustrations in all!), this book provides the easiest way to learn computer networking and to implement a network. It's a virtually foolproof, visual guide to networking concepts and functions, including architecture, tools, and administration and security issues."

In addition to the two reference materials listed on the Barnes and Noble online bookstore Web site, this URL (**http://www.cisco.com/univercd/**

cc/td/doc/cisintwk/ito_doc/) is from a document found on Cisco's Web site, "Internetworking Technology Overview."

This document's associated table of contents contains hypertext links for various other online Web pages which discuss related topics including: internetworking, bridging and routing, network management, and a variety of other networking topics.

This URL also contains a link to a list of other recommended reading. As some of the listed materials may be particularly useful to you when you are studying for the Network + Certification test, we have included some here as they were listed on the Web page:

❖ Black, U. *Data Networks: Concepts, Theory and Practice*. Englewood Cliffs, NJ: Prentice Hall; 1989.
❖ McNamara, J.E. *Local Area Networks*. Bedford, MA: Digital Press.
❖ Miller, M.A. *LAN Protocol Handbook*. San Mateo, CA: M&T Books; 1990.

Suggested Reference Materials for Learning About the OSI Model

The Amazon.com Web site lists books specifically about the OSI model. Two books you may find useful for learning more about the OSI model are:

❖ Black, Uyless D. OSI. *A Model for Computer Communications Standards*. Englewood Cliffs, NJ: Prentice Hall; 1991. ISBN: 0-136-37133-7.
❖ Stallings, William. *Handbook of Computer Communications Standards. The Open Systems Interconnection* (OSI Model and OSI-Related Standards) Prentice Hall; 1990. ISBN: 0-024-15521-7.

The Barnes and Noble Web site includes, in addition to the two books Amazon lists, *Encyclopedia of Telecommunications: IEEE 802.3 & Ethernet Standards to Interrelationship of the Ss7 Protocol Architecture & the OSI Reference Model & Protocols*, Vol. 9 Ed. Fritz E. Froehlich and Allen Kent. New York: Marcel Dekker, Inc.; 1994. ISBN: 0-824-72907-2.

The document found at **http://www.uchsc.edu/csa/is/hd/hdstand.htm** contains an interesting discussion on the various layers of the OSI model. It is the University of Colorado Health Sciences Center's standards document as based on the OSI model. As such, it is a good example of how the OSI model relates to the IT professional's working environment.

Suggested Reference Materials for Learning About TCP/IP

There are many books on TCP/IP. Mike Oliver, the individual who maintains the TCP/IP Frequently Asked Questions HTML page at **http://www.dc.net/ ilazar/tcpipfaq/faq-1.htm#books**, states that the two following books are always recommended reading:

❖ *Comer, Douglas E. Internetworking with TCP/IP Volume I (Principles, Protocols, and Architecture)* Prentice Hall; 1991. ISBN 0-134-68505-9. This is an introductory book which covers all of the fundamental protocols, including IP, UDP, TCP, and the gateway protocols. It also discusses some higher level protocols such as FTP, Telnet, and NFS.

❖ Stevens, W. Richard. *TCP/IP Illustrated, Volume 1: The Protocols* Reading, MA: Addison-Wesley; 1994. ISBN 0-201-63346-9. This book explains the TCP/IP protocols and several application protocols in exquisite detail. It contains many real-life traces of the protocols in action, which is especially valuable for people who need to understand the protocols in depth.

    This book is listed on Amazon.com. It contains 576 pages and has an average customer review ranking of 41/2 stars. According to Amazon.com, individuals who bought this particular book also bought two other TCP/IP related books:

❖ Wright, Gary R. (Contrib.) *TCP/IP Illustrated, Volume 2: The Implementation.* Reading, MA: Addison-Wesley; 1995.

❖ Stevens, W. Richard and Wright, Gary R. *TCP/IP Illustrated, Volume 3: TCP for Transactions, HTTP, NNTP, and the UNIX Domain Protocols* (Vol 3) (Professional Computing Series); Reading, MA: Addison-Wesley; 1996.

McGraw-Hill's online bookstore (**www.bookstore.mcgraw-hill.com**) offers Adam, Kelli. *TCP/IP with CDROM*, Indianapolis, IN: New Riders; 1998. Although written primarily for MCSE candidates, this includes good information about TCP/IP, and sample test questions and exercises to provide additional practice answering TCP/IP related questions.

New Riders publishing lists several books which cover TCP/IP. Of special interest is Siyan, Karanjit. Inside *TCP/IP, 3rd Ed.*, Indianapolis, IN: New Riders; 1998. Of particular interest therein is information about troubleshooting TCP/IP.

There are also several Internet sites useful information about TCP/IP. To find more, use a Web search engine and use TCP/IP as the keyword for the search.

Suggested Reference Materials for Learning About Security

The Barnes and Noble Web site lists the following books about network security.

❖ Benton, Chris. *Mastering Network Security*. Alameda, CA: Sybex, Inc.; 1998. ISBN: 0-782-12343-0.

 "Now that most companies are networked, security is the topic that keeps network administrators awake at night. With up to the minute information on the latest technologies, including Virtual Private Networks and intrusion detection, this book covers all major network operating systems. CD-ROM includes evaluation and demonstration versions of commercial firewalls, intrusion detection software, a variety of hacker tools for testing user's own networks, and much more."

 "Do you need to secure your network? Here's the book that will help you implement and maintain effective network security, no matter what size your network is or which NOS you're using. Packed with practical advice and indispensable information, this book systematically identifies the threats that your network faces and explains how to eliminate or minimize them. Covers all major network operating systems—NT, NetWare, and UNIX—and all aspects of network security, from physical security of premises and equipment to anti-hacker countermeasures to setting up your own Virtual Private Networks. The CD-ROM includes evaluation and demonstration versions of commercial firewalls, intrusion detection software, and a variety of hacker tools for testing your own network."

❖ Strebe, Matthew. Perkins Na, Charles, and Moncur, Michael. *NT Network Security*. Alameda, CA: Sybex, Inc.; 1998. ISBN: 0-782-12006-7.

 "NT Server is rapidly becoming the network operating system (NOS) of choice, with approximately 1 million copies sold in 1996. Featuring case studies on security implementation, here is a complete, practical guide to assessing network security needs and implementing effective solutions. The CD-ROM contains tools for securing NT networks."

The Amazon.com online bookstore lists the following books that either concentrate on network security, or include information about network security.

❖ Ford, Warwick. *Computer Communications Security: Principles, Standard Protocols and Techniques*. Englewood Cliffs, NJ: Prentice Hall; 1994. ISBN: 0-137-99453-2.

The publisher of Prentice-Hall ECS Professional says the following about this book:

"This book identifies and explains all the modern standardized methods of achieving network security in both TCP/IP and OSI environments—with a focus on inter-system, as opposed to intra-system, security functions. Part I is a technical tutorial introduction to computer network security; Part II describes security standards, protocols and techniques. It covers such topics as cryptography, authentication, access control, and non-repudiation; describes a wide range of standard security protocols and techniques, drawn from international, national, government, and Internet standards; and considers areas such as network and transport layer security, local area network security, security management, and security for applications such as electronic mail, directory services, EDI, and banking. "

The author adds this information:

"There is no such thing as 100 percent hackerless security There are just levels of insecurity. This is what I have tried to point out in my book but have make security easier for you to understand and use."

❖ Pooch, Udo W. (Contrib.), White, Gregory B.; Fisch, Eric A. *Computer System and Network Security*. Boca Raton, CA: CRC Press; 1995. ISBN: 0-849-37179-1.

"This unique reference/textbook clarifies fundamental and advanced concepts in computer security. covering a wide range of security issues. It includes case studies with information about incidents involving computer security, illustrating the problems and potential damage that can be caused when security fails. Includes exercises, summaries, reference lists, and extended bibliographies."

❖ Atkins, Derek (Ed.), Sheldon, Tom; Petru, Tim; Snyder, Joel. *Internet Security: Professional Reference*. Indianapolis, IN: New Riders; 1997. ISBN: 1-562-05760-X.

Dorothy Cady has this to say about *Internet Security: Professional Reference*: "I have written many books on networking technology for New Riders Publishing. I'm familiar with the quality of their publications, and often choose New Riders' publications when looking for technology books. This book includes a comprehensive overview of network security and the problems associated with it. One of its particularly interesting features is the fact that not only does it explains the problems of and concepts associated with network security, but it also provides information on what to do about those problems."

Suggested Reference Materials for Learning About Remote Connectivity

Although both Amazon.com and Barnes and Nobles list the following book about remote connectivity, the reference is from the Barnes and Nobles Web site.

❖ Salamone, Salvatore L. LAN *Times Guide to Managing Remote Connectivity*. Berkeley, CA: Osborne-McGraw. ISBN: 0-078-82267-X.

"This guide examines the technical and business issues network managers face when they must give remote and mobile users access to databases, internal electronic mail systems, critical business applications, the Internet, and other corporate resources. The author discusses the services and technologies required to give users access to network resources and helps the reader develop strategies and a business model for remote connectivity."

Suggested Reference Materials for Learning About Installing Networks

Many reference books will help you learn about installing a specific type of network operating system such a Novell's NetWare 5 or Microsoft's NT Server. If the network installation information you need to know relates to hardware or otherwise needs to be more of a general good reference on networking hardware, then look at the books listed here.

You can also go to Web sites such as Amazon.com and do a search on for the term "networking hardware." If you do, you'll see several references returned. The two top books on Amazon.com's list are:

❖ Shafer, Kevin. *Novell's Guide to Networking Hardware*. San Jose, CA: Novell; 1998. ISBN: 0-764-54553-1.

"Advanced network administration requires a fundamental understanding of networking hardware, which this book provides. The guide has been lavishly illustrated with detailed renderings of hundreds of hardware components. The CD-ROM includes a searchable Adobe Acrobat version of the book.

❖ Tanenbaum, Andrew S. *Computer Networks*. Upper Saddle River, NJ: Prentice Hall; 1996. ISBN: 0-133-49945-6.

"Computer Networks excels in its elucidation of the seven-layer Open Systems Interconnect (OSI) network model, dedicating a section of the book to each layer. In the physical layer section, for example, you'll find in-depth discussion of cabling of various kinds and cellular radio and satellite connections. The section devoted to the network layer also covers Internet Protocol, including IPv6, ATM networks, and congestion control.

You won't find any screen shots in *Computer Networks* (conceptual drawings are the order of the day) since little attention is given to actual network operating systems and applications, such as Windows NT and UNIX. Instead, this book focuses on the concepts behind network operation."

Suggested Reference Materials for Learning About Managing and Maintaining Networks

There are some books designed specifically to provide information about managing and maintaining a network, and there are others written for a different overall purpose, which contain useful information about managing and maintaining a network. Barnes and Noble's Web site contains the following books you are likely to find useful when learning about managing and maintaining networks:

❖ Chellis, James; Perkins, Charles; Strebe, Matthew. *Networking Essentials Study Guide* (with CD-ROM). San Francisco, CA: Sybex, Inc.; 1998. ISBN: 0-782-12220-5.

"Here's the expanded and updated second edition of the best-selling MCSE *Networking Essentials Study Guide*! This Microsoft Certified Professional Approved Study Guide provides complete coverage of all the objectives Microsoft has defined for the Networking Essentials exam, one of the four core requirements for the MCSE certification. Special Real-World Problem sections challenge you to apply the concepts of networking to real-life situations and help you learn. The CD includes a practice test for the Networking Essentials exam, together with information resources."

❖ York, Dan. *Networking Essentials Exam Guide*. Indianapolis, IN: Que; 1997. ISBN: 0-789-71193-1.

"This guide offers complete preparation for exam #70-58, Networking Essentials, a key test required for MCSE certification. Written by a team of experts, the book covers all tested areas and includes case study questions to help readers build real-world savvy while studying for the exam. The CD offers integrated skills assessment tests, chapter review tests, and a final exam."

Booknews also had the following comments about this book on the Barnes and Noble Web site:

"A book/CD-ROM aid to preparing for the Networking Essentials Microsoft Certified Systems Engineer Exam, presenting essential information on installing and supporting computer networks. Sequential chapters include skills prerequisites, key concepts, notes, and tips. Appendices offer lab exercises arranged by topic, sample tests, a glossary, a certification checklist, testing tips, Microsoft contacts, and print and electronic resources. The CD-ROM contains review questions and a practice final exam. Assumes familiarity with computers, their components, and Windows products. Annotation © Book News, Inc., Portland, OR.

The following suggested reading reference for learning about managing and maintaining your network was found at Amazon.com.

❖ Andrews, Jean. *A Guide to Managing and Maintaining Your PC*. Cambridge, MA: Course Technology; 1998. ISBN: 0-760-05083-X.

Amazon.com's book description and synopsis state:

"This text contains all of the material necessary to prepare you for the new A+ exam, available in 8/98. The text goes beyond simple exam preparation, however, and enables you to develop skills required to become a proficient PC support technician.

Serving as a comprehensive exam prep study guide for both hardware and software technologies that are non-vendor specific, this book includes coverage of the general "core" concepts module, DOS/Windows module, key Macintosh topics, and printer and monitor topics. The book features real-world examples, interactive activities, and over 100 hands-on projects that reinforce key concepts and help prepare for the exam. The CD-ROM includes practice exams."

Suggested Reference Materials for Learning About Troubleshooting and Repairing Network Problems

The following is a list of troubleshooting books found on the Barnes and Noble Web page. Two cover network troubleshooting in great depth. Since the synopsis or brief overview does not give any idea of the depth of information contained withihn these books, the table of contents for these two books is shown in Figure 6.8 following the reference.

❖ Feldman, Jonathan. *Teach Yourself Network Troubleshooting in 24 Hours*. Indianapolis, IN: Sams, 1999. ISBN: 0-672-31488-6.

"Hands-on solutions for anyone who has to troubleshoot a network. Emphasis is in imparting practical diagnostic techniques and principles, giving readers a list of troubleshooting approaches that come from all fields of discipline.

❖ Allen, Neal. *Network Maintenance and Troubleshooting Guide*. Everett, WA: Fluke Corp.; 1997. ISBN: 0-963-86501-3.

❖ Brenton, Chris. *Multiprotocol Network Design and Troubleshooting*. San Francisco, CA: Sybex Network Press; 1997. ISBN: 0-782-12082-2.

From the publisher:

"Plan, configure, and troubleshoot multi-NOS and multiprotocol networks. This book provides the information you need to get your servers and clients communicating efficiently. You'll find in-depth coverage of the protocols used by the NOSes for communication, discussions of all current and upcoming networks topologies, and detailed information on the troubleshooting tools available for the network operating environments. You'll also find step-by-step procedures for advanced troubleshooting and diagnostics, such as tracing mail problems, locating renegade systems, and isolating performance bottlenecks.

Now that the Internet and Web are a vital part of the corporate desktop, multiprotocol networking is a necessity. Almost every company with a network now needs to integrate TCP/IP with its network operating system to provide Internet and Web connectivity, and all network professionals need to know how to design, implement, and troubleshoot multiprotocol environments. This book covers all aspects of multiprotocol networking with NT Server, NetWare/IntranetWare, Unix, and Lotus Notes and the following protocols: TCP/IP, IP, NCP, IPX/SPX, UDP, DDP, ATP, NetBIOS, and NetBEUI. Contains quick-reference appendixes packed with NetWare/IntranetWare, NT, and Unix connectivity commands."

Table of Contents

Sams Teach Yourself Network Troubleshooting in 24 Hours

- INTRODUCTION: GETTING READY TO TROUBLESHOOT

PART I - GETTING YOUR HOUSE IN ORDER

- HOUR 1 - THE TELEPHONE ANALOGY: BECOMING FAMILIAR WITH BASIC NETWORKING CONCEPTS
- HOUR 2 - YOU CAN'T HAVE TOO MUCH DOCUMENTATION, MONEY, OR LOVE!

PART II - "BLACK BOX" TROUBLE-SHOOTING STRATEGIES

- HOUR 3 - THE DELTAMETHOD: IDENTIFYING NETWORK CHANGE
- HOUR 4 - THE NAPOLEON METHOD: DIVIDE AND CONQUER
- HOUR 5 - THE SESAME STREET METHOD: ONE OF THESE THINGS IS NOT LIKE THE OTHER
- HOUR 6 - THE SOAP METHOD: SUBJECTIVE DATA, OBJECTIVE DATA, ANALYSIS, AND PLAN
- HOUR 7 - THE SIMPLE SIMON APPROACH

PART III - THE CARE AND FEEDING OF NETWORK APPLIANCES

- HOUR 8 - HARD BASICS: GUIDE TO BEING A HARDWARE GEEK
- HOUR 9 - ETHERNET BASICS
- HOUR 10 - TOKEN-RING BASICS
- HOUR 11 - WINDOWS NETWORKING BASICS
- HOUR 12 - UNIX NETWORKING BASICS
- HOUR 13 - NETWARE NETWORKING BASICS
- HOUR 14 - ROUTER AND SWITCH BASICS
- HOUR 15 - FIREWALL AND PROXY SERVER BASICS

PART IV - IN THE TRENCHES

- HOUR 16 - BEAUTY IS CONSISTENCY DEEP: SAVING YOURSELF TROUBLE
- HOUR 17 - WHERE DO I START?
- HOUR 18 - "LOTS OF DIFFERENT PEOPLE IN YOUR NEIGHBORHOOD": IN-DEPTH APPLICATION TROUBLESHOOTING
- HOUR 19 - INTERNET/INTRANET TROUBLESHOOTING
- HOUR 20 - NETWORK TROUBLESHOOTERS JUST WANNA HAVE FUN
- HOUR 21 - TELL ME ABOUT YOUR NETWORK: NETWORK ANALYZERS
- HOUR 22 - WHO WATCHES THE WATCHMEN? NETWORK MANAGEMENT TOOLS
- HOUR 23 - THE NETWORK IS SLOW! GETTING A DEFINITIVE ANSWER TO A SUBJECTIVE QUESTION
- HOUR 24 - REVERSE-ENGINEERING SOMEBODY ELSE'S NETWORK
- APPENDIX A - GLOSSARY
- INDEX

FIGURE 6.8 Abbreviated table of contents for Johnathan Feldman's *Teach Yourself Network Troubleshooting in 24 Hours*

As this book is quite detailed, an abbreviated table of contents is included on Figure 6.9.

Introduction

Chapter 1   Introduction to Multiprotocol Networking

Chapter 2   Transmission Media

Chapter 3   Network Topology

Chapter 4   Networking Hardware

Chapter 5   The OSI Model and Protocol

Chapter 6   Protocols

Chapter 7   IntranetWare

Chapter 8   Windows NT Server

Chapter 9   Unix

Chapter 10   Lotus Notes

Chapter 11   Connectivity Options

Chapter 12   Troubleshooting Tools

Chapter 13   NOS-Supplied Network Tools

FIGURE 6.9   The table of contents for Chris Brenton's *Multiprotocol Network Design and Troubleshooting.*

❖   Miller, Mark. *Troubleshooting TCP/IP. 2nd ed.* New York: Henry Holt & Co.; 1996. ISBN: 1-558-51450-3.
   "*Troubleshooting TCP/IP, 2nd Edition* teaches skilled programmers to use TCP/IP with the Internet, incorporate broadband architectures with

TCP/IP and the Internet protocols, and troubleshoot the Local Network connection including Ethernet, Token Ring, and FDDI LAN. *Troubleshooting TCP/IP, 2nd Edition* also explains common troubleshooting procedures for the Internetwork connection including, IP, RIP, and OSPF. Plus, the CD-ROM contains over 1,000 Internet documents."

Reviewing Basic Study Skills Useful for Taking Technical Examinations

There are several good books on the market to help you prepare to take tests. Silver, Theodore. *The Princeton Review "Study Smart"*. New York, NY: Villard Books; 1992. (ISBN 0-679-73864-9) does a good job of pointing out the difference between studying to learn, and studying to pass a test.

As a network professional, you must learn what you need to know to get your job done. That does not mean that you will necessarily have to learn everything there is to know about each of the 15 job categories outlined on the CompTIA Network+ Certification examination blueprint, however. It is not uncommon for IT professionals to specialize in a specific area. That is one reason why many different professional certifications are available.

If you read Anne Martinez. *Get Certified and Get Ahead*. New York: McGraw-Hill; 1998. (ISBN 0-07-041127-1) you will learn about 160 different certifications. Each of these certifications falls into one of four categories: vendor-specific, multiplatform, hybrid, or vendor-neutral.

Vendor-specific certifications are offered by hardware and software companies. They are designed to let others know that you have at least a minimum level of knowledge about the company's product. Some of the certifications that fall into this category include:

❖ Novell Inc.'s CNA (Certified Novell Administrator), CNE (Certified Novell Engineer), CNI, (Certified Novell Instructor), and other Novell certifications

❖ Lotus Development Corporation's CLP (Certified Lotus Professional) and CLS (Certified Lotus Specialist)

❖ Compaq Computer Corporations' Compaq ASE (Accredited Systems Engineer) and Compaq Associate ASE

Multiplatform certifications are certifications for different platforms or areas of knowledge. For example, if you obtain a Compaq ASE certification as well as a Novell CNE certification, you will have multiplatform certifications. In this example, one is a hardware platform certification, the other a software platform certification. If you are working in an environment where the networking hardware consists mostly of Compaq computers, and the network operating system software is Novell NetWare 5, having this particular multiplatform certification fits your knowledge requirements quite effectively.

Hybrid certifications are those which combine vendor-specific knowledge with vendor-neutral knowledge. For example, a hybrid certification may present hardware and software information from more than one vendor, and blend that knowledge with general knowledge that does not necessarily require a specific vendor. These types of programs are generally developed and sponsored by training companies. They are often the best illustrations of a blending of the types of knowledge in the market. It is logical for the companies to develop and create these types of programs in their effort to ensure the market has the required training.

As Anne Martinez points out in her book on page 109:

> Novell has recently ventured into this market segment as well by creating the Novell Certified Internet Professional (CIP) designation. Professionals can choose from five tracks, including Internet business strategist, Web designer, Web developer, intranet manager, and Internet architecture.

Vendor-neutral certifications are generally sponsored by professional associations and industry organizations. They focus on certification based on an individual's knowledge of technologies as opposed to knowledge of a specific product. A vendor-neutral certification may well be the most long-lasting of the certifications.

The Novell CNA certification concentrates on the basics of a given Novell NetWare platform. A CNA certification has been offered for NetWare 3, NetWare 4, and NetWare 5. As companies outgrow the older version of a particular software product (such as NetWare 3), and upgrade to the newer versions (such as NetWare 4 and NetWare 5), the older certification becomes obsolete. Therefore, often require that you update your certification to the newer technology if you want to remain certified.

Certification obsolescence is less likely to be the case with vendor-neutral certifications than it is with vendor-specific certifications, particularly software certifications. As a rule, the technologies themselves change less drastically than the software products that take advantage of them. For example, the basics upon which the TCP/IP technology was developed have not changed significantly in several years, even though the software which depends on it has changed a great deal.

The point is that you can obtain one or more specialized certifications and be very competent at your job as an IT professional without having to know everything there is to know about the networking industry. However, if you want a general, wide-ranging knowledge of that industry, and want to prove to others that you have such knowledge, the Network + Certification is good to obtain. To get this certification you must pass the Network + Certification examination. The process of successfully studying for that test is not necessarily the same process you would go through to learn, retain, and be able to apply the networking knowledge you need to succeed as an IT professional.

As noted, network professionals must learn what they need to know to get their job done. That may mean, for example, becoming a specialist in Cisco routers, bridges, and other related hardware, but it does not necessarily mean that you will have to learn anything about the Windows NT network operating system software. Unfortunately, if you are a specialist in Cisco routers, NetWare 5, Compaq computers, or any other particular networking technology area, that does not mean you know enough about each of the 15 job categories outlined on the CompTIA Network + Certification examination blueprint to pass the test.

Because you bought this book to help you pass the Network + Certification exam, the study techniques discussed in this chapter are those which will best help you learn the information so that you can pass the test. However, a brief overview of general study techniques to help you learn the materials and later be able to apply them to your work as an IT professional is also included. The general study techniques are presented first, followed by the more specific suggestions for studying with the sole purpose of passing the Network + Certification examination. Read both areas of information, or skip the general study information and read only the specific suggestions for studying for the test.

Preparing Your Network+ Certification Examination Study Plan

Whether you have chosen to study to be able to apply what you learn to your work as an IT professional, or to pass the Network+ Certification test, you will find that a study plan is a useful tool. It will help you more efficiently apply the study time you have available. It will also help you concentrate on those areas where your knowledge is weakest.

To ensure you get the best out of your study time and thus out of your study plan, this section provides general information about study plans and how to create and use them. It also provides an example of what a study plan for preparing to pass the Network+ Certification program might include.

A study plan is a systematic approach to developing the skills and learning what you need to know to meet one or more goals you have set. It helps organize your study and preparation, and make sure you are ready to reach your goal on the date you set for doing so.

In this case, the study plan you want to create should meet the goal of ensuring you pass the Network+ Certification examination. Therefore, the content of your study plan to meet this goal will be based around the examination's blueprint created by CompTIA.

Material content is not the only thing your study plan needs to include. It also needs to set the date on which you want to accomplish that goal. Since your goal is to take and pass the Network+ certification exam, you need to find out where the nearest testing center is located, then contact the center to find out when the test is offered. In many cases, you will be told when the test is scheduled to be available (if it has not yet been released), and what times and days you can take the test.

Many testing centers will let you take the test during any of their regular business hours. However, because you must generally sign up ahead of time to take the test, you have to choose the best day and time to take the test. That date then becomes the date around which your study plan is based. Once you know when you want to take the test (be realistic), the next step in creating a study plan is to obtain a calendar, and mark on it the date on which you plan to take the test. All of the other scheduling and planning revolves around that date.

The next step in preparing a study plan is to make a general determination of what you already know, and what you do not know. The 150 questions in

Chapter 7 of this book are designed to help you do just that. As an assessment test, these questions will give you an idea of what areas of networking technology and practice will require more study time than others.

To help you determine those areas, the test questions are divided into the same 15 categories as the Network + Certification examination blueprint. Once you have taken the assessment test, you will know what categories the questions apply to. Those categories where you correctly answered all or most of the questions then become the categories where less of your study time should be devoted. Those categories where you missed several or most of the questions should be the categories on which you concentrate your study efforts. Although you should spend some time reviewing and practicing to answer test questions in all 15 categories, your study plan should begin by having you spend the most time on the categories about which you know the least.

So that you can use the questions in Chapter 7 as a post-study assessment test as well, the questions have been organized so that you can take only half the test as the pre-study assessment test. To do so, answer only the odd-numbered questions or the even-numbered questions the first time you take the test. Use the results of that test to prepare your study plan. Once you have completed the studying you outlined in your study plan, answer the other half the questions to determine whether there are still some areas in which you can use additional study time.

However, you can also take the entire test twice, once before and once after you implement your study plan. That gives you additional practice at answering questions, but the second time you take the test the questions will be ones you have already seen, and to which you have read the answers.

Regardless of which approach you choose when assessing your current level of knowledge, the answers to each question on the test are more than simply the letter corresponding to the correct choice. In addition, a brief explanation of why the correct answer is the correct choice, and in some cases, of why the other answers are not correct is also included. This lets you see where you strayed when answering the test and should help you determine what you need to study. It does one other thing as well: it shows you how various questions might be worded so as to mislead or confuse you. With some practice, and these 150 test questions will give you at least some practice, you will be able to discern when questions have been written and answers chosen so as to determine whether you do in fact know the material as well as the test writers hope you do.

Now that you know the date you will be taking the test, and you have taken and scored your pre-study assessment test, it is time to determine what topics (categories) you should spend more time studying. As noted, the arrangement of the test questions is by category, so this helps to simplify the task.

In general, if you missed more than 20 percent of the listed questions for any given category, consider this one of the categories you must study. Go through each of the category test questions and determine what percentage of the test questions you missed. (Dividing the number of questions you missed in a given category by the number of questions that exist in that category will give you the percentage of missed questions.) On a sheet of paper, list each category in which you missed 20 percent or more of the questions.

Now, go back to Chapter 5 in this book. For each category of knowledge that you wrote on your list, look up the percentage of the total test questions on the Network+ Certification examination assigned to each category.

For example, if you missed more than 20 percent of the TCP/IP Fundamentals category questions when you took the pre-study assessment test, you would write 12 percent next to that category on your list.

When you have done this for each category of knowledge in which you missed more than 20 percent of the test questions, prioritize the list of categories. Rewrite it from the highest percentage to the lowest. For example, if your list includes the following three categories, then they should be arranged on your list as follows:

❖ TCP/IP fundamentals (12 percent)
❖ Troubleshooting the network (11 percent)
❖ Security (6 percent).

This list lets you know what percentage of the test's questions for any given category you probably would not have passed if you had been taking the actual test. It also tells you what categories are the most important to study (see Figure 6.10).

NOTE This 20 percent figure was chosen as being the most test questions for any given category that you should miss and still assume you know a lot about a given category. It is not the same percentage used to determine whether you pass the actual test or not. In fact, at the time this book was written, CompTIA had not determined the scoring and percentages to be used for the test, as it had also not yet released the beta version of its test. It is the beta version and the scores from beta test takers that CompTIA (and most companies or individuals who design and assess tests) use to determine what the required minimum score for passing is to be.

Sample Study Plan

Scheduled Test Date	June 7
Total Available Study Hours	42

Topics to Study:	**Total Hours for Each:**
TCP/IP Fundamentals (11%)	4.62
Troubleshooting (12%)	5.04
Security (6%)	2.52

Planned study days/times

Mondays	7:00-8:00 PM
Wednesdays	7:00-8:00 PM
Saturdays	5:00-8:00 AM

FIGURE 6.9   Example of a Network+ Certification test study plan

Now that you know what categories are most important to study, you need to determine what percentage of your study time you will allocate to each category. (Figure 6.11 is a form you can use for quickly calculating these percentages. The information presented in the next few paragraphs is a description of the process, and information about why you want to go through this particular process when preparing your study plan.)

Since you have not yet decided how much study time to dedicate to this examination, you will at this point be calculating the amount of study time as a percentage of 100, rather than as a given number of hours.

To calculate the study time for each area, determine what percentage of 100 the total percentage of questions equals. To do this, make two calculations. How to do so is explained using the previous example in which you had three categories you needed to study.

First, of the three categories you determined you would need to study, the associated questions will account for 12 percent, 11 percent, and 6 percent of the total number of questions on the test. Together, these areas of knowledge will account for 29 percent of the test's total questions (12 percent + 11 percent + 6 percent = 29 percent), but will account for 100 percent of your available study time.

Worksheet for calculating study times for each category on the test

1. Circle the percentage under the "Percent of Test Questions" column for each of the categories of networking knowledge for which you missed 20% or more of the pre-assessment test questions you answered in chapter 7; Assessing Your Level of Networking Knowledge.

Category	% of Test Questions	Study %
Basic networking technology knowledge	16	_____
Physical layer of the OSI model	6	_____
Data link layer of the OSI model	5	_____
Network layer of the OSI model	5	_____
Transport layer of the OSI model	4	_____
TCP/IP fundamentals	12	_____
TCP/IP Suite Utilities	8	_____
Remote Connectivity	5	_____
Security	6	_____
Implementing the Installation of the network	6	_____
Administering the change control system	4	_____
Maintaining and supporting the network	6	_____
Identifying, assessing, and responding to problems	6	_____
Troubleshooting the network	11	_____

2. Add the percentages you circled. Write the total in the space provided below.

   TOTAL _____

3. Divide the total you calculated in step 2 by 100, and put the result here: _____

4. Multiply each of the percentages you circled in step 1 by the results of step 3. Write the result for each multiplication on the line next to the percentage under the column titled **"Study %"** in step 1. You now have the percentage of your total study time that you should spend studying the information associated with each of the categories in which you missed 20% or more of the pre-assessment test questions.

FIGURE 6.11 Form for calculating percentage of study time to apply to each category of knowledge

---

NOTE In this example, you already have a great deal of networking knowledge so you do not need to spend time studying the other categories. If you do need to spend time on all 15 categories of knowledge, however, then the percent-age of your study time will exactly equal the percentage of test questions listed for each category. (That is, if a category will account for 12 percent of the test questions, then you should allocate 12 percent of your study time to that category.) That's a lot easier to figure out, but wastes much of your study time if you already know some of the material. You want to know exactly how much of your available time you should spend studying each category, which means that you have to go to the next calculation.

Now that you know the total percentage of test questions whose categories you must study (29 percent in this case), you need to know what percentage of your total study time each category should be given. To calculate that, you have to know what percentage of 100 percent of your study time the com-bined categories account for. You calculate it this way.

First, divide the total percentage of test questions for which you must study (29 percent in this example) by 100 percent (29 percent divided by 100 percent equals 2.9 percent). That tells you what percentage of 100 percent a single percent of the test questions you must study equals. Next, you take the percentage assigned to each category for which you must allocate study time, and multiply that percentage by the answer to the first calculation. So, in this example, you multiply each of 12 percent, 11 percent, and 6 percent for the three categories you must study, by 2.9 percent. For example, multi-ple 12 percent times 2.9 percent. The answer is 34.8. Rounded up, this means that you must spend 35 percent of your study time on the category whose questions account for 12 percent of the test questions.

Now that you know what percentage of time you should spend on each category, you should determine how much study time you actually have available. You will base this on factors such as whether you work, attend school, or have other commitments which must come first. For example, if you work 40 hours per week, then you know that is 40 hours a week you do not have available.

When determining your commitments and the hours they consume that you already have, also consider time you may need and want to spend with your family, any promises or commitments you have already made to others, and anything else which requires some of your time (including proper rest).

Now that you know what time you do not have available, do some calcula-tions and figure out what time you *do* have available. Once you have done that, apply the following recommendations to figure out what days and hours you will spend studying between now and the date you have set for the test.

❖ Choose the days of the week and the hours of the day during which you generally feel the best. Don't wait until the end of the day, an hour before your normal bedtime to study if during that time you are generally too tired to concentrate.

❖ When you have identified the best times and days, let everyone know that is time during which you are not to be disturbed for other than emergency (or at least very important) reasons.

❖ Choose a place to study. Look for one that has adequate light and space, and provides a comfortable chair to sit in (not the recliner in the living room). Also, a desk is often useful. It gives you a place to spread out multiple reference materials so that you can refer to them simultaneously if you need to.

Also, try to choose a place to study that is away from noise and other distractions. As a rule, most people do better if the TV or radio is not playing. However, that may not always be the case. I write every one of my books with the radio playing quietly in the background. I find that it tends to act as a white noise to buffer other distractions. However, I have to be careful to put on a station that plays music that will act as white noise, and not one to which I find myself singing or humming along.

Now that you know where you are going to study, and how much time you have to study, schedule that study time. Take the calendar on which you circled the date you will be taking the exam, and for each day you choose to study, mark the study time on it as if it were any other type of appointment. Then, keep those appointments and don't let others (or even your own desires to "do anything but study") distract you from your goal.

Now that you have marked the calendar, take another look at it. Add up the total number of hours you have available for study time. Then, for each category you must study, figure out what percentage of your total study time should be devoted to that category. To do that, simply multiply the number of available study hours by the percentage you entered into the " percent Study" category on the form in Figure 6.11. This tells you how many hours of your total available hours should be spent studying information associated with each of the categories.

Your study plan is now complete. All you must do is carry it out. To do so, keep the study plan where you can easily find it so that each time you sit down to begin your studies, you will know what you are supposed to be studying. Also, as you study, track the hours you are spending on each category so that the time is correctly allotted.

One other suggestion is to know ahead of time which category you will be studying next so that you can gather the needed study materials before you sit down to study. That will help ensure all your study time is spent studying, not looking for reference or other study materials.

If you are using multiple reference books, this can become a little complex. If you are attempting to learn a great deal about networking technology so that you can implement that knowledge in your daily work life, there may be no getting around all the researching and studying you will have to do. Multiple references will probably be required. However, if you are studying for the sole purpose of passing the exam, then I suggest you limit your study materials. Supplement only those categories you study with additional study material when you feel that what you already know combined with what is covered in a book such as the Meyers book is not sufficient, or not as understandable as you had hoped. (We all learn differently, and have different knowledge needs. That does not make any one book bad, it simply means that while a single book may tell you all you need to know, you may not feel that what you have learned from it is enough, and may decide to supplement your knowledge with additional materials.)

Study Techniques That are Particularly Useful for Studying Technical Materials

As part of creating your study plan, several general study techniques were outlined. Recommendations such as choosing a quiet, well-lighted location in which to study, and always using that area for studying are generally study techniques. For studying technical material, there are also some specific recommendations. All of these techniques are ones the authors have repeatedly used in the course of studying for various certifications obtained, as well as for studying for knowledge.

When you sit down at each study session, use the following techniques to help you get the most out of the time you have available:

1. Quickly skim the materials you will be studying during this session. That gives you an overview of what the material is about.

2. Read through any questions related to the material. For example, many study books have questions at the end of each chapter to help you see how much of the material you remembered. Reading through these questions before you start reading the chapter helps alert you to what the author believes is the most important information you should gain from the chapter.

3. Go through the chapter again and look more closely at any figures, bullet lists, numbered lists, and headings the author has used. This gives you an idea of what key points will be covered, and shows you what the author believes is important enough to want to make it stand out for you.

4. Prepare to take cryptic notes about the most important information. You can do this any way that works best for you. I generally use index cards (without lines), but regular unlined paper will work just as well.

   The reason I used unlined cards or papers is so that I can write my notes very small. Doing so makes the notes themselves seem less overwhelming when it comes time to spend time memorizing them. It also makes them easier to carry around so that I can study whenever a small "snatch" of time is available.

5. Read through the section or chapters you have chosen to work with during this study session. As you read, make small, cryptic notes about the important items of information.

6. When you have finished reading and taking notes for this study session, close up the study materials. Then, take a short break (15 minutes at the most). During that break, do not read anything, or watch TV, or otherwise do something "mental" which will distract your mind from what you have been studying.

7. After taking your break, pull out the study notes you took and read through them again. There are three reasons for doing this. First, you want to make sure that the notes you took aren't so cryptic or written so small (or sloppily) that you cannot read them. If they are, fix the problem. Second, you want to put this information into the front of your mind again so that it is fresh. And third, repetition is an effective way to memorize, even if it is boring. (This technique makes it much less boring, however.)

8. Now, this study session is over, but your studying is not. There is one more thing you need to do. Before you go to bed that night, take out

your notes from today's study session, as well as the notes from each of the other days' study sessions, and read through all of them. As you read through them, make sure they make sense to you. That is, make sure you still understand what they mean. Also, try to remember as much associated information from your previous studying as you can.

For example, if you wrote a cryptic note that simply listed each of the layers of the OSI model and their main functions, try also to remember as many of their other functions as you can. Also try to remember them in the correct order. If the study materials you used showed any graphics, charts, etc., try to remember what they looked like and what the basic idea or main information associated with them was.

Now you know the basic study process to follow. There are also a few tricks you can use that will help you when it comes time to take the actual examination. To make this discussion easier, I will use the term "unit" to apply generically to whatever grouping of information you chose for your studies. For example, if during one study session you read two chapters in a reference book, each chapter could be considered a unit. As could even a section of a chapter if one section is all you read during that particular study session.

For each unit of study, apply the following techniques (in addition to those already suggested) to help you do better when it comes to taking the actual Network+ Certification examination:

- ❖ If questions have been created to help you review the unit you studied, answer those questions. Also, look up the actual answers to see if yours were correct. Then, for those questions you did not answer correctly, restudy the related section. Also, study the question to see if you can determine why the answer you chose was not correct, and why the correct answer is correct.
- ❖ For those units with associated questions, see if your study notes cover the material about which the question was written. If your study notes do not cover the material, add it. If your study notes are not correct based on what you learned by studying the question and its correct answer, modify your study notes until they are correct.
- ❖ If any unit of information is not clear to you when you study it, study it again. If studying it a second time does not make it clear enough to you, then find additional research material to review to make sure you understand the material. Add the new or revise the existing related

information on your study notes. You want to make sure that your study notes are correct.

❖ After you finish each study unit, go back through the unit and write your own test questions. Format them in the same manner in which the test questions have been written for the actual Network+ Certification test. For example, write multiple-choice questions with only four answers to choose from, since most, if not all, of the questions on the Network+ Certification exam will be multiple-choice. Use the questions in this book to help you understand how to format your own questions. Also, when writing these questions, choose the topics which are of the most importance in the unit you studied.

How do you know what is most important? Follow the author's lead. Is there a section heading? What is the main point of the information associated with that section heading? Also, look at the information contained in any charts and graphics in the unit. If a summary is provided at the end of the unit, use it to help pick out key items of information.

When you write these questions, also be sure to write down the correct answers, but not next to the questions. Keep them separate so that you can go through the questions later, and answer them from your learned knowledge, rather than from the answer sheet.

❖ Once you have finished studying all units that you chose to study for passing the entire Network+ Certification examination, review your notes one final time. A week or two before the test is a good time for you to do this "final" review.

❖ Rest a day. Do no studying.

❖ During your next scheduled study period, pull out all the test questions you have written. Then, in an environment that as closely matches the expected testing environment as you can manage, which means at the very least you match the number of test questions and the allotted amount of time, pull out the test questions you wrote and give yourself a test. When you finish taking the test, grade it. If you didn't correctly answer 95 percent or better of the test questions you wrote yourself, you should do a little more studying. Determine what questions you missed and why. It is not a big deal if you simply marked the wrong answer when you knew the correct one and meant to mark it. But if you did not know the correct answer, be sure you find out what it is and why. Adjust your study notes to include the related information if needed.

❖ Now that you once again know what knowledge you are missing (and it should be substantially less than when you created your study plan), study only what you still need to know until three days before it is time to take your test.

❖ Two days before test time, review all your notes once again. Do it two or three times during the day if possible, and again before you go to bed that night.

❖ The day before the test, do no studying. Rest. Relax. Make sure you get a good night's sleep the night before the test.

❖ Next day, take your notes with you to the testing center. (No, you aren't going to use them to take the test.) Before you go into the testing center (that means you have to arrive a few minutes early) pull out your notes and read through them one last time. (This will help give you confidence in your level of knowledge. Confidence is useful at test-taking time.) Then, go into the testing center, sign up, take the test, and pass.

Consider another useful bit of information. Although it costs somewhere around $90 to take the average certification test, if you do not pass it the first time, you should deem it money well spent. Taking the actual certification test, whether you pass it the first time or not, lets you see the real test questions. And although it is very unlikely that you will see the same test questions the next time you take it, you will know what the testing program and database itself determined as those areas of knowledge in which you still may need additional studies. As a rule, the results of the test are presented to you after it is scored.

As most certification tests are computerized, once you tell the system you are finished, it scores the test and tells you whether you passed or not. If you did not pass, the system generally presents you with details about how well you did on each section of the test. A printed copy of this information is usually also given to you. You then take that information, go back and redo your study plan to concentrate on those areas, and study again. (Do not forget to keep reviewing all of the notes you made the first time. You do not want to become proficient in the sections you missed the first time you took the test, only to miss questions on other sections of the test because you simply have not reviewed the material recently.

So, if you do not pass the certification exam the first time, don't give up. Many professionals have taken certification tests more than once in order to pass them. Sometimes it is the "luck of the draw" on the questions you get that determines whether or not you pass. That is particularly true when you know you have been studying and thought for sure you were ready to take the test and pass it. As the results of your test are not given to anyone but you, you will be the only one who really knows whether you passed it the first time or not, so don't worry about it if you do not pass. There is no shame (just a little extra money since you have to pay again to take it again) in not passing it the first time, only in giving up altogether. If you don't pass the first time, remember that someone has to help keep those testing centers in business. It is downright nice of you to help them out like that.

While reading all the reference materials and following all the study suggestions in this chapter will not guarantee that you will pass the Network + Certification test the first time you take it, you will pass it eventually if you don't give up. In the process, you will have gained a great deal of knowledge about networking technology.

To determine whether you currently know enough about networking to have a good chance of passing the Network + Certification examination, the following chapter presents a sample test of 150 questions for you to take. It is designed as a pre-study assessment and a post-study test. Chapter 7 contains the test and provides more information about how to get the most out of the test.

CHAPTER
7

Assessing Your Level of Networking Knowledge

This chapter presents 150 sample Network+ Certification examination questions. Its purpose is to help you determine your current level of networking knowledge so that you can decide how close you are to being ready to take the Network+ Certification test. The chapter and the test questions in it are also designed to give you practice at answering the types of questions you can expect to see on the Network+ Certification test.

The sample questions in this chapter are not the actual test questions (although some of them may be close to the real test questions). Therefore, you probably should not assume you know all there is to know about networking just because you can correctly answer each of these questions. These sample test questions are, however, as close in format as possible to the actual test questions. Working with these sample test questions should help you become more comfortable with answering the types of test questions you will have on the actual test, and thus help you be more comfortable and relaxed when you take the exam.

In addition, reviewing how well you answer these questions, and which ones you answered incorrectly should give you an idea of the areas of networking technology and networking practice with which you are already familiar. It should also help you determine which areas you should spend more time studying.

The test questions in this sample test are arranged by Network + Certification examination knowledge category. This arrangement will make it easier for you to determine what areas of knowledge you should spend more time studying, and prepare your study plan accordingly.

The number of sample test questions in each of these groups of test questions was determined by the percentage CompTIA assigned to each category of knowledge. For example, if a category of knowledge was identified by CompTIA as being 5% of the total networking knowledge needed to pass the official Network + Certification examination, then 5% of the total number of questions on this sample test are based on that same category. However, because this sample test contains 150 questions, and the actual Network + certification test will contain approximately 80 test questions, each knowledge area on this test contains approximately double the number of actual test questions you are likely to see on the official Network + certification exam. Since we cannot write a fraction of a question, there may be one question less or one question more than the percentage would actually indicate for any given category of knowledge.

In addition to the test questions, this chapter contains relevant answers. Where appropriate and helpful, a brief explanation or useful, related information is also included with the answer to help you better understand why the chosen answer is the correct one.

You will also notice as you go through this chapter that although the categories change, the question numbers are continuous. This was done deliberately to make finding the answers to the questions easier.

Sample Test Questions

This test is designed so that you can take it before you begin to study for the Network+ Certification test, and perhaps even before you actually decide whether you are going to pursue the Network+ certification. It is also designed for you to take it a second time once you think you may be ready to take the Network+ Certification test. However, if you prefer, you can also take only half the test before you begin your studies, and then take the other half once you believe you have completed your studies and are ready to take the actual Network+ Certification test.

This sample test is one continuous list of 150 questions and not two lists of 75 questions, however. In addition, the 150 questions on this test are grouped together by category.

That makes studying a little easier, but can make splitting the 150 questions into two tests just a little more difficult. Therefore, in order to take only half the test at a time and still get a variety of questions from each of the areas of required knowledge that are outlined in the CompTIA blueprint for the examination, you must modify your normal test-taking approach. To take only half the sample test at a time, answer either all the even-numbered questions, or all the odd-numbered questions the first time you take the test. Then, answer the other 75 questions when you take the test the second time.

There are two added benefits to taking only half the test each time. First, each test will contain a different set of questions, ones that you have not already seen. When you take the actual certification test, you will not have seen the questions before either. Second, this approach also allows you to simulate the approximate number of questions you can expect to be given when you take the actual Network+ Certification test. That will make it seem as though you have practiced taking the test twice. The main drawback is that you do not get as much test taking practice, even though you are answering the same number of questions.

If you do 150 questions twice, you get practice at answering 300 questions. However, 150 of them are duplicates. If you do 75 questions each time, you only get practice at answering 150 questions, but none of them are duplicates. You have options. Choose the one that works best for you.

Basic Networking Technology Knowledge

1. When examining the topology for a given network, if each device connects to a central point via a point-to-point link, which type of network are you examining?
   A. Star
   B. Bus
   C. Mesh
   D. Ring

2. If you have a few computers on your network which place a heavy load on the network, which network topology makes it possible for you either to isolate those computers, or to distribute them to better balance the network load?
   A. Star
   B. Bus
   C. Mesh
   D. Ring

3. If extra cabling hasn't been incorporated into the network to prevent it, in which topology will a single break in the cabling disable the entire network?
   A. Star
   B. Bus
   C. Mesh
   D. Ring

4. In Figure 7.1, which topology is displayed?
   A. Star
   B. Bus
   C. Mesh
   D. Ring

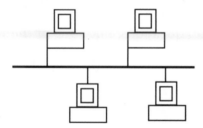

5. What type of connector is displayed in Figure 7.2?

   A. UTP
   B. RJ24
   C. BNC
   D. Dix

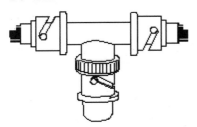

6. Which of the following network operating systems is based on the CCITT X.500 standard?

   A. LANtastic
   B. Novell Netware 4.x and above
   C. Microsoft NT
   D. UNIX

7. Which Internet protocol provides non-guaranteed, connectionless delivery of packets at the transport (host-to-host) layer of the Internet model?

   A. IPX
   B. IP
   C. TCP/IP
   D. NetBEUI

8. What is the main function of the IPX protocol?

   A. Control data flow
   B. Establish connections
   C. Emulate a terminal on a host-based network
   D. Route packets

9. What name is given to the fault tolerance feature of a server containing two hard disks, when one exactly duplicates the other, allowing users to access the secondary hard disk if the primary one fails?

   A. Mirroring
   B. Duplexing
   C. Stripping
   D. Routing

10. Which of the following statements about STP cabling systems is not true?
    A. It is more expensive and harder to install than UTP cabling systems.
    B. STP cabling requires physical continuity of the shielding to ensure proper functioning.
    C. To use STP cabling for low-frequency signals, you must ground it at both ends.
    D. STP cable that is not properly grounded can be a source of interference on a network.

11. Which of the following network access methods can be used in almost any network topology?
    A. Star
    B. Token Passing
    C. Polling
    D. Carrier Sensing

12. Which of the following is a disadvantage of the mesh topology?
    A. Redundant paths may be incorporated into the network.
    B. All devices on the network require multiple network boards.
    C. If each workstation has routing abilities, multiple paths may be established.
    D. Multiplexing may be used.

13. What term best describes the part of a network in which the network traffic sent from one workstation or server is received by all other workstations or servers?
    A. Node
    B. Segment
    C. Backbone
    D Topology

14. Which protocol did IBM specifically introduce to be used by LAN workgroups of 20 to 200 computers thus designing it to be small, efficient, and fast?
    A. IPX
    B. IP
    C. NetBEUI
    D. OSI

15. What is the name given to the database that contains descriptions and related information for all entities on a network?
    A. Message Handling System
    B. File Transfer, Access, and Management
    C. Directory Services
    D. Network Interface Card

16. Using Figure 7.3 below, identify which model displays the OSI layers in the correct order.
    A. Model A
    B. Model B
    C. Model C
    D. Model D

Application	Application	Application	Network
Presentation	Session	Data-Link	Presentation
Session	Transport	Session	Session
Transport	Network	Transport	Transport
Network	Presentation	Network	Physical
Data-Link	Data-Link	Presentation	Data-Link
Physical	Physical	Physical	Application
Model A	**Model B**	**Model C**	**Model D**

17. This type of cable cannot be tapped, each one is as thin as a human hair, and it is limited in its carrying capacity primarily by the technology of the encoders and decoders it uses. Which type of network communications cable is the previous statement referring to?
    A. Coaxial
    B. Fiber optic
    C. UTP
    D. STP

18. Which fault tolerance feature shares data among multiple drives, allows the data to be read from all of the drives, and is particularly effective when used with parity?
    A. Mirroring
    B. Duplexing
    C. Stripping
    D. Backing up

19. What is the name of the fault tolerance feature requiring two controllers as well as two matched hard disks?
    A. Mirroring
    B. Duplexing
    C. Stripping
    D. Backing up

20. Which of the following best describes a WAN?
    A. Multiple local area networks connected together.
    B. One or more LANs in different geographical areas communicating across the Internet
    C. Computers organized into a network within a specific region
    D. None of the above

21. Choose the word that best represents a PC that has been specifically configured to be able to access the network.
    A. Client
    B. Workstation
    C. Peripheral
    D. Device

22. What of the following most correctly describes broadband?
    A. Ability to avoid collisions on the transmission media
    B. Transmission of data one bit at a time
    C. Dedication of the entire channel's bandwidth to a single signal
    D. Capacity to carry multiple signals simultaneously

23. What of the following most correctly describes baseband?
    A. Ability to avoid collisions on the transmission media
    B. Transmission of data one bit at a time
    C. Dedication of the entire channel's bandwidth to a single signal
    D. Capacity to carry multiple signals simultaneously

24. Which describes a network node functioning as an interface between different types of networks?
   A. Gateway
   B. Modulator
   C. Station
   D. Host

Physical Layer of the OSI Model (6%)

25. If a user still cannot connect to the network after you have replaced their workstation's Ethernet network interface card (NIC), which step might be the next most logical choice?
   A. Verify that the configuration settings on the board match the system's settings in the configuration file.
   B. Run a diagnostic utility to verify whether the board can see the network, even though the user may not be able to.
   C. Add the PREFERRED SERVER = statement to the Shell.cfg file.
   D. Remove the NIC and install a different one.

26. Which of the following work at the physical layer of the OSI model?
   A. Bridge
   B. Gateway
   C. Router
   D. Repeater

27. Which layer of the OSI model is concerned with transmitting raw bits across the communication channel?
   A. Physical
   B. Data Link
   C. Network
   D. Transport

28. Which of the following is not associated with configuring a network interface card?
   A. IRQ
   B. DMA
   C. EPROM
   D. I/O Base Address

29. Which device contains relays to short out nonoperating network workstations thus helping to prevent other workstations on the ring from being affected by the problem?
    A. Repeater
    B. MAU
    C. Hub
    D. IRQ

30. If you must add a workstation to a network even though you know the cable distance is so great that the signal may be too weak at the other end, what component can to restore the strength of the signal?
    A. MAU
    B. Hub
    C. Repeater
    D. Transceiver

31. If you need to physically change some aspect of the configuration of a NIC, which one of the following might you have to use?
    A. Jumper
    B. EPROM
    C. HUB
    D. Repeater

32. Which network device relies on collision detection to help prevent corruption of transmitted data?
    A. MAU
    B. Hub
    C. Repeater
    D. Transceiver

33. Of the following, which is least likely to give you the help you need when trying to resolve a hardware conflict on a network workstation?
    A. Reading the original documentation that came with the system.
    B. Running an appropriate diagnostic utility.
    C. Using the Device Manager on a Microsoft Windows 95 computer.
    D. Reviewing the network documentation associated with configuration of this specific type of hardware.

Data-Link Layer of the OSI Model (5%)

34. Which of the following is a function of the data link layer of the OSI model?

    A. Routing

    B. Controlling access to the network

    C. Providing uniform user interface

    D. Reliable data transfer

35. Which of the following is not a primary function of the data-link layer?

    A. Routing

    B. Defining frames

    C. Error detection/correction

    D. Flow control

36. What is the main function of the MAC address?

    A. To connect unlike networks to each other

    B. To provide connectionless transport on an Ethernet network

    C. To function as the interface between the NIC and the transport layer of the OSI model

    D. To uniquely identify each node on a network

37. Which of the following is one of the sublayers of the data-link layer of the OSI model?

    A. MAC

    B. DDC

    C. DLC

    D. CLL

38. Which of the IEEE 802 standards relates to network management?

    A. 802.2

    B. 802.3

    C. 802.5

    D. None of the above

39. Which of the IEEE 802 standards is the general standard for the data link layer of the OSI model?
   A. 802.2
   B. 802.3
   C. 802.5
   D. None of the above

40. Which of the IEEE 802 standards defines the MAC layer for token-ring networks?
   A. 802.2
   B. 802.3
   C. 802.5
   D. None of the above

41. Which of the IEEE 802 standards is the basis for the Ethernet standard?
   A. 802.2
   B. 802.3
   C. 802.5
   D. None of the above

Network Layer of the OSI Model

42. Which of the following is not a function of a router?
   A. Route messages
   B. Handle packets
   C. Ensure reliability
   D. Be efficient

43. If your network needs to send packets over the most efficient route and the packets cannot be routed, what device can you use instead of a router?
   A. Brouter
   B. Repeater
   C. Transceiver
   D. Hub

44. When you must add a device to your network that can dynamically adjust its table to re- optimize a previously chosen path, which network device would you need?
A. Brouter
B. Router
C. Transceiver
D. Repeater

45. Which term applies to a router that is capable of actively monitoring the state of the network, and of choosing the best route over which to send a packet?
A. Static
B. Dynamic
C. Interpretive
D. Repetitive

46. To which device do the terms RIP and OSPF commonly apply?
A. Gateways
B. Hubs
C. Dynamic routers
D. Bridges

47. What (shaded) device is at the center of the network shown in Figure 7.4 below?
A. Brouter
B. Bridge
C. Hub
D. Gateway

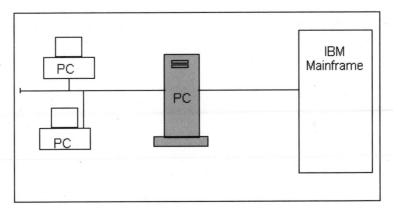

48. Which of the following is an example of the use of a default gateway?
  A. When the gateway sends general network traffic
  B. When the gateway sends IP traffic from itself
  C. When only a single route through the network is needed
  D. None of these are examples of the use of a default gateway

Transport Layer of the OSI Model

49. Which layer of the OSI model is responsible for ensuring the data delivered between processes on two network computers are reliable?
  A. Physical
  B. Transport
  C. Network
  D. Session

50. If reliable delivery of packets on the network is paramount, which delivery system should be used?
  A. Connectionless transport
  B. Connection transport
  C. Either method is sufficient
  D. Neither method is sufficient

51. Which of the following services provides flow control?
  A. Connectionless transport
  B. Unacknowledged connectionless transport
  C. Non-responding connection-oriented transport
  D. Connection-oriented transport

52. Which service is not provided by connection-oriented services
  A. Flow
  B. Error control
  C. Sequence control
  D. None of the above

53. Which connection-oriented service is responsible for rearranging the smaller pieces of the original message when they are received?
 A. Error controlling
 B. Virtual circuitry
 C. Segment sequencing
 D. End-to-end flow control

54. Why does the transport layer use acknowledgments?
 A. To reduce error control
 B. To resequence segments
 C. To detect corrupt segments
 D. To manage end-to-end flow control

TCP/IP Fundamentals

55. Which protocol of the TCP/IP suite can be used to speed up the delivery of data if the network has already proven to be reliable?
 A. UDP
 B. WINS
 C. DHCP
 D. DNS

56. If the terms NetBIOS, IP address, p-node, b-node, and NBT are used, which TCP/IP suite protocol is being referred to?
 A. UDP
 B. WINS
 C. DHCP
 D. DNS

57. Which application protocol dynamically translates an Internet name such as **http://www.keylabs.com** to its numeric address used by IP?
 A. DNS
 B. DHCP
 C. WINS
 D. FTP

58. What protocol allows you to transfer documents and programs from one computer to another?
   A. DNS
   B. DHCP
   C. WINS
   D. FTP

59. If you send queries and commands from a network management station to an agent service running on a target system so as to collect information about event notifications, which TCP/IP application protocol are you likely to be using?
   A. UDP
   B. POP3
   C. SNMP
   D. HTTP

60. To move Web pages across an internet, which protocol is commonly used?
   A. UDP
   B. POP3
   C. SNMP
   D. HTTP

61. What is another name for the list of IP addresses to which a network is connected?
   A. Default gateway
   B. Internet domain name server
   C. Proxy service
   D. Subnet mask

62. To decipher the IP address of other network computers, what binary number does your network computer use?
   A. Default gateway
   B. Internet domain name server
   C. Proxy service
   D. Subnet mask

63. Which subnet class is being used if the subnet number is 255.255.0.0?
A. Class A
B. Class B
C. Class C
D. None of the above

64. With the popularity and growth of the Internet, which of the following is most appropriately used for securing your network.
A. Default gateway
B. Internet domain name server
C. Proxy service
D. Subnet mask

65. Which protocol is commonly referred to as the electronic mail engine used between network hosts?
A. UDP
B. POP3
C. SMTP
D. HTTP

66. When network computers are to have an IP address assigned to them at the time it is needed instead of permanently, which of the following is probably being used?
A. FTP
B. DHCP
C. POP3
D. WINS

67. If the first part of an IP address ranges from 0 to 127, which IP network class is it?
A. A
B. B
C. C
D. None of the above

68. Which set of formats and procedures is used to assign names that relate to the IP address of a location on the Internet?
    A. POP3
    B. DNS
    C. Default gateway
    D. IP proxy

69. Which of the following can be described as a 32-bit, four-section representation of a network location?
    A. Default gateway
    B. IP proxy configuration
    C. Host name
    D. IP address

70. Which of the following protocols relies on ports?
    A. SMTP
    B. IP
    C. UDP
    D. DHCP

71. Which port number is commonly used for SMTP?
    A. 21
    B. 25
    C. 53
    D. 137

72. If an application references port 41, what type of application is it likely to be?
    A. Graphics
    B. Quote of the day
    C. Telnet
    D. SQL service

TCP/IP Suite Utilities

73. Which TCP/IP protocol translated an Ethernet packet's IP address to a MAC address?

A. ARP

B. FTP

C. Telnet

D. NETSTAT

74. Which of the following is important to accurately delivering data?

A. ARP

B. FTP

C. Telnet

D. NETSTAT

75. To view a UNIX server's network functions, which tool might you choose?

A. Telnet

B. NETSTAT

C. Ping

D. Tracert

76. To view real time network status data using Netstat on a UNIX server, which of the following must you use?

A. Netstat -A

B. Netstat -B

C. Netstat -C

D. Netstat -U

77. Which of the following is considered a basic Internet management tool?

A. Telnet

B. NETSTAT

C. Ping

D. Tracert

78. To measure round-trip delay on a network, which tool might you choose?
    A. Telnet
    B. NETSTAT
    C. Ping
    D. Tracert

79. Why use NBTSTAT?
    A. To view protocol statistics using NetBIOS over TCP/IP
    B. To verify network continuity
    C. To view IP physical address tables
    D. To view user connections

80. Which parameter should you use with NBTSTAT if you want to reload the LMHosts file without rebooting NT 4?
    A. /?
    B. –R
    C. –C
    D. \%

81. On a TCP/IP network, which utility can you run to view all of the current TCP/IP configuration information?
    A. NETSTAT
    B. Nbtstat
    C. Tracert
    D. IPconfig

82. Which TCP/IP utility lets you see the route a packet takes from one PC to a remote computer?
    A. NETSTAT
    B. Nbtstat
    C. Tracert
    D. Ipconfig

83. Which TCP/IP utility relies on TTL periods to identify the route a network packet takes?
    A. NETSTAT
    B. Nbtstat
    C. Tracert
    D. Ipconfig

84. To view the DHCO address on a TCP/IP network, which utility can you use?

    A. NETSTAT

    B. Nbtstat

    C. Tracert

    D. IPconfig

Remote Connectivity

85. Which Internet protocol's primary benefit is security of transferred data?

    A. PPP

    B. PPTP

    C. SLIP

    D. IRQ

86. To exchange IP packets using serial lines, which protocol is appropriate?

    A. PPP

    B. PPTP

    C. SLIP

    D. IRQ

87. Which protocol eliminates the cyclic redundancy check and the destination address to simplify data transmission?

    A. PPP

    B. PPTP

    C. SLIP

    D. IRQ

88. When a digital transmission is used, which of the following services supports it?

    A. SLIP

    B. IRQ

    C. I/O address

    D. ISDN

89. Which of the following frequently uses POTS for data transmission?
   A. IRQ
   B. I/O address
   C. ISDN
   D. PSTN

90. Which service has a data transfer rate that is comparable to leased lines?
   A. ISDN
   B. PSTN
   C. POTS
   D. SLIP

91. When you make a telephone call to Aunt Mary, which service do you generally use?
   A. PSTN
   B. POTS
   C. SLIP
   D. PPP

Security

92. Of the following, which is not a true statement regarding network security?
   A. Hiding a directory is one way to protect access to network data.
   B. All users should be required to have a password.
   C. Batch files containing passwords simplify user access and help protect the network.
   D. Users passwords can be required to have a minimum number of characters.

93. Which of the following statements about network security is true?
   A. A call-back modem can be programmed with a list of authorized users.
   B. Leaving logged-in workstations unattended is only a security breach if the building itself is unlocked.
   C. Encrypted passwords can still be read from the NOS password file.
   D. All of the above are true statements.

94. Which of the following is a frequent user security violation?
   A. Repeatedly using the same password
   B. Leaving their computer logged in when they aren't present
   C. Writing their password down
   D. All of the above

95. Of the following, which is not designed to protect the network from viruses?
   A. TSRs that check memory for viruses before loading programs
   B. Regularly backing up the network
   C. Using a call-back modem
   D. Removing access to floppy drives with a user menu

96. What do menu programs, regular backups, and call-back modems all have in common?
   A. They allow networks to share devices.
   B. They are network security options.
   C. They all function at the network layer.
   D. Nothing

97. Which of the following cannot contain a virus?
   A. Memory
   B. Partition tables
   C. Boot sectors
   D. Network Interface Cards

98. To restrict a remote user's access to the network, which of the following can you use?
   A. Remote modems
   B. Dial-up modems
   C. Network modems
   D. Call-back modems

99. Daily network backups is an example of which network management task?
   A. Remote connectivity
   B. Security
   C. Installation
   D. Troubleshooting

100. Of the following, which does not apply to user security on a network?
- A. Creating accounts and IDs
- B. Managing groups
- C. Setting a default document
- D. Managing passwords

Implementing the Installation of the Network

101. When you are looking at a user's workstation setup, which of the following is most likely to be a potential environmental hazard to the user's computer?
- A. Plants on a windowsill
- B. Books stacked next to the monitor
- C. A radio playing in the cubicle next door
- D. Closed window blinds

102. Which of the following environmental factors should the network administrator consider when designing a new network?
- A. Server console security
- B. Location of heat/air ducts in the building
- C. Internet access
- D. Number of network users

103. What is the common name for a standard connector that is used for RS-232-C wiring, and that consists of one top row of 13 pins and a bottom row of 12 pins?
- A. DB-9
- B. DB-25
- C. RS-232
- D. RS-449

104. Which of the following accurately describes a common and important difference between and RJ-45 connector and an RJ-11 connector.
   A. The RJ-11 connector can be connected to a NIC for either voice or data transmission.
   B. The RJ-45 connector is designed to be used specifically for voice connection.
   C. The RJ-11 connect contains either four or six pins and is designed for normal voice communication.
   D. The RJ-45 connector contains eight pins and is designed for network communication using shielded twisted-pair wire.

105. When you are adding a workstation to the network, which of the following, if overlooked, can result in the new workstation's having physical problems accessing the network?
   A. The length that patch cables add to the maximum allowed cable length for the type of cable being used
   B. The user's network ID and password
   C. A server located too far from the user
   D. None of the above

106. Of the following, which will you probably not need to have at the time you perform an installation of network operating system software on a file server?
   A. IP addresses
   B. User passwords
   C. At least one administrative account
   D. IP configuration information

107. Which of the following is not a true statement about serial ports?
   A. They use two types of communication: synchronous and asynchronous.
   B. They divide bytes into eight bits, arrange them, then transport them.
   C. Their configuration is defined by the Electronics Industry Associations RS-232C standard.
   D. None of the above statements about serial ports is true.

108. Which device contributes most to the efficient use of network peripherals?
A. Print server
B. Print queue
C. Application server
D. Brouter

109. What does the shaded box in Figure 7.5 below represent?
A. Hub
B. Mainframe
C. Router
D. Gateway

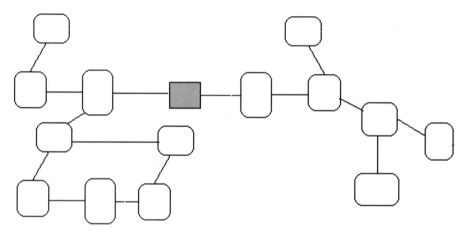

Administering the Change Control System

110. When a user complains of inability to log in to the network since installing a software program on a workstation, which of the following might be the most useful?
A. A network tape backup
B. An updated driver
C. A baseline for the workstation
D. A single-folder replication on the network

111. If the network server has limited disk space but the users' workstations must be backed up, which is the best option?

A. Tape backup

B. Folder replication to a network drive

C. Removable media

D. None of the above

112. If you are working with a subset of the OSI protocol tuned to better suit a company's needs, what are you working with?

A. Profile

B. Right

C. Saps

D. Permission

113. To ensure a user has needed network access, what must be provided?

A. Policies

B. Rights

C. Groups

D. Profiles

114. To simplify network administration, particularly when dealing with users' network access, which of the following should you implement?

A. Policies

B. Rights

C. Groups

D. Profiles

115. To ensure consistency in network administration, which of the following should a company have in place before implementing network changes?

A. Drive mappings

B. Profiles

C. Administrative utilities

D. Policies

Maintaining and Supporting the Network

116. To prevent users and others from loading potentially problematic programs onto the network, what can you do?
A. Load Rendir
B. Load Server.exe
C. Load backup tapes
D. Load antivirus software

117. What is the next logical step for a network administrator to perform if the user's workstation functions fine as a standalone, but cannot access the network?
A. Check the video cable
B. Make sure the printer is turned on
C. Check for a network cable or NIC problem
D. Set up a service appointment for the workstation

118. If a user has successfully demonstrated a problem for you, what is the next most logical step for you to take?
A. Identify the exact issue
B. Recreate the problem
C. Isolate the cause
D. Formulate a correction

119. What should be your first goal when troubleshooting a user's network-related problem?
A. Identify the exact issue
B. Recreate the problem
C. Isolate the cause
D. Formulate a correction

120. Which of the following is a true statement?
A. If another user on a different workstation can recreate the problem, the problem is probably the result of operator error.
B. When a second operator cannot recreate the problem on a second workstation, the problem is a network problem.
C. When a second user can recreate the problem on the same workstation, the problem is not operator error.
D. All of the above are true.

121. What should you check for when a user complains of an error message stating that no server can be found?
   A. Blinking lights on the NIC
   B. Error logs
   C. Performance monitors
   D. All of the above

122. To prevent repeated data loss due to power failure, which is the best choice?
   A. Bridge
   B. Patch panel
   C. UPS
   D. Media filter

123. If the user is following correct procedures, the cable is connected to the NIC, and software configurations are correct, what should you check next when trying to determine why the user cannot log in to the network.
   A. The NIC itself
   B. The cable
   C. The bridge
   D. The server's status

124. Which of the following is not a potential resource for network troubleshooting?
   A. Vendor documents
   B. Technical support
   C. WWW
   D. /T

Identifying, Assessing, and Responding to Problems

125. Of the following, which is the most serious network problem?
   A. One user cannot see the first network drive.
   B. No user can see one particular file server.
   C. The file server is displaying an error message but only the administrator notices.
   D. Only the network supervisor or administrator can log in.

126. Which network-related problem would you handle last?
    A. One user cannot see the first network drive.
    B. No user can see one particular file server.
    C. The file server is displaying an error message but only the administrator notices.
    D. Only the network supervisor or administrator can log in.

127. Which action is likely to be most appropriate when a user following correct log in procedures still cannot see the network?
    A. Information transfer
    B. Hand holding
    C. Technical service
    D. None of the above

128. Four hours of downtime due to a software bug could have been prevented, if the network administrator had done which of the following?
    A. Installed anti-virus software
    B. Updated older anti-virus software
    C. Established network installation policies
    D. Obtained and installed patches

129. In which of the following is an information transfer action most appropriate?
    A. The user's workstation functions independently but not as a network workstation.
    B. The user can log in to the network but cannot see a specific file server.
    C. The file server sent the user an error message.
    D. None of the above

130. It's a new employee's first day on the job and he has never logged in to a network before. Which type of action may be most appropriate?
    A. Hand holding
    B. Information transfer
    C. Technical service
    D. All of the above

131. A small number of users throughout the network are having trouble running a specific application. Which of the following types of actions should be the administrator's first?

A. Hand holding
B. Information transfer
C. Technical service
D. All of the above

132. Of the following, which problem should be handled first?

A. A non-essential network file server is down.
B. All users in a workgroup cannot access an application they could access yesterday.
C. One user's PC will not boot.
D. The network backup did not run last night.

133. Which type of service is being provided when a network administrator conducts a training class for new users?

A. Hand holding
B. Technical
C. Information transfer
D. Both B and C

Troubleshooting the Network

134. If you have determined that a specific problem is not isolated to a single computer or network segment but that it instead affects most or all of the network, what is the next logical step to take?

A. Have someone recreate the problem to verify that it is a true problem.
B. Formulate a correction.
C. Document the problem and its resolution.
D. None of the above.

135. Of the following, which is not considered a standard troubleshooting method?

A. Gather basic information.
B. Isolate plan.
C. Create a baseline.
D. Document the solution.

136. Once you gather needed information regarding a network problem and hypothesize its potential cause, which is the next logical step?
A. Identify the exact issue.
B. Recreate the problem.
C. Isolate the cause.
D. Formulate a correction.

137. Which of the following is the troubleshooting step you are executing when you reference prior trouble report logs?
A. Identify the exact issue.
B. Recreate the problem.
C. Isolate the cause.
D. Formulate a correction.

138. When you ask another user to perform the same task on the problematic workstation that the original user was doing when the problem occurred, what are your trying to determine?
A. Whether the problem is attributable to the operator or system.
B. What the exact problem is.
C. How to formulate the best correction.
D. Whether the problem is related to a user's network rights.

139. Once you've had the complaining user attempt to recreate the problem for you on his workstation, which is the next best step to perform?
A. Have a second operator perform the same task on the problematic workstation.
B. Have the complaining user perform the same task on a workstation other than the problematic workstation.
C. Have a different operator perform the same task on her own workstation.
D. Formulate a correction.

140. When attempting to identify the extent of a problem, which step should you complete first?
A. Determine whether the problem exists across the network.
B. Determine whether the problem is isolated to a single workstation, LAN, or network segment.
C. Determine whether the problem is consistent and replicable.
D. Use standard troubleshooting methods.

141. Which of the following does not apply only to attempting to determine the extent of a network problem?

A. Determine whether the problem exists across the network.

B. Determine whether the problem is isolated to a single workstation, LAN, or network segment.

C. Determine whether the problem is consistent and replicable.

D. Use standard troubleshooting methods.

142. Of the following, which does not help identify a problem as being a physical problem?

A. Blinking link lights

B. Error displays

C. UPS devices

D. Performance monitors

143. What do dark or blinking link lights on a network connection device generally indicate?

A. An error message received from the server

B. A physical problem with the device

C. The server has exceeded its licensed capacity.

D. The network server is down.

144. Which of the following is not a typical resource you locate on the WWW for troubleshooting information?

A. Virtual help desks

B. E-mail document libraries

C. Vendor reference materials

D. Professional vendor training materials

145. To test the power of a signal through an optical cable, which of the following tools would you use?

A. Voltmeter

B. Scanner

C. Optical power meter

D. Optical time domain reflectometer

146. Under what circumstance would you use a token-ring media filter?

A. To connect a UTP cable to a DB-9 connector

B. To reduce "line noise" caused by excessively long ring cable

C. To activate UPS monitoring software

D. To isolate VPC connections

147. When users on one hub cannot access resources or see users connected to a second hub on the same network, what might the cause be?
    A. Firewall
    B. Bad patch cable
    C. Malfunctioning bridge
    D. None of the above

148. Which device can check remote loopback on a line?
    A. DSI
    B. DSU
    C. CSU
    D. DSC

149. Of the following, which will not generally cause a noticeable power fluctuation or drain on the network?
    A. A brownout
    B. A UPS with a bad battery
    C. A user powering down a workstation for the day
    D. None of the above

150. Which of the following tools is used most often only when installing a network or adding a workstation?
    A. Voltmeter
    B. Crimper
    C. Tweezers
    D. Patch panel

Answers to Sample Test Questions

The answers to each of the 150 sample test questions follow. The numbers for each of the answers match the number given to its question. The correct letter choice for the answer is given first, and is displayed in parenthesis.

A brief description associated with the topic of the question, or an explanation of why the specified answer is the correct one for that particular question is provided. In addition, the answers are divided into the same categories of knowledge as their associated questions. As with the questions, this arrangement should make it easier for you to see where you need to gain more knowledge before taking the Network+ Certification examination.

Basic Networking Technology Knowledge

1. (A) In a star network, multiple devices are connected to a single point. That single point can be a hub, a multipoint repeater, or a concentrator, and the central single point can either be passive (routes traffic without enhancing the signal) or active (routes the traffic and enhances the signal).

2. (A) Because the star topology is hierarchical, you can separate the heavily used computers from the rest of the network, or you can distribute them throughout the network to even the flow of traffic.

3. (D) A ring is a physical, closed loop. Each computer on the ring functions as a repeater. When the cable breaks or becomes disabled, it prevents the entire network from functioning since each node on the ring must take its turn at receiving the transmission, amplifying it, and passing it on.

4. (B) In the bus topology, all network devices are attached to the same cabling system (transmission media).

5. (C) The BNC connector is displayed in this figure. Because of its appearance, it is sometimes referred to as a bayonet connector.

6. (B) The OSI DS is also derived from the CCITT X.500 standards, but this is not one of the listed options.

7. (B) The IP (Internet Protocol) provides non-guaranteed, connectionless delivery of packets at the transport layer of the Internet model.

8. (D) Packet routing and addressing from the source node to the destination node is the main function of the IPX (Internet Packet Exchange) protocol.

9. (A) Duplicate disk drives with a single controller used for both drives is known as disk mirroring.

10. (C) STP cabling systems must be grounded at both ends only when used to transmit high-frequency signals. Otherwise, you can ground the STP cabling system at only one end.

11. (C) Polling, the process by which the one primary device controls access to the network for each secondary device, can be used in almost any topology.

12. (B) Each device on the network must have a network board for every other device on the network. This limits the practical size of the network.

13. (B) A network segment can be defined as the part of a network on which all traffic is common to all devices attached to it. Therefore, if a signal is broadcast from one device on the segment, all devices on the same segment will receive the transmission. Even in a token ring network where the transmission goes from one workstation to the other, all workstations still see the transmission (unless they are faulty or not operating).

14. (C) IBM introduced this protocol in 1985 assuming that LANs would consist primarily of small segments with only 20 to 200 computers on them, and that gateways or routers would connect these networks. NetBEUI provides the fastest communication for small networks, but it is not a routable protocol

15. (C) The directory information database (DIB) of directory services stores all information about devices, such as computers and peripherals, that are part of the network.

16. (A) Model A correctly displays the order of the layers in the OSI model.

17. (B) Fiber optic cable has all of these features and more.

18. (C) Stripping allows data to be stored on and read from multiple hard drives. With parity, this is a particularly effective approach to providing fault tolerance.

19. (B) Duplexing uses duplicate hard disks, but unlike mirroring which requires only one controller, duplexing uses two controllers. Duplicating the controllers as well as the hard disks provides better protection against equipment failure.

20. (A) Multiple local area networks (LANs) connected together form a WAN. They often cover large geographical regions, and while their users may access the Internet, the Internet is not the medium they use to communicate.

21. (B) PCs configured to access a network are also called workstations. While they can be called clients as well, so can any device that is attached to the network and capable of providing resources to users (such as printers attached to the network cable).

22. (D) Broadband uses the communication channel to transmit multiple signals simultaneously.

23. (C) Baseband is a form of transmission that dedicates the entire bandwidth of the communication channel to only one signal.

24. (A) Of the choices, only a gateway functions as an interface between different types of networks.

Physical Layer of the OSI Model

25. (B) Although each of the other options is a possibility, B is the best choice. Most NICs are now plug-and-play. You do not have to configure the NIC's settings manually. If the system requires a PREFERRED SERV-ER= statement, it should already be in the Shell.cfg file since all you changed was the NIC. And, although it is possible that the new NIC is not functioning properly, this is not the most likely cause.

26. (D) Of the choices presented, only the repeater works at the physical layer.

27. (A) The physical layer of the OSI model concerns itself with transmitting data. Your first reaction might be to choose the transport layer, but its function is to take the data it receives from the session layer, and break them up as needed to pass them to the network layer.

28. (C) EPROM (Erasable Programmable Read Only Memory) is a chip which is programmed by and stores information using an electrical charge.

29. (B) The MAU (Media Access Unit) is a token ring network device to which network workstations attach. If one of the workstations is not operating, the MAU can sense it and route network traffic so as to ignore that workstation.

30. (C) A repeater amplifies electrical signals, thus restoring the weak signals to full strength.

31. (A) When you have physically to change a NIC's configuration, you change one or more jumpers—removable wires or plugs.

32. (D) The transceiver is both a transmitter and a receiver and physically connects a device to a LAN. Ethernet networks uses transceivers to transmit network packets and to detect signals from other network devices in an effort to avoid packet collisions.

33. (A) Although the original documentation can be of some use, the default configuration information found in those documents frequently differs from the actual settings on the NIC. That is particularly true with plug-and-play cards.

Data-Link Layer of the OSI Model

34. (D) The data-link layer includes information about when a workstation can transmit, and organizes incoming bits of information into logical frames.

35. (A) The data-link layer ensures reliable transfer of data across the network. It checks the bits it receives for errors and corrects them where possible, creates frames from the bits it receives, and manages the flow of data between network devices to prevent fast senders from causing problems for slow receivers.

36. (D) The main purpose of the MAC address is uniquely to identify each node on a network.

37. (A) Only the MAC (Media Access Control) layer is a sublayer of the data-link layer of the OSI model. The other sublayer is the LLC (Logical Link Control) layer. On networks that do not conform to the IEEE 802 standard, the node address is called the Data Link Control (DLC) address.

38. (D) The IEEE 802.1 standard relates to network management.

39. (A) An Internet search of the IEEE standard will answer this question for you if you cannot find a reference elsewhere.

40. (C) There is a great deal of information about the IEEE 802 standard available. You should be familiar with what each of the specified standards defines.

41. (B) Information on the OSI model makes reference to the IEEE 802 standard, so you should be sure you understand the standard.

Network Layer of the OSI Model

42. (B) Routers do not ensure the reliability of data. Routers function at the Network layer of the OSI model. Only hardware such as a gateway which functions at the transport layer is responsible for reliable data delivery.

43. (A) A brouter (bridging router) can do both routing and bridging.

44. (B) Routers can dynamically adjust their routing table to reoptimize a previously chosen path.

45. (B) Dynamic routers are capable of actively monitoring the state of the network, and of choosing the best route over which to send a packet. Static routers always send the packet over the same route.

46. (C) RIP (Routing Information Protocol) and OSPF (Open Shortest Path First) are two common protocols capable of monitoring the state of the network so that the dynamic router can choose the best route over which to send a packet.

47. (D) Gateways are commonly used to connect two networks of completely different formats such as a PC-based network and an IBM mainframe environment.

48. (B) The use of a default gateway generally has no effect on how general network traffic is forwarded, although it may slow the network down somewhat. The default gateway is typically used when the gateway sends IP traffic from itself, such as when a device on the network sends a trap.

Transport Layer of the OSI Model

49. (B) At the transport layer, communication now concerns itself with processes, rather than with the physical components.

50. (B) Only connection-oriented services ensure reliable delivery of packets.

51. (D) Only connection-oriented services provide flow control.

52. (D) Connection-oriented services provide all three of these services.

53. (D) End-to-end flow control is responsible for rearranging the smaller segments of the original message when they are received.

54. (D) The transport layer use acknowledgments to manage flow control.

TCP/IP Fundamentals

55. (A) If your network is highly reliable, the UDP protocol of the TCP/IP suite can be used to speed up network packet delivery acknowledgment.

56. (B) Windows Internet Naming Server (WINS) is a database containing a PC's NetBIOS and IP address, both of which are used to locate the PC on the network. For more friendly names to be available to, NetBIOS over TCP/IP (NBT) is used.

57. (A) DNS takes the human-readable Internet address and changes it to the IP-readable address.

58. (D) File Transfer Protocol (FTP) is a hypertext interface that lets you transfer files and programs to any computer in the world.

59. (C) The SNMP (Simple Network Management Protocol) protocol is used to collect information about event notifications on a TCP/IP network.

60. (D) HTTP (Hyper Text Transfer Protocol) is the protocol used to move Web pages across a TCP/IP based internet.

61. (A) Gateways connect TCP/IP networks and control the flow of packets between networks and subnets. Each network keeps a list of its own IP addresses. That list is known as the default gateway.

62. (D) The subnet mask is a 32-bit binary number used by one network computer to decipher the IP address of another network computer.

63. (B) Class A uses 255.0.0.0; Class B uses 255.255.0.0; Class C uses 255.255.255.0

64. (C) A proxy is the power (or authority) to act on behalf of another. In networks, a proxy service allows information exchange between networks while maintaining security for individual computers.

65. (C) Simple Mail Transfer Protocol (SMTP) is the electronic mail engine used between network hosts on a TCP/IP network.

66. (B) Dynamic Host Configuration Protocol (DHCP) dynamically allocates IP addresses to networked computers.

67. (A) Class A IP networks have a value range of 0 to 127 in the first part of the IP address.

68. (B) Domain Name System (DNS) defines how names are assigned to locations on the Internet.

69. (D) Each of the four sections in a 32-bit IP address is called an IP address segment or octet.

70. (C) Both TCP and UDP rely on ports.

71. (B) Some common port numbers are 20 and 21 used by FTP for data and control respectively, 25 for SMTP, 53 for DNS, and 137 for NNS.

72. (A) Graphics commonly use port 41, while SQL uses 156, quote of the day uses 17, and Telnet uses 23.

TCP/IP Suite Utilities

73. (A) Address Resolution Protocol (ARP) uses an address resolution table to translate IP packet addresses to MAC addresses (the physical addresses of network devices).

74. (A) ARP translates an IP address to a MAC address, therefore it is important to accurate delivery.

75. (B) Netstat is a tool used to view statistics for network functions on a UNIX server.

76. (C) Use-c with Netstat to see real-time, full-screen network status data for a UNIX server.

77. (C) Ping is a basic network management tool.

78. (C) Ping can measure round-trip delay but if used repeatedly, can also load the server.

79. (A) Nbtstat is a utility that displays protocol statistics and current TCP/IP connection information.

80. (A) Use the /? With Nbtstat to prevent NT from rebooting when the LMHosts file reloads.

81. (D) Ipconfig without parameters displays all TCP/IP configurations including subnet masks, WINS, and DNS configuration.

82. (C) Tracert documents the route a packet travels.

83. (C) Time-To-Live (TTL) periods are used to create a router count (hop count) when using Tracert to document the route a packet travels.

84. (D) IPconfig displays all current TCP/IP network configuration information including the DHCP (Dynamic Host Configuration Protocol).

Remote Connectivity

85. (B) The Point-to-Point Tunneling Protocol's (PPTP) main benefit is its secure transfer of data across the Internet.

86. (A) Point-to Point Protocol (PPP) lets you send IP packets and other frames over serial lines.

87. (C) SLIP can simplify transmission by eliminating the CRC and destination address fields in TCP/IP.

88. (D) Integrated Services Digital Network (ISDN) lines transport data using digital.

89. (C) One of the advantages of ISDN is that it can use the Plain Old Telephone System (POTS).

90. (A) The data transfer rate of ISDN compared to that on leased lines is one of its advantages.

91. (B) POTS is the correct answer.

Security

92. (C) Batch files can be easily viewed by unauthorized users, so putting passwords in them is a breach of network security.

93. (A) Call-back modems allow only users identified in the list to have remote network access.

94. (D) All of these are common user security violations.

95. (C) Call-back modems help prevent unauthorized access to the network, but are not specifically designed to prevent a virus from getting into the network.

96. (B) These are all ways you can help secure a network.

97. (D) NICs and other boards do not contain viruses.

98. (D) Call-back modems let the user dial in, provide a password, and be called back if the user is listed in the modem's list of authorized users.

99. (B) Backups are done to secure network data and programs.

100. (C) Setting a default document helps users view at least some document when the one they've requested is not available, but it is not a security issue.

Implementing the Installation of the Network

101. (A) Because of their physical closeness to the computer, books can block the air flow to the computer, causing it to overheat. The plants and radio are potential problems, but as long as they are not close to this computer, they are not as likely as the books to cause problems.

102. (B) Only the location of heating and air conditioning ducts in the building is an environmental factor included in the answer choices.

103. (B) The DB-25 connector is a standard connector used for RS-232-C wiring. It contains two rows with a total of 25 pins.

104. (D) The RJ-45 connector contains eight pins and is designed for network communication using shielded twisted-pair wire.

105. (A) The patch cables' length must be considered when determining whether a workstation added to the network causes the maximum cable length specification to be exceeded.

106. (B) Even though you may set up user accounts when installing NOS software, users must set their own passwords. IP information such as addresses and configuration requirements, as well as an administrative account are all more likely to be required when you perform an install.

107. (D) All of these statements about serial ports are true, which makes answer D the only correct one.

108. (A) Print servers make it possible to share expensive printers on the network.

109. (C) A router, bridge, or modem could be depicted in this figure and used in this scenario.

Administering the Change Control System

110. (C) A baseline for the workstation will allow you to reset the workstation's configuration. Just uninstalling the software may not be sufficient.

111. (A) Tape backup is the simplest solution that will not put added strain on the server's limited disk space.

112. (A) Subsets of the OSI protocol are called profiles. GOSIP is an example.

113. (B) Rights determine a user's access.

114. (C) The use of groups allows you to set rights and restrictions specific to a given set of requirements. You then assign users to the group, and all members of the group then have the same rights and restrictions without having to provide them separately to each individual user.

115. (D) Policies help ensure network changes are made consistent with management requirements.

Maintaining and Supporting the Network

116. (D) Anti-virus software helps prevent virus programs from damaging your network.

117. (D) Software patches fix software problems that can cause potentially serious network problems.

118. (C) If the user shows you the problem, it has been successfully recreated (although you may choose to recreate it again in a test environment). The next step is to isolate the cause.

119. (A) Before taking steps to solve a problem, make sure you know exactly what the problem is.

120. (C) If someone other than the original user can recreate the problem on the same or a different computer, the user is most likely not the cause.

121. (A) If the network cannot be found, checking for an active physical connection is indicated.

122. (C) An Uninterruptible Power Supply (UPS) helps protect against the damage that can be caused by power failures as it gives you enough time to correctly close out files and shut down the network.

123. (A) A bad NIC is generally more likely than a bad cable. If no one else is having problems, the NIC is the most likely choice of the available answers provided for this question.

124. (D) All of the others are potential sources of information. So too is the /? Or Help option available with some software. There is no /T option for seeking information, however.

Identifying, Assessing, and Responding to Problems

125. (D) This means the network is non-functional for everyone else.

126. (C) If the administrator is the only one noticing the error, then the problem isn't currently affecting users. It probably can wait until the other problems are solved.

127. (C) A network connection that cannot be established when a user is following correct log in procedures is more likely to be an equipment problem than a user problem.

128. (C) There probably is nothing wrong with the PC itself if it can function without network access. The NIC or cable is more likely to be the problem.

129. (C) If the user receives an error message, it is likely the user has done something incorrect. It may just need to show the right way to do it.

130. (A) Walking the user through the log in process the first time may be the best approach because the user is inexperienced.

131. (C) In this instance, the administrator should verify that these users have the needed rights and drive mappings. As multiple users are having the problem, it is probably not just a matter of training them.

132. (B) When other problems are not critical, solve first those problems that affect the greatest number of users.

133. (C) Although technical information may be provided during the training, the training itself is a type of information transfer.

Troubleshooting the Network

134. (B) Now that you have narrowed down the problem, the next logical step of the provided choices is to formulate a correction.

135. (C) Creating a baseline should be done when the network is first brought up and is running satisfactorily, then again any time important changes are made. Use the baseline to help troubleshoot, but it is not a troubleshooting method as such.

136. (D) You have determined the potential problem by doing the other three steps. Now you must formulate a correction.

137. (A) One method available for identifying the exact problem is that of referencing previous related documentation.

138. (A) If the problem is not repeated when circumstances other than the user change, the problem is likely to be user-oriented.

139. (A) This helps identify whether the problem is centered around the user or the workstation.

140. (A) The best way to identify the extent of a problem is to start wide and then narrow it down.

141. (D) Standard troubleshooting methods are used for more than just determining the extent of a network problem.

142. (C) UPS devices help protect the network from power failures, but do not help identify a network equipment problem.

143. (B) No lights on a device indicates a physical problem such as no active connection or no power.

144. (D) While much material is available on the Web, professional vendor-developed training materials are generally not available there (although you may be able to use the Web to place an order for them).

145. (C) The optical power meter measures the strength of the signal in decibels.

146. (A) Connecting a UTP cable to a DB-9 cable is the purpose of a token ring media filter.

147. (B) Patch cables can be used to connect hubs. If two hubs connected together do not interrelate, the problem can be a faulty patch cable.

148. (C) A Channel Service Unit (CSU) is one component of data communications equipment. One of its functions is to test remote loopback on the communications cable.

149. (C) One user turning a PC on or off will not noticeably affect network power levels.

150. (B) Crimpers are used to attach connectors to cables, so they are used mostly when installing a new network or adding a new user workstation to an existing network.

Primary References Used to Create the Sample Test

Multiple books were references to help create a variety in the questions included in this chapter. In addition to some of the suggested reading materials included elsewhere in this book, the following books were used, and in some instances, can be a good source of study material for you.

As a rule, most of these books have information about only one or more topics covered on the Network + Certification examination; they do not generally cover those topics in detail. Consequently, most of the books listed here are not books you would read from cover to cover in order to study for the test, but are books you may find useful for reference purposes.

Additional books referred to specifically for creating the sample test questions in this chapter are:

❖ Brier, Doug; Cady, Dorothy; Heywood, Drew; Niedermiller-Chaffins, Debra; and Stein, William. *Novell CNE 4 Study Guide*. Indianapolis, IN: New Riders Publishing; 1996.

❖ Cady, Dorothy; Heywood, Drew; and Niedermiller-Chaffins, Debra. *CNE 4 Short Course*. Indianapolis, IN: New Riders Publishing; 1994.

❖ Cady, Dorothy; Heywood, Drew; Niedermiller-Chaffins, Debra; and Wilhite, Cheryl. *Networking Technologies*. 2nd ed. Indianapolis, IN: New Riders Publishing; 1994.

❖ Feibel, Werner. *Novell's Complete Encyclopedia of Networking*. San Jose, CA: Novell Press; 1995.

❖ Holderby, William. *Real-World Networking with NT4*. Scottsdale, AZ: Coriolis Group Books, Inc.; 1996.

❖ Jenkins, Neil; Schatt, Stan. *Understanding Local Area Networks*, 5th ed.: Indianapolis, IN: Sams Publishing; 1995.

❖ Mueller, John; Williams, Robert. *The CNA/CNE Study Guide*. Intranetware ed. New York, NY: McGraw-Hill; 1998.

❖ Petrovsky, Michele. *Optimizing Bandwidth*. New York, NY: McGraw-Hill; 1998.

❖ Sasser, Susan B.; McLaughlin, Robert. *Fix Your Own LAN*. 2nd ed. New York, NY: MIS:Press; 1994.

Now that you have read the chapters in this book, you should have a better understanding of the Network + Certification program, its creation, the need for certification in this industry, and the benefits of this program. You should also have a better understanding of why obtaining the Network+ Certification is in your own best interest. In addition, you should have a good idea of the extent (or limit) of your own knowledge of networking principles and practices, as well as a good general idea of what you still need to learn if you want to pass the Network+ Certification examination. You also should know what you need to do to prepare for the exam, and you should have a pretty good idea of what materials are available to help you study for that exam.

We hope that you have found in these pages not only the information you need to help you understand and begin preparing to take the Network+ Certification examination, but the inspiration to follow through with becoming Network+ certified. To that end, we wish you good luck on your test as well as with your career in networking.

INDEX

Note: Boldface numbers indicate illustrations

About the Authors

DOROTHY CADY is an award-winning former senior technical writer for Novell, Inc., who currently works as an independent consultant. She has written many technical books on networking technologies, including McGraw-Hill's recently published *Accelerated NetWare 5 CNA Study Guide* and *Accelerated NetWare 5 CNE Study Guide*. She is also a Certified Novell Engineer (CNE), Certified Novell Instructor (CNI), and a Certified Novell Administrator (CNA).

NANCY CADJAN is a technical writer for Novell, Inc. She has worked on documentation for such products as the Novell Client, Novell Internet Access Services, and NDS for NT.